C0-ALN-037

Sorry I Don't Dance

Sorry I Don't Dance
Why Men Refuse to Move

Maxine Leeds Craig

OXFORD
UNIVERSITY PRESS

OXFORD

UNIVERSITY PRESS

Oxford University Press is a department of the University of Oxford.
It furthers the University's objective of excellence in research,
scholarship, and education by publishing worldwide.

Oxford   New York

Auckland   Cape Town   Dar es Salaam   Hong Kong   Karachi
Kuala Lumpur   Madrid   Melbourne   Mexico City   Nairobi
New Delhi   Shanghai   Taipei   Toronto

With offices in

Argentina   Austria   Brazil   Chile   Czech Republic   France   Greece
Guatemala   Hungary   Italy   Japan   Poland   Portugal   Singapore
South Korea   Switzerland   Thailand   Turkey   Ukraine   Vietnam

Oxford is a registered trade mark of Oxford University Press
in the UK and certain other countries.

Published in the United States of America by
Oxford University Press
198 Madison Avenue, New York, NY   10016

© Oxford University Press 2014

Library of Congress Cataloging-in-Publication Data
Craig, Maxine Leeds.
Sorry I don't dance : why men refuse to move / Maxine Craig.
pages cm
Includes bibliographical references and index.
ISBN 978-0-19-984527-9 (hardcover : alk. paper)—ISBN 978-0-19-984529-3 (pbk. : alk. paper)
1. Male dancers—Social conditions. 2. Men—Social life and customs.
3. Masculinity. 4. Gender identity in dance. 5. Dance—Sociological aspects.
6. Dance—Anthropological aspects. I. Title.
GV1588.6.C73   2013
792.8081'1—dc23   2013025939

To Mitch

CONTENTS

ACKNOWLEDGMENTS

This has been a far-reaching project and I have many people to thank. When I set out to write this book I was not sure that men would be willing to tell me about their experiences with dance. Talking about dance meant telling me about how they felt about their bodies, their interactions with partners, and about their perceptions of living in a world structured by inequalities. I owe a profound debt to the fifty men who opened up to me and helped me to understand an embodied experience that is not my own. They made this book possible. Though they must go nameless, I am deeply grateful to them for their willingness to give me their time and to recall experiences that were sometimes embarrassing or painful. I listened to them to try to understand the structures that weigh upon all of us, though in different ways.

I am very fortunate to have friends and colleagues who generously helped me to develop the project. Their encouragement kept me going and their critical comments made it a better book. Jessica Fields and Aziza Khazzoom are sharp, critical listeners and helped at the earliest stage when the project was little more than a half-baked talk. Rita Liberti and Nina Haft shared their wisdom about the politics of bodies and offered crucial suggestions about how to design the project. Mona Abdoun and Rosa Klein-Baer provided skilled research assistance collecting periodical citations about dancing men.

Eileen Otis, Kathy Sloane, Tyson Smith, Susan Kaiser, and four anonymous reviewers read the manuscript and gave me extensive and valuable comments. I am extremely grateful to them for their generosity and thoughtfulness. I have been buoyed by the constant enthusiasm Amina Mama, the director of my institutional home, the Women and Gender Studies Program at UC Davis, has shown for my work. My ever-supportive writing buddy, Stephanie Sears, read multiple versions of the drafts that eventually became this book. I cannot remember how many years ago we met and began talking about dance, race, and gender, but her astute judgment and steady support have been essential to me. Telephone conversations with Betsy Wheeler, my kindred spirit and fellow boogying intellectual, were nourishing. Betsy always knows exactly what I mean.

This book allowed me to bring together parts of my life that had previously remained separate. My sister Beverly Gina Leeds was my earliest dance partner. Dancing, talking, and thinking with her is always a way to return home. I thank the many dance teachers who encouraged my love of movement. When I was a little girl, Rose Arons, director of Dnipro Dance Ensemble, taught me how to dance like a Ukrainian, an early lesson in my understanding that ethnic movement cultures can be learned by anyone. Anna Dal Pino, a brilliant modern dancer and teacher, and "Rodson" De Souza, a fantastic Brazilian dancer and teacher, showed me that I still have plenty to learn about dance.

As I entered the world of dance scholarship, Lynn Garafola, Julie Malnig, and Barbara Cohen-Stratyner were generous guides. I could not have written this book without the extraordinary collections and skilled assistance of the librarians at the New York Public Library for the Performing Arts, the Special Collections of the Langson Library at the University of California, Irvine, the Library and Archives of the Hoover Institution, the Oakland History Room of the Oakland Public Library, and the San Francisco History Center of the San Francisco Public Library. Jeff Thomas of the photo desk at the San Francisco History Center was especially creative, patient, and enthusiastic as he helped me to locate photographs of dancing men.

I benefited from a California State University, East Bay, Faculty Support Grant, which contributed to covering the cost of travel to archives and the expense of conducting interviews and having them transcribed. I am grateful to The University of California, Davis Division of Humanities, Arts and Cultural Studies for providing support to defray costs associated with the book's illustrations.

When this project was barely a notion I mentioned it to Susan Ferber of Oxford University Press. Her encouragement at that stage was crucially important to me. James Cook has been a superb editor. He understood the project from the beginning and gave me exactly the guidance I needed to find my way through substantial revisions. I am grateful to Oxford University Press for providing the copy-editing services of Katherine Ulrich. I enjoyed reading her thoughtful questions. She appreciated the spirit of my writing but caught all the places where I went astray.I dedicate the book to Mitch, who asked me to dance nineteen years ago and still keeps up with me on the dance floor.

Sorry I Don't Dance

CHAPTER 1

The Search for Dancing Men

Hi everybody
I'm Archie Bell of the Drells
From Houston, Texas
We don't only sing but we dance
Just as good as we walk

—Archie Bell and Billy Buttier, "Tighten Up"

When I was a young girl in Bedford-Stuyvesant, Brooklyn, I spent many weekends in the basement of my cousins' brownstone house listening to records and practicing dancing. We trained ourselves in the art of looking good while moving to music, and we practiced perfect parodies of bad dancing. Acquiring the art of comic exaggeration was part of the way we turned ourselves into dancers who knew the limits of good form. We brought each other new named steps that somehow appeared and circulated in our schools: The push and pull, the four corners, the tighten up. As a result of these hours of practice we were confident when dancing, polished and fluent, yet our fluency did not distinguish us among our friends. It only made us competent within a culture in which, it seemed to me at the time, everyone danced.

I was thirteen when I went to my first teenaged party, given by one of my older sister's friends. There were white kids at our junior high school but none of them were at this party. I sat on a sofa, too socially awkward to make conversation, but completely prepared in case someone asked me to dance. Either out of kindness or curiosity or because he had more nerve than the others, Arthur, a well-dressed, brown-skinned, popular young man asked me to dance when someone put Archie Bell and the Drell's

"Tighten Up" on the record player. The recording's funky bass line and snappy beat had briefly propelled it and the dance that went with it to the heights of popularity that year. The tighten up is a good dance for parties given in small spaces. It stays in one place. A couple of dancers face each other and just lift alternating heels off the floor to raise and twist their hips to one side and then the other, accenting each side with a little bounce. When Arthur asked me to dance, I knew exactly what to do. I had perfected the tighten up in my cousin's basement. My social debut was a success.

This is a book about masculinity and everyday dance, and it seeks to understand why many men do not dance.[1] Arthur was able to cross a living room and ask me to dance. It was a simple accomplishment, but something many young and even adult men cannot do. Like me, Arthur had learned how to do the tighten up. No one is born able to do the tighten up, the lindy hop, or any era's popular dance. Dancing is not an innate skill; it is a learned accomplishment that begins to look natural after hours of practice. Still, people who dance well are often perceived as naturals; it seems natural when women dance, and just as natural when men do not. There is a word for non-dancing women at a party, but the wallflower has no masculine equivalent.[2] They are not wallflowers, they are merely men standing around while others dance. The popular assumption that women dance and men do not, and that women will want to dance and men will not, allows, or perhaps even encourages, many men to avoid dancing.

But Arthur danced. The supposition that dance is feminized, and that men do not dance, was never about all men. This is one of those places in descriptions where "men" has stood in for non-Hispanic, white, heterosexual men. The belief that men do not dance shapes not only the way men experience gender, but how they experience race, ethnicity, and sexuality as well. Particular individuals are commonly considered natural dancers, but so too are categories of persons. Within the historical record, popular and "expert" assertions about the racial origins of dance talent are common. Contemporary observers, however, are just as likely to discuss dance talent as innately tied to race. These popular linkages persist even during an era when color-blindness is a speech norm.[3] This may be because dance is deemed unimportant, since for the average person the ability to dance has little economic value, compared to, for example, literacy or quantitative skills.[4] Yet assumptions about a seemingly unimportant talent form the base of a chain of signifiers that support long-standing racist associations between blackness, femininity, sensuality, the body, emotional expressiveness, and lack of control, on the one hand, and between white masculinity and the opposite characteristics of rationality, intellect, and emotional control, on the other.[5] If we pay attention to dance within everyday contexts, we can see the social production of that which is perceived as natural. We can view the roots of essentialist thinking.

Much can be learned about masculine norms by looking at practices they exclude. The following chapters explore masculinity and dance by examining dance as it is practiced, imagined, and represented in order to raise the following questions: Why do some men dance while others do not? And why do so many accept, as common sense, that white heterosexual men are unlikely dancers?

WHERE THE BOYS WEREN'T

In the early stages of this project I searched the sociology of masculinity and histories of American masculinity for descriptions of dancing men and could not find them.[6] I read social histories of the emergence of public nightlife in the beginning of the twentieth century for accounts of dancing men. Detailed descriptions of dancing men were rare. Men were present in these studies of nightlife as the apparently less interesting partners of women, whose entry into nightlife commanded more attention.[7] An important exception is Paul Cressey's 1932 study of "taxi" dance halls where men paid women to dance with them. This exception, however, proves the rule. Cressey identified nine types of men who patronized taxi dance halls.[8] Filipinos, who according to Cressey bore an "invidious racial mark," were the largest group of customers. Unassimilated European immigrants were the second largest group. The rest were a dishonored collection of men whose "matrimonial ventures had ended disastrously," varieties of transients, disabled men, and criminals on the run. All of the men were in some way distinguished from the normative, white, able-bodied, middle-class, heterosexual man who is the subject of general studies of masculinity. General histories and sociological studies of men have little to say about dancing. Either the men they describe did not dance, or their dancing escaped the chronicler's attention. There have been studies of masculinity and professional or semiprofessional dance, but ordinary dancing men are uncommon figures in contemporary social science accounts of masculinity.

I looked for dancing men in the novels that have defined modern western masculinity.[9] Did Tarzan dance? In Dashiell Hammet's *The Thin Man*, did suave detective Nick dance with his wife Nora? Did John Updike's anguished working-class male character, Rabbit, bring his frustrated physicality to the dance floor? Masculine fiction allows occasional glimpses of dancing. Apes danced in *Tarzan of the Apes*, and Tarzan, the noble white man they adopted, danced with them. Nora danced, but was partnered by a disreputable man, not Nick. The only dancing in Updike's *Rabbit, Run* took place among the children a despondent Rabbit watched in the televised Mickey Mouse Club show. In westerns and hard-boiled detective fiction "dance" was what a cowering man did when his options ran out. A vigilante pointed his gun at a cornered criminal in Max Brand's *Destry Rides Again* and yelled "Hold him while I make him dance, the chicken stealin' little son of a gun!" and when the femme fatale in James M. Cain's *The Postman Always Rings Twice* turned on the man she had embroiled in her husband's murder she warned him that "It don't cost me a thing to make you dance on air. And that's what you're going to do. Dance, dance, dance."[10]

Whose real and imagined masculinity is chronicled in narratives in which heroes and "normal" men do not dance? The non-dancing men in these narratives are adult versions of the All-American boy. They represent white, heterosexual, able-bodied, morally sufficient men. Though white dancing men are nearly absent from general histories of masculinity and rare in male fiction, I suspected that they were more common in real life. I looked for accounts of dancing men in newspapers in the 1910s and 1920s, a period when dancing was enormously popular. I found dancing men in accounts that begin as reports about women's affairs: a woman's dinner dance, a bad girl's romance, and a romance that led to murder. I found good male dancers who were bad men in afternoon tango teas, a time when good men were out of place on a dance floor. I sought glimpses of men dancing in the minutes of meetings of a dance hall regulation organization, in newsletters for folk dance enthusiasts, and in periodicals written for World War II–era servicemen. I read descriptions of white men dancing in relation to the less rare descriptions of racially and ethnically marked men who danced. I was interested in the place of dance in contemporary men's lives and interviewed Asian, black, Latino, and white men about their high school proms and about what it is like to dance with their wives at weddings. I found and heard accounts from All-American boys who danced with enthusiasm and finesse.

THEORIZING MASCULINITIES

Dance, when it is practiced or avoided in everyday settings, sheds light on processes by which men make masculinities. In the 1980s and 1990s historians and sociologists began to conceptualize masculinity as a changing social construct. While, in general, men's dominance over women has endured, popular understandings of the basis of male dominance and social expectations for men's behavior have changed over time.[11] Sociologist

Raewyn Connell has proposed that gender is a hierarchal social structure, which takes relatively stable form as a "gender regime."[12] Within societies characterized by male domination, masculinity, in general, is deemed superior to femininity, and particular ways of being a man have greater social value. Under a gender regime, hegemonic masculinity exists as a privileged ideal in relation to alternative, stigmatized masculinities. The definition of the ideal man varies over time and in different places. In one era the ideal man may be defined by his ability to physically dominate others, in another by his relative wealth.

Masculinities are in many ways things produced on the surface. Men work to appear masculine to other men. However, this work not only creates an appearance but changes the body below the surface. Gender becomes embodied even though it is not innate. For example, even when exemplary masculinity is primarily defined by wealth, wealth will in some ways distinguish the hegemonic masculine body. Class privilege may be visible in the cultivation of the body's movements, in the absence of a worker's calluses, or in a toned and trim body developed through class-aligned fitness activities. The masculine body is never merely the natural outcome of male genes. Rather, it is acquired through what Connell has described as "a personal history of social practice."[13] Masculine bodies are the product of work and leisure, deliberate and inadvertent acquisitions of physical competencies, and socially supported patterns of consumption.

Connell has characterized hegemonic masculinity as a "project" that many but not all young men actively take on as their own.[14] The project of masculinity provides a socially supported way to act in the world and it has consequences for bodies. James Messerschmidt argues that boys and girls use their bodies as the media through which they produce gender. In a study of high school students he found that youths "literally constructed a different body," as they worked at producing gendered selves.[15] One of the ways a boy may gender his body is through the acquisition of habitual ways of moving. Depending upon the movement habits he inadvertently and deliberately acquires, he becomes cool, or "gay," or known as a jock, a nerd, or a stud. As a boy develops embodied habits and movement capacities he positions himself within a gender regime.

According to Connell "the most important feature of hegemonic masculinity is that it is heterosexual."[16] Therefore a large reason why men shun dance has to do with perceptions of sexuality. Avoidance of the appearance of homosexuality is central to normative masculine embodiment. The fear of appearing gay constrains men as they walk and gesture. It prohibits them from partnering with each other. It determines how men dance and prevents some men from dancing at all. In an ethnographic study of high school students, sociologist C. J. Pascoe found that it was the vagueness of the epithet "fag" that made it so threatening.[17] Teenagers used the epithet compulsively but inconsistently, and so a boy could never be sure of what behavior would warrant it in the judgments of his peers. The uncertainty of interpretation makes any boy's body an unreliable instrument with which to convey a sense of self. What will his movement reveal? Many decide that the best strategy is not to move too much. Boys learn habits of controlling entire regions of their bodies. Their chests are stiff. They do not move their hips.

Since at least the beginning of the twentieth century professional dance has been associated with homosexuality in the United States.[18] The association arises from a bundle of false assumptions. One of these is the belief that gay men are necessarily feminine, and that feminine men are necessarily gay. Another is a limited conception of what may constitute masculine embodiment. Underlying both of these is the stigmatization of same-gender attraction. Dance historian Ramsay Burt has argued that if a man's appearance on stage is "desirable, he is, from the point of view of a male spectator, drawing attention to the always-already crossed line between homosocial bonding and homosexual sexuality."[19] For men unwilling to acknowledge the pleasure of gazing at another man, the man who dances is an uncomfortable sight.

Watching men play sports, however, is an entirely different matter. It is a comfortable sight for men and a thrilling one. When men watch athletics, they gaze upon the creation of male heroes, whose existence bolsters the general idea of male supremacy.[20] Sports such as football promote strength, toughness, and the capacity to prevail as broad cultural values; cultivate these qualities in men; exclude women; and contribute to the belief that such qualities are inherently male. To the extent that the nation celebrates sports heroes, displays of masculine dominance in sports naturalize men's domination in other realms. Few if any men possess the characteristics associated with hegemonic masculinity, but many support the legitimacy of that masculine ideal, and benefit from the status that accrues to men as a result.

While the athlete is a masculine ideal, the man who dances professionally risks being perceived as the perfect example of a type of failed masculinity. Men who dance on stage labor under the assumption that professional male dancers are gay, and therefore are belittled within a homophobic society for being the wrong sort of men. In the dancer's performance, appearance rather than domination is the goal. It is telling that in b-boying, a form of dance currently popular among young men, which is performed to hip-hop music, dance is framed as a battle. B-boys attempt to dominate opponents through displays of daring, inventiveness, and physical technique. The majority of staged dance performances are not organized primarily as man-to-man competitions. Still, those who wish to legitimate men who dance often minimize what is distinctive about dance and emphasize its athleticism.[21] Just as perceptions of athletes establish powerful ideals with consequences for gender in everyday life, so the perception of professional dancers provides boys with information about what is cool, what is not, and how they should carry their bodies.

Sociologists Candace West and Don Zimmerman have argued that gender is not something we are, it is something we do.[22] Their theorization of gender has gained wide acceptance among sociologists as the "doing gender" model.[23] We do gender, not entirely as we please, but, to use Connell's terminology, within the constraints imposed by a gender regime. West and Zimmerman argue that we are held accountable for the production of normative gender within everyday interactions. Their theorization of gender focuses on its production and reinforcement at the interactional level. Gender arises in situations, including those in which we touch, hold, move with, support, give our weight to, approach, or keep our distance from other people. In doing so, we signal how much we may be touched and by whom, and whether we are leaders or followers, strong or weak. Dance is an intimate interactional practice, and it is this very quality that can make it difficult for men who have learned to limit public physical intimacy.

Men can be held accountable for appropriately doing gender in any situation. They adopt gendered bodily practices in order to execute credible masculine performances. Some men do masculinity on the periphery of the dance floor, drink in hand, watching others dance. Arthur did masculinity, by asking me to dance, and doing the tighten up like he was born to it. If doing masculinity can mean either refusing to dance or mastering a dance step, a theoretical model of a singular dominant masculinity, which serves as an exemplar for all men, will not help us understand the lived experiences of masculinities. Everyday dance is a subject that requires theorization of masculinities, not a singular masculine ideal.[24] This book adopts a model of gender embodiment that assumes that the gendered meanings of bodily practices vary across communities.[25]

By conceptualizing gender as something actively "taken up" or "done," Connell, Messerschmidt, and West and Zimmerman are arguing that a lot of work goes into the construction of gender. How does gender end up looking so natural? While Connell theorized the larger gender regime, and West and Zimmerman the way in which such a regime structures interactions, sociologist Pierre Bourdieu explained how social structure, including gendered structure, gets into our bodies. Bourdieu theorized the "habitus" as a socially produced set of embodied habits, emotions, and dispositions that result in strategies for action. "Bodily habitus," he argued, "is what is experienced as most 'natural', that upon which conscious action has no grip."[26] Bourdieu showed how enduring gender and class inequalities become established in bodies in postures, in emotions such as shame or confidence, and in the habitual use of gaze, voice, and gesture.

Bourdieu studied the consequences of socially derived habitus in rural Algeria and in rural and urban France. In each of these settings habitus was the root of social reproduction in that it provided strategies for action that tended to thwart social mobility. In an early ethnography he studied the predicament of rural French peasants, condemned by social and economic circumstances to live as celibate bachelors. He used the concept of habitus to explain their discomfort in urbanizing settings. At dances in town the rural bachelors stood as clusters of rejected men, out of place and refusing to dance. Bourdieu described their bodies as well adapted to farm labor but poorly equipped to perform the latest dances, and therefore to participate in the social life in towns.[27]

Bodily habitus is experienced as natural and yet the body, through training, can acquire new habits. Sociologist Loic Wacquant built on Bourdieu's concept of habitus in a study of lower-class black men who trained in a neighborhood boxing gym. Wacquant described the development of a "pugilistic habitus," a "set of bodily and mental schemata," habits of movement and ways of thinking and feeling that are the ways of a "natural" boxer.[28] Wacquant's analysis powerfully shows the social production of what appears to be natural. Training made his subjects boxers, but socially derived class, race, and gender dispositions led some persons rather than others to the gym, and made them receptive to the interactional demands they found there. Structures of class, race, and gender affected the way their trained bodies would be perceived by others.

This study draws on the theoretical frameworks built by Bourdieu, Wacquant, Connell, Messerschmidt, and West and Zimmerman and employs them in an analysis that is always attentive to issues of race, gender, sexuality, and class. The strategies generated in the habitus are enacted in interactional contexts in which race, gender, sexuality, and class matter. Men acquire gendered bodily habits because, as West and Zimmerman have argued, they are repeatedly in interactional contexts that hold them accountable for appropriate gender performances. However the limits of appropriate gender performances, and what they imply about sexuality, are never unidimensionally about gender. Men respond to racialized, class-located gender constructs in bodies that are publicly identified in terms of gender, race, and class. Feminist theorists use the term intersectionality to describe the

ways in which gender is always co-constructed with, inflected by, and perceived through race and class.[29] The co-construction of gender, race, class,
and sexuality is especially visible when we consider everyday forms of
dance. As a man moves on the dance floor, or stays away from it, he positions himself within intersecting gender, race, class, and sexual regimes.
This is a study of the development of the dancer's habitus and its opposite,
the habitus of the sitter-out. These embodiments are formed in contexts in
which bodies, movements, and the use of interpersonal and public space
are coded by those who act and those who watch them act in terms of race,
gender, class, and sexuality.

What will we see when we look at men in and around dance floors in the
United States? According to literary critic Marjorie Garber "the All-American boy doesn't have a body."[30] Where is his body? What happened to it?
And what of Archie Bell from Houston, Texas, who boasted in the "Tighten
Up" lyrics that the Drells "dance just as good as we walk?" Is he not All-
American? An intersectional analysis of race, gender, sexuality, and class
can help us understand the differing embodiments of the All-American boy
and Archie Bell. In an analysis of basketball player Michael Jordan as a cultural figure, cultural critic Michael Eric Dyson wrote that "stylization of the
performed self" is a defining characteristic of African American aesthetics.[31]
Black men who value style express flair on basketball courts, on dance floors,
and in everyday movement. In contrast to Archie Bell's style, the All-
American boy typically develops a form of embodiment that queer theorist
Judith Halberstam has termed "anti-performative."[32] That form of embodiment eschews the appearance of cultivation. The All-American boy has no
swagger in his walk.

This book will take a long look at boys who refuse to acquire style and
men who do not dance. To do this it uses an intersectional approach to
study white masculinity. Feminist theorists developed intersectional theoretical frameworks in the 1980s in order to bring greater complexity to
what had been one-dimensional studies of gender or race. Earlier studies of
gender commonly excluded consideration of race, and studies of race often
neglected gender. Race, class, and gender have gained recognition as the
basic units of analysis in studies that include women of color, yet too often
studies of dominant groups remain one-dimensional studies of gender or
of class in which the whiteness of the subjects is noted in a footnote but
not given analytical attention. Studies of dominant groups also require intersectional analyses. Arlene Stein and Ken Plummer have argued that
queer theory has taught sociologists that it is important to "to study the
center and not just the margins" and to ask queer questions about those in
the center, to mark the usually unmarked positions in the center, and to

look at the social construction of heterosexuality.[33] As cultural studies scholar Richard Dyer wrote, "we need . . . to make heterosexuality strange."[34] This book asks readers to consider it strange that so many straight white adult men do not dance.

Projects of masculinity are relational. The awkward middle-class heterosexual white man is produced in opposition to images of the graceful straight woman, the rhythmic black man, the sensual Latino, the gay ballet dancer, and the parodied working-class ethnic white man at the disco. Through this study I hope to make visible the acquisition of at least some part of the physical sense of masculinity, of whiteness, of heterosexuality, and of the embodiment of a middle-class position and thereby contribute to the denaturalization of their dominance.[35]

GRACEFUL MEN?

Today grace is a defining characteristic of femininity, and therefore is an attribute whose absence defines masculinity. This was not always so. Delicate movement was once important for the bodily aesthetic of powerful aristocratic men.[36] When ballet developed in French and Italian Renaissance courts, noblemen employed it to flaunt their possession of the traits associated with their social positions.[37] That way of embodying dominance is difficult to imagine today, when delicate steps are as unacceptable for men as lace cuffs. When ballet traveled from palaces to the stage it developed into a different sort of spectacle. Mid-nineteenth-century ballets attracted men to theatres by showcasing ballerinas, not danseurs. Men in the audience may have appreciated the ballerina's artistry and technique, but also enjoyed the pleasure of gazing at a woman's body made beautiful through dance training. Dance historian Ramsay Burt argues that men who could easily enjoy watching a scantily clad woman could not publicly enjoy the spectacle of another man's physical charms.[38] Ballet was feminized in the nineteenth century, in ways that stigmatized male dancers and minimized the choreographic opportunities available to them.

Ballet is perceived as feminine because of its eroticism and its delicacy, both of which can be troubling embodiments for white middle-class men. Though a ballerina must be quite strong, ballet technique masks the effort involved in her performance and professional norms for extreme thinness, which grew more stringent in the twentieth century, contribute to the illusion of her frailty. By the beginning of the twentieth century the public additionally associated stage dance with gay men. Historian George Chauncey has argued that gay and dominant cultures are dynamic and mutually constitutive.

Heterosexually identified men constitute "themselves as 'normal' only by eschewing anything that might mark them as 'queer'."[39] When ballet became feminine and queer, men who wished to be perceived as normal stayed away from ballet studios and stages.

The gender coding of dance, and its association with men's homosexuality, has long been treated as a problem by dance advocates who felt that a feminized art form, and one associated with gay men, lacked legitimacy. Twentieth century dancers and dance instructors anxiously worked to align dance with what were perceived to be masculine traits.[40] For the early twentieth-century defenders of men who danced, controlled energy was the distinguishing characteristic of masculine grace. This formulation sought to make dancing men acceptable by dissociating grace from delicacy while fusing it to power. W. G. Anderson, director of the Yale University gymnasium at the beginning of the twentieth century and proponent of the inclusion of dance instruction in education described the difference between graceful and awkward men. The graceful man "conserves his physical energy, he spends just enough to make the movements accord with some standard that exists in the human mind. The other, performing the same evolutions, wastes his energy, is, in short, awkward."[41] In his "A Defence of the Male Dancer" modern dance pioneer Ted Shawn blamed the "decadent" and "freakish" Nijinsky for propagating the misconception that dancing must be effeminate.[42] Shawn dedicated his life to proving the manliness of dance through writing, interviews, the establishment of an all-male dance company, and the choreography he developed for them, which simulated hard physical labor. The dancers in Shawn's company clenched their fists to signify masculine power and bodily control as they moved between stiffly held poses.[43] In Shawn's choreography, grace was firmly linked to power, a coupling that appealed to dance critics. In Dallas, Texas, a reviewer told readers that Shawn's dancers were not "sissies" but rather were men with "extraordinary physiques, litheness, and power and grace."[44]

Defenders of men who danced masculinized grace by welding it to control, but their strategic yoking of grace and power failed to secure credibility for male dancers or to make grace acceptable for men. They were never able to remove dance's feminine taint.[45] A 1931 *American Dancer* article entitled "Control Not Grace" profiled actor Richard Cromwell who studied dance to improve his stage presence. "He had to overcome his awkwardness," the reporter wrote. "His thoughts immediately flew to the one solution—dancing. But, to study the ballet was out of the question, for he despises 'graceful' men and would on no account be one of them."[46] Even in the pages of the dance press, masculinity could be seen as incompatible with grace.

New York Times dance critic John Martin dismissed the effeminate dance staging of "self-expression, emotional unrestraint, chiffon waving, lamentations over dead birds, and sentimental prettiness," whether it was performed by men or women.[47] Dancers, regardless of gender, would have to eliminate eroticism and feminine forms of expression if dance were ever to be taken seriously. According to Martin, men's psychological constitution meant that they could, more easily than women, escape the pitfalls of eroticism, excessive emotion, and sentimentality and restore dance to its rightful position as "a man's art." Throughout the 1930s the dance trade publication *American Dancer* regularly denounced effeminate dancing as it offered highly conditional support for men who danced professionally. In its 1938 "In Defense of the Male Dancer," a contributor declared "Any dancing which is effeminate is bad dancing!"[48]

The large-scale mobilization of men into military service during World War II diluted the stigma associated with male dancing.[49] Wartime publications represented dancing men as the admirable bearers of U.S. culture abroad. The jitterbugging GI became a symbol of healthy heterosexual leisure as dance was promoted as a state-sanctioned substitute for the commercialized sex that the military feared would arise to serve soldiers. Even on stages, when the stages were attached to the war effort, men who danced provided entertainment for the troops, and their dancing was praised for its skill rather than denounced for its effeminacy. When the war ended, in the increasingly homophobic postwar period, the specter of the effeminate man who danced arose with renewed vigor. *Dance Magazine*, the successor to *The American Dancer*, returned to providing suggestions to dance teachers regarding instructional techniques that would circumvent the association of dance with effeminacy.

In 1964 a newspaper reporter asked Gene Kelly about dance's gender problem. Kelly, a dancing star in Broadway shows and Hollywood films in the 1940s and early 1950s, was known for an athletic and natural-appearing dance style that was frequently celebrated for its masculinity. The reporter opened the conversation by noting that "unless he's a Gene Kelly or a Fred Astaire, a man is a little suspect if he's a good dancer." Kelly responded by drawing on the grace with power convention to prove the masculinity of dance. "Dancing is a man's business" he explained, "but women have taken it over. In America, we equate grace with fragility and femininity. Actually, a woman cannot be as graceful as a man because she's not as strong. And strength is grace."[50] The reporter noted Kelly's virility at age fifty-one and showed readers that he was no mincing salad-eater. Kelly, the red-blooded man, ate chopped sirloin during the interview. Between bites he explained that he had not intended to become a dancer, but was pushed into it. "I came to New York in the '30s to be a director. But my talents were unnoticed by Broadway producers. The only way I could make a living was to perform." The happenstance of his professional dance career was central to representations of Kelly as a masculine dancer. It was the way his career was explained in a *New York Times* obituary, which quoted Kelly saying "I didn't want to be a dancer. I just did it to work my way through college. But I was always an athlete and gymnast, so it came naturally."[51] Like many other men who danced professionally, Kelly publicly attested that he had arrived at the career by chance and the irrepressible force of his talent.[52] Narratives of unintended dance careers are common in male dance autobiographies and serve to remove a man's accountability for having chosen a feminized profession.

DANCE AND CONTEMPORARY POPULAR CULTURE

Dance-themed television programs have proliferated in the past decade, often taking the form of competitions. *Dancing with the Stars* and *So You Think You Can Dance* have won huge audiences. Much of the dance presented in these programs involves heterosexual partners who perform choreography that stages romantic passion. The extent to which viewers are likely to experience these breathless, acrobatic romances as models of either everyday dance or love is questionable. The dancers on these programs are quite unlike their viewers. The would-be stars flaunt perfect bodies as they perform exhilarating choreography yet still face elimination as they are compared to even more dazzling competitors. These programs are very different from *American Bandstand* and *Soul Train*, the most popular dance and music programs of the 1960s, 1970s, and 1980s. *American Bandstand* and *Soul Train* brought parties into the nation's living rooms and invited viewers to join them. Though talented and attractive, their televised dancers still appeared to be ordinary people performing the kinds of dances people performed at parties. Viewers rose from their couches and danced in front of their television sets. The current shows do not invite viewers to dance, but only to electronically vote for their favorites and to exclude the losers from further competition. These programs have contributed to the popularity of dance as spectacular entertainment but do not make dance accessible as an everyday practice.

Nonetheless, in everyday life, many men continue to dance. Men and boys eschew stage dance but certain forms of popular dance are less troubling for them. The codified steps and often archaically polarized gender roles of highly structured forms such as tango tend to reduce masculine dance-floor anxiety. They provide men with a way of moving that can be mastered and set patterns for interaction. The emergence of hip-hop music and its associated dance styles have led to a resurgence of interest in dance among young men. Many of the dance styles performed to hip-hop music involve gymnastic feats and stylized aggressive gestures and are therefore perceived as masculine forms, even when they are performed by women.[53] Slam dancing, the style of dance performed at punk clubs, is another way of moving to music that is recognized as a masculine practice. It provides violent cover for dance's intimate interactions. "Freaking," also known as "grinding," a dance form in which couples sensuously move in close proximity to each other, can be a way for a young man to demonstrate sexual conquest.[54] In the performance of freaking among heterosexual pairs, women are expected to perform more of the erotic labor, and so gender difference is accentuated in the dance.[55] These varied dance forms provide solutions to the problems that dancing presents for masculinity. It is easier for many men to dance when dance is associated with physical intimidation, athleticism, or heterosexuality.

STRUCTURE OF THE BOOK

The perspective of the first half of this book is historical, covering the period from the beginning of the twentieth century through the 1970s. The book's second half addresses masculinity and dance in the present. The historical chapters identify which men danced in a given era, how they danced, and how they were perceived by their contemporaries. Chapters 2 and 3, which discuss periods ending in 1945, rely on archival and published sources. Beginning with chapter 4, which focuses on the post–World War II period, I bring in data from interviews I conducted with fifty men aged eighteen to eighty-six and from my participant observation in a college dance class. Interviews provided access to men's subjective accounts of the physical experience of and emotions evoked by dancing in public, perspectives that are more difficult to draw from archival records. Chapter 5's focus is sexuality; chapter 6 provides accounts of how contemporary men become dancers or non-dancers. Chapter 7 examines how race, as it is lived and imagined, shapes men's experience of dance.

The book begins with historical accounts as a way to provide critical distance from current assumptions about the bodies of Asian, black, Latino, and white men. A basic question motivated my initial historical explorations. Were there periods in the United States when most people assumed that white men could dance? The short answer is yes, for example, around

1914. At that time there was nothing exceptional about young white men wanting to dance, dancing well, and dancing often. At a minimum, that history unsettles contemporary truisms.

Beyond challenging the cliché that white men cannot dance, there is an additional reason to analyze historical shifts in public beliefs about race, gender, and dance. Groups have voiced dispositions toward dance to position themselves within social hierarchies. Their assertions had particular consequences and resonances because they described embodied talents, habits, and stances, and therefore appeared to be descriptions of natural differences. The history of public perceptions of the dancing man is complex. Beliefs about bodies are, like any ideology, contradictory agglomerations. While it is true that control has been central to popular understandings of masculinity, masculinity was also associated with passion, playfulness, and wild rebellion. These contradictory discourses, and the imperfect fit of any of them with what men actually did on dance floors, opened a great space for debate. The first half of the book shows how the public debated the meaning of race and gender categories as they learned new steps, refused to dance, campaigned for dance hall regulation, praised dance floor skill, or ridiculed finesse.

Chapter 2, "Who Killed the New Man?" looks back to 1900 and follows the ascendancy of dance as a popular amusement in the 1910s and 1920s. Even when dance was the most popular form of mixed-gender recreation, questions might be raised about a man's character if he danced the wrong way, at the wrong time of day, in a suspect place, when too young, or too old. These questions were raised by elites who worked to secure their positions through claims about the meaning of dance and the character of dancers. They promoted conceptions of normative adult masculinity that depended on its distance from an array of masculinities that they marked as immature, feminized, foreign, or immoral. By the end of the 1920s these problematic associations surrounded dancing men and kept many men, who wished to be seen as mature and dignified, off the dance floor.

During the Swing Era that followed, from 1935–1945, an athletic, partnered dance style known as the jitterbug gained great popularity among youth nationwide. Chapter 3, "Dancing in Uniform," examines representations of dancing men during the war years 1941–1945 when the military and associated civic organizations sponsored dances as recreation for soldiers. It traces how the meaning of male dancing shifted from effeminate, foreign, and dangerous to masculine and emblematically American when the nation's young men went to war. A national propaganda effort and the context of war muffled the contradictions surrounding the embodiment of masculinity, as dancing received the government's endorsement as wholesome recreation for soldiers.

Chapter 4, "Sad Sack's Sons: Dancing in the Postwar Years" examines transformations in the way dance was practiced and represented from 1946 through the rise and fall of disco. The gender conservatism and homophobia of the 1950s tightened constraints on men's movement, and then the rebellion of the 1960s appeared to release them. However, it was in the 1960s and 1970s that the truism that white men cannot dance became firmly established. The chapter explores how changes in postwar family life, enduring beliefs about masculine bodies, and the racial polarization of music and dance cultures combined to produce a new common sense about race, gender, and dance.

The analytical approach taken in the historical chapters, in which public assertions regarding men's bodies and dance are read for what they say about prevailing norms of social categorization, is applied to contemporary men in chapters 5, 6, and 7. Issues of sexuality, race, ethnicity, and class are present in every chapter of this book, but chapter 5, "Sex or 'Just Dancing,'" foregrounds sexuality as it examines the meanings attached to men's bodies, to bodily movement, and to dance. Many non-dancing men associate dance with sexuality and shrink from the possibility of appearing sexual in public. The chapter shows how the social constraints of heteronormativity produce men who are unmoved by the sound of music.

Chapter 6, "Home Schooling," chronicles how men learn to dance or learn to avoid dance. It shows that dancers and non-dancers are made at home, where they soak up cultures that informally teach boys to move or cultures that model masculinity as stolid and non-sensuous. Home cultures interact with the social expectations boys meet in neighborhoods and schools regarding how and how much they should move. The chapter considers the problems that rehearsing dance, being looked at, and looking may present for boys and men within gender regimes in which many men are expected to look but not to be the object of another's gaze.

Chapter 7, "Stepping On and Across Boundaries," considers the interplay between imagination and everyday performance in order to explore how race shapes masculine embodification. When talking about dance, men often referred to imagined others. They imagined those who danced easily and others who were predestined to physical awkwardness. Men described their own feelings on dance floors, judged the performances of other men, and made assumptions regarding the feelings other men have while dancing. As they spoke about physical grace and its absence, men employed racial and class terms. They placed their own bodies in racial, ethnic, or class categories, even if they did so to ultimately resist the popular meanings attached to the categorization. Imagined categories shape practice, and practice reconfigures the ways categories are imagined. When men practiced dance steps at home or performed them in public and when they ridiculed or praised others about the ways they moved, they defined membership in communities, imagined authenticity, and stretched, hardened, or denied the existence of social boundaries.

Together the historical and contemporary chapters describe two kinds of stance-taking in relation to dance. One is more collective, external, and voiced, the other individual, internal, and embodied. The historical chapters consider anti-dance campaigns as well as representations in newspapers, popular fiction, and propaganda efforts and highlight the first way of taking a stand regarding whether men should dance. This sort of stance-taking reveals how groups position themselves within race, gender, and class hierarchies by adopting a stance towards dance. The chapters on contemporary men show us men refusing to enter dance clubs, or entering but staying at the bar, staggering drunk to the dance floor and dancing with wild abandon, or dancing with great style. They show us men using their bodies to take stances toward dance as dancers, reluctant dancers, or sitters-out.

By studying how men have danced and how dancing men have been represented, this book traces long, unfolding, and interconnected processes of racialization and gender reconfiguration. It looks at how the problem of masculine embodiment is presented to and solved differently by different groups of men. Masculinity is not a natural way of being, or an unchanging set of behaviors, or a singular ideal. At any given moment and in any place it is a set of ways of being that have taken shape in relation to other past and present ways of being masculine and in relation to femininity. Nor is whiteness a natural way of being, an unchanging set of behaviors, or a singular ideal. It is a category in formation, shaped in relation to past and present racial categorizations. White heterosexual masculinity has a history during which the categories of white, heterosexual, and masculine became associated with particular forms of embodiment. White heterosexual masculinity is a continually reenacted project for those who claim it as their own. This study of dance seeks to uncover that history and set of contemporary experiences as part of the larger project of explaining how over and again race, gender, sexuality, and class change yet continue to appear timeless and natural.

CHAPTER 2

Who Killed the New Man?

Twentieth Century man thinks he does not like the new woman. But he does.
—Minnie J. Reynolds, *New York Times*, August 30, 1903

Never was there such a time. Emancipation is the password. The New Woman flings in the teeth of the tyrant Man her determination to "live her own life."
—Charles Willis Thompson, *New York Times*, September 20, 1925

Athletic and outspoken, hair cut into a short "bob," the new woman was a symbol of the gender and generational changes of the first two decades of the twentieth century. Dance halls were especially good places to watch her push the boundaries of feminine deportment.[1] In the 1910s and 1920s new dance steps allowed her to move independently of her partner's control or when connected to a partner, hold him scandalously close, placing her feet between his. The new woman's freedom was vividly and publicly displayed when she danced, but who was the new woman's partner? Was he a new man?

Men who unreservedly moved to jazz rhythms and danced cheek-to-cheek were undoubtedly experiencing their bodies in new ways, yet their new masculine embodiments went unnamed. More precisely, there was no new man who was unmarked by race or ethnicity. There were "new Negroes," whose unmarked gender was often male and whose unmentioned sexuality was sometimes gay, but the newness in the new Negro popularly signified a change in the meaning of race, not gender or sexuality.[2] There were also new Americans, European immigrants who were disproportionately male. Social workers and industrialists worked to melt their nonconforming masculinities into the pot. New women, new Negroes, and new Americans existed, but no new men.

Part of the explanation for the absence of the new man was that the white middle- and upper-class man's freedom to take part in the sexualized culture of nightlife, even in transformed public amusements, was assumed. His absence may also be seen as part of the effort to maintain the unmarked and dominant position of white masculinity at a moment when new women, new Negroes, and new Americans threatened white masculine privilege. Contemporary commentary about masculinity at the beginning of the twentieth century was largely defensive. Observers who noticed new ways of being masculine treated them as threats to the social order or symptoms of social decline. Rather than seeing newness in men's dancing, the middle class assimilated modified forms of dance into existing models of masculinity, ridiculed that part that could not be easily assimilated as sissified, or policed it as a dangerously foreign form of feminized menace. New ways of being masculine were displaced onto a set of disparaged unmanly men. New men who appeared on the scene were called "powder puffs" or vilified in xenophobic portrayals of swarthy, tango-dancing gigolos. These varied responses maintained the dominance of the old man over the new woman, white men over racial and ethnic others, and middle- and upper-class men over the poor.

In the 1910s and 1920s dancing men were everywhere, yet they left few traces in print. This chapter reads existing scholarship, archival sources, and fiction for glimpses of dancing men. It traces the meanings attached to masculine dancing and identifies dance as a practice through which dancers and observers sought to stabilize meanings of masculinity. At the beginning of the twentieth century there was an explosion of interest in dancing among youths who began to do relatively full-bodied and sensual dances that were known collectively as the animal dances—the bunny hug, the grizzly bear, and the turkey trot. By the 1910s these were replaced by the fox trot and other similarly subdued dances. Dancing continued to be a popular amusement through the 1920s.[3] Women have been the primary focus of historians of popular dance of the 1910s and 1920s.[4] These scholars found rich material in the records of social workers who sought to either reform or eliminate public dance halls. Primarily concerned with protecting women's chastity, social workers left records that are foremost accounts of the behavior of women. Men have a sketchy presence in these records as the victimizers of women, as social reformers who worked alongside the women leaders of dance hall reform campaigns, and very occasionally as vulnerable young men whose futures were placed at risk by the purported depravity of dance halls.[5]

Dancing men also skirt through the edges of masculine fiction at the beginning of the twentieth century. *The Virginian*, the novel that in 1902 established the western as a principal fictional genre for male readers, opens with a raucous all-male dance. Though most remembered for his singular jungle yell, Tarzan, the hero of the enormously popular series first published in 1912, also danced. Penrod, a character who first appeared in publication in 1913, was popular with young readers, and typified the "Good Bad Boy."[6] Like the earlier Tom Sawyer, or the later Dennis the Menace, Good Bad Boys are fictional characters who combine innate goodness with naughtiness to form ideal representations of young masculinity. Penrod lacked social graces, stepped on toes when on the dance floor, and charmed readers through his bad behavior. Sinclair Lewis published *Babbitt* in 1922 and introduced George Babbitt, the embodiment of middle-class masculine success and disappointment. Bad dancing was one of his many failings. These novels presented ideals of masculinity for popular consumption by boys and men.[7]

Dance is expressive movement. When an author sets a man in motion, his masculine character is revealed. The Virginian danced with other men, Tarzan with apes. Both Penrod and Babbitt found themselves in situations where they had to dance as part of a mixed-gender couple, and sunk in the occasion. What did dancing well or poorly say about fictional men and, by implication, about masculinity? Were they manly men or "sissies"?[8] Could white middle-class men dance at the beginning of the twentieth century without being considered sissies and, if so, when did the notion that dance was feminizing arise? This chapter answers these questions by drawing primarily on sources that purported to describe the actions of actual men. The Virginian, Penrod, Tarzan, and George Babbitt cut into the narrative from time to time to solve, in their own ways, the puzzle of white middle-class masculinity that presented itself at the beginning of the twentieth century.

The first part of this chapter will describe the fears that emerged in the early part of the twentieth century regarding the perceived dangers of boyhood dancing. By the beginning of the twentieth century physical education had become a regular part of public school education, and dance was often part of it. Some physical educators, however, began to question the pedagogical value, and social and psychological risks, of organized boyhood dancing. Others defended dance and attested to its physical, psychological, and social benefits for all children. Their debates unfolded amid larger concerns about the feminization of boys and masculinization of girls and eventually contributed to the feminization of dance. School policies also contributed to the infantilization of certain forms of dance, particularly gymnastic and folk dance, forms that the early physical education teachers distinguished from social dancing. Physical educators began to regard these forms of dance as wholesome exercise for girls of any age and for young boys, but as either a waste of time or moral hazard for older boys (fig. 2.1). As they educated immigrant children in public schools, they helped to shift European folk dance from a form of recreation open to all ages into an activity for children.

While curricular changes at the beginning of the twentieth century meant that fewer older boys would practice dance as part of physical education, young men of all classes found amusement and a way to meet women in dance.[9] Not only were more men dancing in the early decades of the twentieth century than in the nineteenth century, but the way in which men danced radically changed. The second part of this chapter looks at the meaning of dance in the lives of adult men of the 1910s and 1920s. As dance styles proliferated and allowed more individual expression, meanings proliferated as well. Couple dancing became synonymous with youthful heterosexual courtship and was most acceptable when performed by middle-class youth. Older white men who danced became subject to ridicule, while dancing could be a stigmatizing sign of degeneracy for ethnic, racialized, and working-class men.

Figure 2.1
School Children Learning a Dance. Washington, DC, circa 1899.
Photograph by Frances Benjamin Johnston. Library of Congress.

SHOULD BOYS DANCE?

The place of dance in physical education was the overarching theme of the 1905 annual meeting of the American Physical Education Association held in April at Columbia University's Teacher's College. Luther Halsey Gulick, a physician who directed physical education for the public schools of New York City, opened the annual convention with the most stirring image of dance he could imagine. He described a large black woman feeling the Holy Spirit in church in Alabama. Through the kind assistance of contacts among the southern clergy Gulick had the opportunity to visit a black church and, he claimed, to sit in the back, "unknown to the audience" so that he could "observe with unusual fullness." He described the effect of rhythmic music and the reiterative cadence of the preacher's voice upon the gathered. At a moment of special intensity "one woman, weighing, I should say, two hundred pounds jump[ed] straight into the air and then fell back into the pew behind the one in which she sat. The combined strength of four men was insufficient" to stop her.[10] Gulick's talk was a version of an "I was the only white there" boast, a white person's account of a visit to a majority-black setting to be the thrilled witness of expressive movement. Though they celebrate black expressivity and physical capacities, "I was the only white there" boasts have always been a way to damn with bold praise. They reinforce associations between blackness and the uncontrolled body and whiteness and rationality. In this case the account served to introduce a talk on the effects of rhythm on the human brain, a phenomenon Gulick formulated as a physiological law: "When rhythmical muscular movements are expressive of emotional states, they tend to intensify the attention." Influenced by the work of psychologist William James on the relationships between muscular action and emotion, Gulick was convinced that muscular action could have powerful moral and psychological consequences and that its potential could be harnessed by educators. Gulick began with the image of the black congregant in order to set up his conclusion. Dance was of special value in educating mentally disabled children. "When we consider the place of rhythm among savage and undeveloped people, it seems reasonable that it should be similarly so among the feeble-minded." Thus Gulick opened the 1905 convention whose purpose was to consider the value and place of dance in education.

Other speakers found value in dance training for all children. Henry Ling Taylor believed that hygienic, rational dance would properly stimulate the mind and body of any child.[11] C. Ward Crampton, who would succeed Gulick as the director of physical education for New York City's public schools, assumed that boys as well as girls should be taught dance through the high school grades and presented a paper on the best method to teach high school boys a basic dance step. There was a report of ballet instruction for young men and women at teacher education courses taught in the summer at Harvard, and W. G. Anderson reported on dance in physical education at Yale. Anticipating debates that would unfold over the next several years, E. H. Arnold's paper compared the degree of emphasis that should be placed on dance in the physical education of men and women.

The conference was a huge success for the association, drawing large audiences of members for the talks and an even larger audience for demonstrations of folk dances in the evening. Journalists covering the conference reported that the experts had decided that dance had an important place in physical education for boys as well as girls.[12] These reports, however, masked controversy surrounding masculinity and dance that had emerged in the meetings. As the editors of *American Gymnasia and Athletic Record* complained, "The daily newspapers have been busy saying many things concerning what the 'physical culture experts' did and decided concerning the efficaciousness of dancing, but half the statements are untrue and most the other half quite unreliable."[13] *American Gymnasia and Athletic Record*'s editors considered Arnold's paper, "Comparative Emphasis of Dancing for the Two Sexes," and the discussion that followed it, the highlight of the conference. Though Arnold allowed that American folk dances, such as the virginia reel, were excellent ways to provide wholesome recreation for the masses and should be encouraged, he argued that men were naturally more graceful than women, and hence it was a waste of time to provide men with dance training in schools. Arnold's conclusion provoked an audience member who rose to object. The differing athletic capacities of the sexes, the speaker countered, were due to the limits placed on women's activities. Their exchange was an early volley in a debate about how best to train boys' and girls' minds, bodies, and morals through physical education. In the evenings following the talks spectators could draw their own conclusions regarding gender and dance. Young men and women performed folk dances, and a group of men in their sixties brought the house down with a vigorous performance of the highland fling.

The discussions at the conference regarding the value of dance in physical education took place within the context of a growing moral panic about the depravity of popular social dances and widespread concern about the feminization of boys and masculinization of girls. The physical educators dealt with the first issue by distancing themselves from the latest social dances. Advocates of dance included only dances considered aesthetic, gymnastic, or folk in their curricula. Though folk dances were certainly sociable and may have involved heterosexual coupling, they were treated, by at least some teachers, as productive, innocent exercise and a valuable way to cultivate knowledge of European culture. Concerns regarding appropriate gender training that lurked in the background of the April 1905 conference subsequently gained greater attention in the professional debates of physical educators.

Educators had been troubled by some of the conclusions formed by a group of British academics led by Alfred Mosely, who had toured the United States in 1903 observing education at all levels from kindergarten through college. Their findings were published in 1904 as the *Reports of the Mosely Educational Commission*. According to one of the visitors, Professor Henry E. Armstrong, the proper goal of education was the production of virile men, a goal that was undermined by the preponderance of women teachers in American schools. He reported that "the boy in America is not being brought up to punch another boy's head or to stand having his own punched in a healthy and proper manner . . . there is a strange and indefinable feminine air coming over men; a tendency towards a common, if I may so call it, sexless tone of thought." Though less than a third of the twenty-six reports in the Mosely Commission volume mentioned the predominance of women teachers in American schools, and among those, only Armstrong was fervently and unequivocally against them, Mosely concluded that there was general "alarm" within the commission regarding the feminization of American boys and promoted this view in summaries of the commission's work.[14] In September 1905 Gulick attempted to address head-on charges that schools produced effeminate boys. Gulick responded to Mosely's concern by conceding that schools civilized boys when they taught them to control their impulses. This was indeed a feminine trait, but a necessary one for boys and men who live in populous cities. He argued furthermore that civilization was only a secondary virtue and one that boys could acquire without losing their primary virtues of "manhood, of independence, resolution, aggressiveness, bravery, individuality and capacity for heroism."[15]

Concern regarding the gender consequences of schooling was not laid to rest by Gulick's response, and he continued to speak publicly on the topic. While downplaying the risk of feminization of boys, he warned that especially vigorous forms of exercise would masculinize girls. Speaking before the Public School Physical Training Society, he explained that girl's athletic abilities declined as they approached womanhood. Strenuous exercise was unnatural for women, a law that became more apparent as girls matured. His proof was that high school girls were better athletes than the young women at Vassar College.[16] A year later, the American Physical Education Association's journal published an editorial comment that stressed the dangers of ignoring women's biological destiny for marriage and mother-hood. "Business life and independence in women tend to develop certain masculine qualities."[17] They urged physical educators to counteract the trend by keeping women out of competitive athletic games.

"Athletics for Girls" was the theme of the Association's next annual meeting, and Gulick's presidential address suggests that he may have been influenced by the dance advocates at the previous year's meeting. In a paper entitled "Exercise Must Be Interesting," Gulick tepidly endorsed a place for folk dance in physical education as a way to encourage exercise for children of the masses.[18] The meeting exposed considerable dissension regarding suitable physical activities for men and women. According to Dudley Sargent, director of the Harvard gymnasium, women's athletics had the potential to dismantle the very structure of society.[19]

> The time may come when effeminate man will succumb to virile woman. To post-pone that time, however, and to strive for the best interest of both sexes in the community at large, I think we should direct our efforts in mental and physical education towards the development of the highest ideals of the manly man and the womanly woman.

Women at the meetings challenged the stark division of physical activities along gender lines. Frances Kellor argued that athletics prevented nervous-ness in women and in fact minimized masculinity in them by discouraging habits of careless dress. Clara Fitch presented research that found that folk dancing was as good for boys as it was for girls.[20]

Folk dance was incorporated into many physical education programs in the 1910s, though mainly in activities for girls.[21] Elizabeth Burchenal was a physical education teacher who traveled to Europe at the beginning of the twentieth century to study and document folk dances. After returning to New York Burchenal was hired by the Girls' Branch of the Public School Athletic League and in 1909 was appointed Inspector of Girls' Athletics by the New York City Board of Education.[22] In each of these positions she promoted folk dancing for girls. She began organizing annual massive demonstrations of girls' folk dancing in Central Park, which grew, in time, to include ten thousand girls. Boys did not dance in these exhibitions, but instead served as security guards.[23] Dance historian Linda Tomko observed that these public performances of multitudes of girls dancing created spec-tacular demonstrations of gender difference.[24]

Boys continued to dance in many elementary schools, and men partici-pated in folk dancing at Y.M.C.A. facilities, but increasingly in the physical education literature, folk dance was presented as an activity for girls. In

1914 this became formalized within one of the nation's largest school systems. Ward C. Crampton, director of physical training for New York City schools, who roughly a decade earlier presented a paper on the best method for teaching dance steps to boys, had apparently by this time been swayed by concerns about the feminization of boys. He published a new standard physical education curriculum for the system, which mandated dance for girls and eliminated it for boys.[25] Excluding girls from some athletic activities and boys from all dancing, the curriculum was shaped by the fear that physical education could undo the natural gender order. It also solved another problem. Some New York City schools were racially integrated. In 1911, a parent in Flushing, Queens, claimed that his white daughter was traumatized after having been forced to dance with a black boy in school.[26] Keeping boys out of schoolyard dancing would maintain white purity.

WHICH MEN DANCE?

At the beginning of the twentieth century effeminate men were disparaged as "overcivilized," men who had been ruined through the combined forces of urban life, education, and indoor employment.[27] Physical educators, believing that curricula shaped gender, felt challenged to stem the feminization of American manhood and eliminated dance from the physical education of older boys. Does this mean that dancing was feminized generally? Was the dancing man always a sissy, or could the rhythmic, sensual, and abandoned act of dancing be a way for men to publicly express masculinity? The answer is a complex one, shaped by the class structure of dancing and the changing styles of movement that emerged in the 1910s (fig. 2.2).

Changes in the character of masculine play were set in motion by changes in masculine work. Middle-class men in the 1910s and 1920s were urban office workers, toiling indoors in increasingly bureaucratized workplaces. Historian George Chauncey notes that "the number of salaried, nonpropertied workers grew eight times between 1870 and 1910" and historian Gail Bederman found that during the same period "the proportion of middle-class men who were self-employed dropped from 67 percent to 37 percent."[28] Bederman argues that what ensued was not a crisis of masculinity but merely masculinity's reestablishment on new grounds. According to Bederman "there is no evidence that most turn-of-the-century men ever lost confidence in the belief that people with male bodies naturally possessed both a man's identity and a man's right to wield power." When independent employment no longer served as the basis for male domination, a belief in a superior masculine essence took its place.

Figure 2.2
Dancing at a Service Club. Washington, DC, World War I.
Library of Congress.

Changes in men's working lives led to changes in male leisure. Historians of masculinity have argued that the loss of autonomy at work led middle-class men to seek fulfillment through consumption, leisure, and self-expression.[29] Male leisure expanded beyond the homosocial contexts available to men in the nineteenth century into mixed-gender restaurants, cabarets, and dance palaces. Within these venues men watched and learned to perform improvisational, expressive, and sensual modern dances as entirely new bodily practices. Yet if men found new possibilities for self-expression in movement, they also encountered dangers there. The dance floor and the controversies that surrounded it were theatres for the contestation of legitimate forms of masculine embodiment. Physical expressivity, sensuality, and grace never became the grounds for a reconstituted masculinity. Dominance over others and physical and emotional self-control continued to be hallmarks of white middle-class masculinity. Countless white men found pleasure in dance in the 1910s and 1920s, but nonetheless, the more a man was associated with dance, the more his masculinity was at risk. Men could dance, but a man whose primary public identity was that he was a dancer was suspect. The very moves professional dancers made to reassert dance as a masculine practice contributed, in the end, to the feminization of dance.

In a study of women in dance halls at the beginning of the twentieth century musicologist Susan C. Cook wrote that social dance is a "bounded sphere" in which women "test boundaries of 'good' and 'bad' sexuality."[30] Which boundaries did men test on the dance floors between 1900 and 1929? Not a boundary between good and bad sexuality but between good and bad men. Merely by having women in their arms, men certified their "good" sexuality, that is to say, their desire for women. Rather than testing the boundaries between good and bad sexuality, men tested gender boundaries marked by ethnicity, citizenship, and class. Between 1900 and 1929 social dance was a bounded sphere in which how a man moved, where, with whom, and at what time of day, tested and marked the boundaries between good and bad men, that is, between white and not-yet-white men, citizen and foreigner, and between men who supported themselves by legitimately masculine or criminally feminized means.

There was not one representative dancing man but an array of types, often popularly mapped to different class locations and racial and ethnic groups. Men who danced included cultivated and culturally dominant members of the upper class, dance instructors who steadily worked to defend their reputations, college students whose popularity rested on their ability to dance, purportedly dangerous paid dance partners, older members of the middle class whose dancing others challenged as inappropriate, and perhaps most numerous of all, "tough dancers": young men who went to public dance halls and performed the latest steps. These steps involved sensual movements and a level of intimate contact with partners that shocked social reformers. Out of all these types no recognizable new man emerged. On the contrary, these cultural representations of normative, failed, or dangerous masculinities stabilized the existing racialized, heteronormative, gender order.

CULTIVATED MEMBERS OF THE UPPER CLASS

At the turn of the century, private dances were the center of elite social life. Socially successful upper-class men danced. This is not to say that all upper-class white men danced. Social columnists frequently remarked on the problem of inadequate numbers of male partners for women who wished to dance. Dance historian Elizabeth Aldrich notes that this problem increased in the last quarter of the nineteenth century as growing numbers of upper-class men spent a greater portion of their leisure time in men's clubs.[31] On February 5, 1893, a *New York Times* reporter wrote, "The man who doesn't dance . . . is so common that his complement, the dancing man, has added value." On July 30 the same year a reporter commented, "Just now there is a scarcity of dancing men at the seaside resorts." In 1896 the *New York Times'* social column reported the good news that there was "no scarcity of dancing men in Washington," but in 1902 another article described the frustration of a society matron whose organized ball was ruined by the young men who would not dance. Many upper-class men refrained from dance, but there was no stigma attached to masculine dancing. On the contrary, dancing was a way to perform credible, upper-class white masculinity. An upper-class man danced as the leading half of a heterosexual couple. His torso remained erect, and his hips were still. He used his arms to guide his partner as his feet took measured steps around the dance floor.

Elisha Dyer was a distinguished member of the upper classes whose main distinction was his dancing ability. In August 1900 at her villa on Rhode Island's Newport Cliffs, Mrs. Ogden Goelet gave a dinner in honor of her daughter Miss May Goelet. A Hungarian band played during and after the dinner when two hundred additional guests arrived to dance a cotillion. In 1900 in the United States the word cotillion was used to describe a choreographed dance in which the movements of all of the couples were coordinated with every other couple to create an overall effect that left no room for improvisation. Such synchronicity was possible because all of the guests had been groomed from childhood to take part in a cotillion. The guests at Mrs. Goelet's dinner arrived ready to follow the direction of the two men designated as the evening's leaders, Mr. Harry Lehr and Mr. Elisha Dyer. Harry Lehr danced with the honored Miss Goelet; Elisha Dyer with Mrs. Cornelius Vanderbilt Jr.[32] This is how the American upper class entertained in 1900. They danced at lavish invitation-only balls, held in the evening in palatial but private homes or in a small number of exclusive restaurants. They danced to live European music, and the hostesses of these balls made efforts to link themselves to past European grandeur. Servants dressed in costumes from the Louis XIV period distributed trinkets to Mrs. Goelet's guests. Following the cotillion, the guests returned to the dance floor to dance in couples to the band's continuous music. Their dancing stopped at daylight.

Elisha Dyer, one of the leaders of the evening's cotillion, led cotillions at many balls. When he died in 1917 his obituary's headline declared "ELISHA DYER DIES; COTILLION LEADER" and noted that Dyer, one of the most popular men in the Newport summer colony, was regarded as the best dancer in Newport society.[33] Though he was a well-to-do stockbroker and the son of a former governor of Rhode Island, leading cotillions was the principal thing for which he was remembered. Elisha Dyer personified the good dancing man at the turn of the century. He was white, married, earned money from money, and danced with women of his own class. He gave attention to his appearance and yet was not characterized as feminine within his social world.[34] Layers upon layers of masculine dominance were structured into upper-class dancing. Within heterosexual couples, men led partner dances that were smaller components of choreographed cotillions commanded by men like Elisha Dyer. These dances took place within private social worlds built upon accumulated masculine wealth. All elements of the dance, including its rigid posture, the heterosexual partnering, the direction of the entire cotillion, and the exclusivity of the setting, reinforced the existing gender, class, and racial order.

The compatibility of the structured dancing of the upper class to a male-dominant gender order is starkly revealed when moved to the world of upper-class fantasy. Owen Wister, author of *The Virginian*, was born into a wealthy East Coast family. He attended exclusive boarding schools, was a classmate and friend of Theodore Roosevelt at Harvard University, and was a graduate of Harvard Law School.[35] He dedicated *The Virginian*, his 1902 novel about crooked card games, cattle rustling, lynching, and skirmishes with Native Americans, to Roosevelt. Its success inspired so many imitators that within time they were recognized as a new literary genre, the western. *The Virginian*'s first chapter title, "Enter the Man" signals the author's intent to tell us about masculinity. The "man" is the Virginian, a cowboy who epitomizes masculinity to the urban, eastern visitor who narrates the tale. He observed the cowboy and thought "in his eye, in his face, in his step, in the whole man, there dominated a something potent to be felt, I should think, by man or woman."[36] The Virginian and the narrator were traveling and had to spend the night, and potentially share beds, at the town's combined saloon and guesthouse with itinerant salesmen. The salesmen were urbanites in the Wild West, "two Jews handling cigars, one American with consumption killer, and a Dutchman with jew'lry."[37] There to hawk goods made by others, and in the case of the Jews, insufficiently white, these men lacked the dominating potency of the Virginian and would be publicly unmanned by the evening's end.

Given the distastefulness of his possible bedmates, the Virginian wagered that he would be able to claim an entire bed for himself. The salesmen went to separate beds early, while the Virginian and other cowboys played cards in the saloon. Later the Virginian climbed into bed with the American, the salesman "that look[ed] like he washed the oftenest." As his fellow cowboys clustered in silence at the door, the Virginian placed his knife and gun under his pillow and cautioned his still awake bedmate that once or twice a year he had nightmares of fighting Indians. If awakened suddenly during one of these episodes, he was likely to grab his knife, and might possibly, while still asleep, use it. The Virginian briefly feigned sleep and then commenced to holler. The terrified salesman sprang out of his bed and ran, unsuspecting, toward the crowd of cowboys at the door. They grabbed him and forced him into passive dance partnership in a virginia reel, an American folk dance in which women are passed from one man to the next. While being flung, undressed, from man to man, the salesman begged to be allowed to put on his boots. Ignoring his pleas, the jubilant cowboys continued the rapacious dance, yelling "feed the machine," and yanking each of the outsiders, including the narrator, into feminized partnership. As the evening wound down, the cowboys shifted to music-making and drinking, and finally went outside, where they went to sleep, uncoupled, on blankets under the open sky. The urban, eastern narrator asked himself, "What world am I in? Does this same planet hold Fifth Avenue?"[38] Though painting them as patently different worlds, Wister transported the masculine order of Fifth Avenue dance to the raucous frontier. In Wister's imagined West, real men dance, and they dominate through dance. Undressed, tricked, being thrown from man to man and made to spin against their will, the salesmen were emasculated for the evening's amusement. Written by Wister as good clean fun, the scene reaffirms a gender order displayed ritually in dance. Dance could be a manly activity when it was used to command a passive partner.

TOUGH DANCERS AND SPIELERS

Wister's narrator might have asked "what world am I in" had he stepped into a working-class dance in New York City. Working-class men and women danced on small dance floors attached to saloons and in rented halls at dances sponsored by fraternal lodges. The couples in these halls danced to jazz music that originated in black communities. Their dances were not choreographed, and often involved close embrace. The syncopated rhythms of the music performed in these halls encouraged playful improvisation as dancers chose to accent different beats. Steps that originated in black dance halls were picked up by white stage performers and imitated in attenuated forms by youth of all social classes. Some of the dances acquired animal names: the bunny hop, turkey trot, and grizzly bear. As these dances spread, reformers called them "animal dances" and used that moniker to describe them as "vicious" in campaigns to close or reform dance halls. They bolstered their attacks on the dance halls with the unsubstantiated but alarming information that nine out of ten unmarried mothers met the father of the child at a public dance, and that even the cleaned-up versions of the turkey trot that were danced by debutantes at society balls were social problems because they gave legitimacy to the unwholesome animal dances performed by the masses.[39] Campaigns like these succeeded in the enactment of hundreds of laws written into municipal and state codes that licensed, limited the hours, and proscribed activities in dance halls, but that ultimately did little to discourage dancing at commercial establishments.[40] After 1910 huge dance palaces opened that kept entrance prices low enough to attract up to three thousand dancers on a Saturday night.[41]

The freer dance styles of the working class spread in attenuated forms to young members of the upper class, for whom improvisational couple dances were more appealing than the rigid conformity of the cotillion, until on July 12, 1912, the cotillion's death was announced in the society pages. "COTILLION ABANDONED" the headline proclaimed; "Society at Newport Gives it up for Less Normal Measures." "Less normal" in this case was the more usual, but unscripted, couple dancing. Mrs. Stuyvesant Fish, one of the most important of society's hostesses, discarded her plans to have Elisha Dyer lead a cotillion at the largest party of Newport's summer season. The less normal had become popular, even among the upper class. Commercial establishments of all types laid down dance floors to create new spaces to accommodate the increased demand for dancing. Cabarets in which exhibition dancers had entertained diners extended their floors to make room for customers who would rather dance than watch.[42]

The new dances and dance halls opened up new ways of moving that changed public physical interactions between men and women. There was more room for individual expression. Improvisation gave women some freedom from the command of their partners' lead. Dancers learned to move their previously still shoulders, torsos, and hips. Unbridled movement not only transformed dancers, but also provided a different group of upper- and middle-class men and women with a new sense of purpose in activism against what they saw as dangerous public obscenity. Dance hall reform campaigns were led by white middle- and upper-class women on behalf of young working-class women.

Campaigns to protect young men from the dangers of dancing were less common. Where they existed, they were often led by men who were inspired by religious conviction to be concerned with the development of proper masculinity. Luther Gulick, who after leaving his position as director of physical education for the public schools of New York City, helped to found both the Boys Scouts and Camp Fire Girls, and direct the Department of Child Hygiene of the Russell Sage Foundation, was exceptional in his concern regarding the moral dangers of the wrong kind of dance for boys. He viewed control of physical sex impulses as a battle that young men must win if they were to develop into healthy Christian men. Strongly influenced by the writing of William James on the relationships between bodily movement and emotion, Gulick advised boys to protect their minds by limiting the experiences of their bodies. Once a youth experienced intimate contact with a woman, the image would linger in his mind as an enemy within. In his 1917 book on the proper development of male character he warned that "dancing can be, and often is, done in a way to bring to consciousness the physical contact" and that sort of dancing must be avoided.[43] While Gulick was director of its Department of Child Hygiene, the Russell Sage Foundation produced an Edison photoplay about "Charlie," a decent young man whose visit to a dance hall led to his rapid moral decline from sober worker to unemployed idler.[44]

Conservative Protestants were among the anti-dance campaigners and linked dance to a disparaged sensuality, which they located primarily in women's bodies. The widely popular early twentieth-century evangelist Billy Sunday preached against dancing. In an anti-dance sermon delivered before a large crowd in 1917 he linked dance with sensuality, and sensuality with effeminacy, to impugn the manliness of men who danced.[45]

They tell you and me that they love to dance for the exercise. It is nothing of the kind. People dance because of the mingling of the sexes—the social attractions. Why don't a man dance with his wife? Why, he would rather stay out all night husking corn in the moonlight. If you made the men dance by themselves and the women dance with each other public dancing places would close up in two weeks.

His tirade appears to associate the sensuality of dance with men and women, but from his pulpit that day, Billy Sunday mimed womanish dancing while condemning dance as an expression of lust. The feminization of sensuality and its disparagement is also present in a pamphlet distributed to recreation directors about the same time by the Mormons. Dancing was permissible but not when embraces were close enough for faces to touch, a position described as the "sissy-boy hold." The phrase feminized physical closeness, even when it involved heterosexual contact. The implication was that real men eschewed public intimacy.[46]

It was much more common for social reformers to wage anti–dance hall campaigns on behalf of endangered women.[47] Belle Israels was a leader of dance hall reform, working at the head of the Committee on Amusements and Vacation Resources of Working Girls.[48] She had great sympathy for young working women and did not blame them for attending dance halls, but viewed commercial halls as public menaces and campaigned against them. In her view the dances permitted in commercial dance halls were by themselves corrupting. "You cannot dance night after night," she argued, "held in the closest of sensual embraces, with every effort made in the style of dancing to appeal to the worst that is in you, and remain unshaken by it."[49] Israels advocated for licensing of dance halls, limiting the sale of liquor and the days and hours of operation, and requiring managers to refuse entry to "questionable persons," a category that was, perhaps, left deliberately vague. She also worked surreptitiously to establish alternative dance halls where young people would dance in policed and sanitized safety, without knowing that the facility had been organized and supervised by social workers.[50]

References to men in anti-dance campaigns generally identify them as the sources of women's corruption. The most common man in the records of dance hall reform movements is the "spieler," a young man employed by the dance hall to dance with women who had no partners. Israels vilified spielers, arguing that they were part of the network that entrapped innocent women and transformed then into prostitutes. "Whether the spieler is part of an organized system for supplying girls to houses of prostitution is questionable, but he is part of that underworld which spreads its network for that most attractive of captures—the young and innocent girl."[51] Journalist and social worker Rheta Dorr characterized the spieler as "not uncommonly a worthless fellow; sometimes he is a sinister creature, who lives on the earnings of the unfortunate girls."[52] The presence of the spieler suggests that there may have been a shortage of unpaid male dancers on the floor. Yet while dancing may have been even more favored by women, dance halls were widely popular with young working men. A survey of working men conducted around 1913 found that almost half of men who worked eight or nine hours a day regularly went to dance halls in their free time and over a third of respondents aged seventeen to twenty-four said they attended dances regularly.[53] The dance halls were undoubtedly filled with young, single, employed men, who danced among a smaller number of professional partners. Louise de Koven Bowen, president of the Chicago Juvenile Protection Association, reported that there were always more men than women at dances.[54] Most reformers viewed men in dance halls as victimizers rather than victims. Relatively progressive reformers like Belle Israels occasionally allowed that some young men in the halls had "no deliberate intention to seek out the girl for wrongful purposes."[55] As she noted these exceptions, Israels commented that the harmless boys were most often the "light-hearted Irish," a remark that left readers with the impression that darker immigrants and black young men were more likely to be dangerous. Less charitable reformers noted no exceptions among the men at dance halls. Chicago reformer Bowen warned that "crowds of young men attend with the sole idea of meeting girls for immoral purposes."[56] Reformers such as Gulick, Bowen, and Israels thought the only lesson a man or woman could learn from the experience of full-bodied or intimate dancing was depravity. Obscured by reformers' focus on spielers and ruined women, thousands of men danced new dances in these halls without producing a new way of seeing masculinity.

DANCE AND CIVILIZATION

In 1912 dance reformers began to focus their reform efforts upward at the dances being performed in the private functions of the upper class. Convinced that the sensual abandon of the dances themselves endangered working women, reformers felt it was important to stop their spread to debutante balls. If accepted by the upper class, the "tough" dances would have greater legitimacy and there would be no way to banish them from the lives of more vulnerable working women. Members of the Committee on Amusements and Vacation Resources of Working Girls began publicizing the shocking news that debutantes were performing tough dances, and Belle Israels planned a media event to raise public indignation. She invited six hundred social workers, clergymen, city officials, and additional guests, whose class position is indicated by reports that they arrived in "silks and fine furs," to a meeting to discuss the problem of tough dancing. To dramatize the vulgarity of the dances to those who may not have had the opportunity to see them performed, two pairs of professional ballroom dancers, including Al Jolson and his partner Florence Cables, demonstrated the intimate contact involved in cheek-to-cheek dancing and the bodily gyrations of the animal dances. It is difficult to know whether the audience, whose reactions shifted from nervous laughter to hearty applause, left outraged by or appreciative of the new dances.[57] Nonetheless the campaigns against the tough dances were beginning to have some effect. Dancers continued to favor the dances, but dance hall owners began to feel pressure to ban them.[58] Maurice Mouvet, a popular dance instructor, wrote a letter to the *New York Times* to protect his reputation by distancing himself from the dances.[59]

I have remained quiet in the face of rather drastic criticism for a long time—or, at least, it seems so to me—but now I feel that I should say something in my own behalf. Will you bear with me, please? I have not brought to America that dance they call the "turkey trot" nor the "grizzly bear" nor the "bunny hug." In fact, until I arrived here I did not know of these dances, and then I find them nothing . . . May I say this: I would not teach any of these dances to a maiden. I have not and would not. My own repertoire is extensive enough, and, I hope, artistic enough, to win me the place I work for as a dancer.

Many among the middle class wanted to continue to dance—in fact dance was their most popular public amusement—but they also felt the need to appear respectable. Lewis Erenberg and Susan C. Cook have chronicled how professional ballroom dancers Irene and Vernon Castle tamed the animal dances to render them respectable.[60] Vernon Castle changed the meaning of dance while leaving conceptions of masculinity intact. Irene and Vernon Castle were the most celebrated exhibition ballroom dancers of the 1910s (fig. 2.3). Vernon Castle's dancing was acceptable to the middle class because it minimized sensuality and emphasized control. As a performer and advocate of social dance forms that minimized shoulder or torso movement, Vernon Castle embodied a style that appeared elegant to middle-class viewers.

His wife and dance partner Irene Castle, an American woman, exuded youthfulness and health. As one of the trendsetters of bobbed hair, she was a new enough woman to be appealing to young women. She was, nonetheless, in many ways conventionally feminine and danced primarily with her husband, and so appealed to older generations of women as well. Vernon was British, thin, and an exceedingly stylish dresser. They were both brilliant social dancers, though Vernon's body and his movement style were sometimes perceived as a bit humorous. A review of one of his early performances reported that "Vernon Castle, a weirdly tall and thin youth, acts as if his legs and arms had gone insane."[61] Irene and Vernon Castle became exhibition ballroom dancers during the height of the early twentieth-century dance craze, when a changing array of dances with frenetic steps, improvisational freedom, pelvic- and shoulder-shaking and partner-hugging shocked older generations. Through their exhibition dances, their New York school, and their published dance manuals, the Castles established versions of these dances that were acceptable to middle- and upper-class whites. The last page of their popular 1914 dance manual plainly states, "Do not wriggle the shoulders, Do not shake the hips, Do not twist the body. Do not hop—glide instead. Drop the Turkey Trot, the Grizzly Bear, the Bunny Hug. These dances are ugly, ungraceful, and out of fashion."[62] Smoothly

Figure 2.3
Irene and Vernon Castle. Circa 1914.
Library of Congress.

gliding and holding his carriage erect, Vernon Castle embodied a manliness that was not visibly sensual, a manliness of men who do not move their hips. It was a performance of masculinity that won the approval of critics of the wilder dances, but which diminished his masculinity in the eyes of the broader public.

At the beginning of 1916, while World War I raged across Europe, Vernon Castle announced his intention to join the British forces as a fighter pilot. Though turning away from his career as a professional dancer, he was initially ridiculed by the American press. "Vernon, the tall, the slender, the fragile and debonair, is to give up dancing and become an explorer of the air . . . his recent life of luxury has unfitted him for the trenches."[63] The derision continued as newspapers mocked him for delaying his departure and linked his hesitancy to his profession.

> Despite his determined efforts to get to the front and stop the war by annihilating the German army, Vernon Castle doesn't seem to be able to get away.

Daily for the past month he has missed a taxicab, a train, a steamer, an airship or some other kind of vehicle chosen to carry this irrepressible, precipitous hero to the warring countries. Almost nightly, his eyes blazing with feverish excitement, he has set forth to put a crimp in the Germans, and something always has happened to hold him at the Hippodrome, the Domino Room, the Beaux Arts or similar places that are strictly neutral. For instance, on Monday evening, Mr. Castle left his apartment, irrevocably resolved to sail immediately for Europe and throw a scare into Teuton forces, but by the worst misfortune his route took him past the New Amsterdam Theatre, where one-stepping tunes from the Ziegfield "Midnight Frolic" caused his feet to go astray, and it was 2 o'clock in the morning before he regained his equilibrium sufficiently to realize that he had missed another battle.[64]

Irene defended his masculinity in interviews, assuring the press that Vernon was confident "in his ability to cross the channel and make the enemy suffer."[65] Two weeks later the *Toledo Blade* kept the scorn alive, in an article that took particular aim at his feminized attention to grooming. Vernon Castle would have been fighting Germans already except for

having to stop to get manicured, or having to turn back and fetch some toilet article he had omitted from his service kit . . . It seems that this time, however, Vernon is really prepared to make his precipitous dash for the front. In St. Louis Mrs. Castle looked over his wardrobe carefully and declared that there was not so much as a silk sock missing from his knapsack, and that he was thoroughly equipped either to wipe out the German army or perform a tango.[66]

Vernon Castle did enter the British air force and tragically died in a crash on February 15, 1918. His death while flying a military plane led to an outpouring of testimonials from the press regarding Vernon's unexpected heroism. In death Castle was recognized as a man because of his military service but despite his thin body, advanced fashion sense, and ability to dance. Susan C. Cook was the first to write about journalists' responses to Castle's death and to note that his military death brought on a chorus of tributes to his masculinity.[67] My analysis of the sources uncovered by Cook differs only in my attention to the stability of the gendered meanings attached to his dancing. The obituaries, which emphasize his manly conduct in war, nonetheless show that by 1918 dancing, at least Vernon Castle's kind of dancing, was characterized as sissy. Days after his death an ode to Vernon Castle appeared in the *Ohio State Reporter*:

How could we tell, who only knew
The empty nimbleness of you?
We saw the lanky harlequin prance,
We watched the fox-trot teacher dance.
We did not dream that you were set
For aught except to pirouette.
How well you hid a doughty heart,
How well you played a mummer part!
While burly slackers who had sneered
At your frail measure, shrank and feared
The battle trench
You did not blench,
Where death called eagles to the clouds
To win their glory and their shrouds

Irene Castle embodied the new woman.[68] Why wasn't her partner, whose form of embodiment was as challenging to conventions as hers, considered a new man? Cook notes that Irene Castle's "thin, boyish figure, so unlike the s-curve look of the earlier bustle period, was regularly commented upon in the newspaper (as was Vernon's thinness) and would become the modern figure of the 1920s."[69] Irene's body established a new ideal for feminine beauty; Vernon's was the source of mild amusement. His marriage to the era's ideal young woman secured his masculine credibility to a limited extent, but as a professional dancer, a physically slight man, and a dandy, he was never considered manly. Vernon Castle was able to establish new norms for dancing, but not for masculinity. His controlled, gliding, and elegant style of embodying masculinity remained suspect among the arbiters of manliness.

Yet Vernon could not have moved otherwise and maintained the white middle-class respectability he and his benefactors sought to establish for dance. Sensual movement, particularly hip movement, signified a disparaged, uncivilized blackness. This connection was made explicit in the advice to dancers offered by dance instructor Edward Scott. He felt compelled to alert unsuspecting white dancers to the African origins of the "alien body actions that more or less infested all" contemporary dances.[70] The movements stemmed from what he described as a characteristically African appreciation of the buttocks. Scott strove to establish a masculine bodily aesthetic that could claim a position of supremacy because of its distance from blackness. The embodiment of respectability that men like Vernon Castle and Scott sought to establish sidestepped one prejudice but was caught by another. Male dance instructors could escape the stigma associated with racialized sensuality by constraining their movements. However by doing so they fell into another trap, that of being seen as men whose overly disciplined bodies made them feminine.

The admired position of the upper-class dancing man disappeared along with the era of the cotillions. When cotillions declined, masculine grace was primarily visible in popular parodies of European, priggish, but ultimately servile dancing masters. In 1913 Booth Tarkington published the first of his Penrod stories. Penrod was a very popular children's series about an endearingly bad Midwestern eleven-year-old boy. In a story published in his first Penrod collection, Tarkington placed Penrod in dance class, under the tutelage of the overly formal Professor Bartet, whose foreignness was indicated in dialect. Penrod fidgeted, scratched, could not keep time, and defied his dance master. Bad dancing and resistance to authority made Penrod a real boy. An illustration depicted Penrod hunched over with a look of surprise as his dance partner rubbed her recently stepped-on toe. In a subsequent story Penrod was invited to a party and there saw Marjorie, the girl on whom he had a terrible crush. Unable to ask her to dance, he stood in the doorway with other shy boys while watching his rich classmate Maurice Levy dance with his secret beloved. Penrod and his friends began pushing and he allowed himself to be shoved into Marjorie and Maurice. Soon the dance floor was a minor riot of pushing and yelling, its composure ruined by boisterous masculinity. Later in the party Marjorie revealed that she liked Penrod the best and the story's lesson is revealed. Real boys don't dance.

Recall, however, that Tarzan danced. Edgar Rice Burroughs began the immediately successful series of adventure books with *Tarzan of the Apes*, published in 1914. Tarzan was John Clayton, Lord Greystoke, a noble Englishman orphaned as an infant in an African jungle and nurtured by apes. Raised lovingly by his adoptive ape mother, Tarzan's noble British blood destined him to develop physical, intellectual, and moral supremacy over apes and Africans. Trained by the apes to swing from trees and to hunt, he developed an extraordinary physique. Burroughs described a ritual dance, which the apes performed each time they killed an enemy. After a killing Tarzan joined the dance and became

> one of the wild, leaping horde. His brown, sweat-streaked, muscular body, glistening in the moonlight shone supple and graceful among the uncouth, awkward, hairy brutes about him. None was more stealthy in the mimic hunt, none more ferocious than he in the wild ferocity of the attack, none who leaped so high into the air in the Dance of Death.[71]

Brown, though only because of a tan, muscular, sweaty, and ferocious, he was so superlatively masculine by the prevailing standards of the 1910s that he could also be graceful. Historian John Pettegrew identified the importance of the image of the brute as an exemplar of masculinity within the United States between 1890 and 1920.[72] Tarzan gave finesse to the brute, and in so doing embodied a racialized and racist masculinity, one that claimed gender and racial superiority. No ordinary brute, Tarzan innately carried civilization to the jungle. Driven by an inborn sense of morality, Tarzan covered his genitals with the skins of the animals he slaughtered. Combining, and even surpassing, the primitive physical power of an ape, with the assumed morality, beauty, and grace of European civilization, he embodied a perfect fantasy of white masculine supremacy.

Vernon Castle, an actual dancer, had too much civilization and barely a drop of the brute. Castle freely admitted that he and Irene translated and modified African American and Latin American dances for North American whites.[73] They regularly visited dance clubs in Harlem to observe black dancers and musicians. Dance historians Marshall and Jean Stearns quoted black dancer Ethel Williams saying that the Castles visited her home to learn new steps.[74] White commentators of the era characterized African American dances and dancers as primitive, lacking technique, and vulgar. This sentiment is captured in a letter from a British peeress originally published in the *London Times* but reprinted in 1913 in the *New York Times*.[75] The new dances were

> scandalous travesties of dancing which are, for the first time in my recollections, bringing more young men to parties than are needed. I need not describe the various horrors of American and South American negroid origin. I would only ask hostesses to let one know what houses to avoid by indicating in some way on their invitation cards whether the "Turkey Trot," "the "Boston," (the beginner of the evil,) and the "Tango" will be permitted.

A reporter, perhaps more attuned to the rapidly changing styles and writing in 1914, noted that the African elements had been removed from the current dance styles. "True it is that the turkey trot, as it was danced hereabout two years ago, when it started as a craze, smacked strongly of the Dahomey-Bowery-Barbary Coast form of revelry, but since then it has been trimmed, expurgated, and spruced up until now it is quite a different thing."[76] The Castles played a major part in expurgating the turkey trot's sensuality. Accompanied by the music of black composer and band leader James Reese Europe, the Castles removed much of the full-bodied expressiveness from black dances but retained elements of their syncopated rhythms to produce a dance style that the middle and upper classes welcomed as fresh but acceptable.[77] The Castles also translated working-class black dances for middle-class blacks. Some middle-class blacks were as dismayed by the sensuality and bodily freedom of popular dances in the 1910s as were their white counterparts.[78] In 1914, the Castles performed their moderated dances at Harlem's Manhattan Casino for an enthusiastic black audience.[79] The Castles' style of controlled dancing propelled them into stardom while failing to reshape conventions of masculinity. Vernon Castle was recognized as a great dancer, but only became a great man when he abandoned dancing to enter a war. In the 1910s the line between the way elites and the working class danced blurred and the dignified, upper-class, graceful man faded from popular imagination. When dance could no longer be perceived as an elite way of embodying adult masculinity, it was vulnerable to being seen as not masculine at all. Two more types round out the array of dancing men in the 1910s and 1920s: criminally dangerous gigolos and fun-loving college students.

GIGOLOS

Before 1912 dance had been an after-dark activity for adults of all social classes. The private balls attended by members of the upper class took place in the evening when businessmen could accompany their wives. Working-class men and women, who were lucky if their workdays were shorter than ten hours, could only attend dances at night. In 1912 a few restaurant owners looking to expand the hours when they could profit from the public's desire to dance opened their dance floors during the day and invited patrons to attend tea dances. Who was available to dance during the day? Wealthy women were permitted daytime leisure, but what sort of man was free to dance during the day? Some of the men who could dance during the day were dance instructors. When the tango teas opened one of the most popular dance instructors was Maurice Mouvet (fig. 2.4). His reputation was such that the *New York Times Magazine* devoted a feature article to him. It told the story of how he traveled to Europe and struggled through poverty, but mastered European social and exhibition dances including the exciting Parisian Apache dance. The dance was a style performed on Parisian stages that simulated domestic violence with choreographed finesse. He ultimately returned to the United States and established himself as a star performer and sought-after instructor whose demanding dance schedule kept him in athletic shape. The *Times* profile concluded with a quote from Maurice, the self-made man. "How did I succeed as a dancer? Because—always—I wanted to arrive! And always I worked! And always I worked alone! Nobody helped me. Never would I listen to anybody. I was always—always

Figure 2.4
Exhibition dancer and dance instructor Maurice Mouvet, dancing with Leonora Hughes.
Library of Congress.

alone!"[80] Mouvet situated his suspect professional identity as a dance instructor inside a conventional masculine narrative of ambition, independence, and unassisted hard work.

The majority of male partners at the tea dances, however, were not dance
instructors. They came with female partners and tended to be middle-class
men whose working days ended early enough and whose working conditions
were clean enough for them to dash to a dance in the late afternoon. A year
after the tea dances opened, they had grown very popular and were the subject of a lengthy article by journalist Richard Barry.[81] He described stockbrokers who rushed to the dances after the market closed and middle-aged men
who went to the dances with their wives to keep their weight down. Most of
the men on the dance floor wore business suits. "These 'teas'," he concluded,
"are the natural and inevitable expression of New York's insatiable demand
for a 'good time.' Like many another popular institution, their support
comes from the vast, indefinable middle class." Middle-class men, he said,

frequented the tea dances because they considered them decent environments. Tea dances appealed to middle-class New Yorkers who were excluded from society balls and feared that they would be "decoyed into compromising acquaintances" at the more heterogeneous dances held late at night.

Not everyone was pleased with the expansion of commercial entertainment in New York. Customers were not only dancing, they were drinking, and the dances they enjoyed were modern. Responding to the demands of social reformers New York's Mayor Gaynor ordered the tea dances closed because the restaurants were not licensed to combine drinking and dancing.[82] The *New York Times* rose to the restaurant owners' defense in an editorial that criticized the mayor for prohibiting the middle class from enjoying the pleasures of dancing at tea dances while the rich danced with impunity at exclusive private dances.[83] The restaurant owners prevailed and the dances continued to be popular middle-class entertainments. One reporter noted that a weak market had driven quite a few former stockbrokers to become dance instructors. They were doing well. Perhaps, he said, the stock market building should be converted to a dance hall.[84]

A year and a half later, on May 23, 1915, a sensationalized court case transformed the meaning of daytime dancing. A young heiress, Eugenia Kelly, was taken to court by her mother who charged her with incorrigibility.[85] She had been attending the tango teas, some of her jewels were found in a pawnshop, and she had withdrawn money from her bank account. Suspicion fell on her male companion at the restaurants, a dancer named Al Davis.[86] Had he accompanied her to the bank as well as the dance floor? Family lawyers brought the case to a hasty conclusion, issuing a statement describing Eugenia's tearful contrition and reconciliation with her mother.[87] Though quickly yanked from the newspapers' front pages, the scandal gave the police and social reformers a new focus in their campaigns against vice. Using undercover officers the police began a broad investigation of restaurants with dance floors, gathering a list of "professional dancers, or young men who make a business of hanging about the trotteries," and investigating their sources of income. Dance hall reformers met the day that the Kelly trial concluded to recommend to the mayor that he abolish afternoon tea dances. The dances, they said, served as the base of operations of "Broadway parasites" and "social gangsters" who supported themselves by ruining misguided young women of the middle and upper classes.[88] The dancing man had become dangerous, and he was a greater danger in the day, when unguarded daughters and wives freely moved around the city. Belle Israels, who had been widowed, subsequently remarried and took the name Belle Moskowitz. The Kelly case gave new energy to her campaign to regulate dance halls.[89] She said, the Kelly case has done good if it has called attention to the danger that lurks in the path of the young woman of today. The principal source of that danger is the afternoon dances, for to these flock the young women whom parental care would ordinarily keep home at night.

Moskowitz conceded that the men danced well but were nonetheless parasites. "The girl of Fifth Avenue," she said, "is exposed to the same danger as her humbler sisters were in the dance halls of the east side." The *New York Times*, which the previous year had written favorably about clever young stockbrokers turned dance instructors, picked up the panicked tone and reported that there were up to two thousand social gangsters, or "tango boys" in the city and that investigators found that at least 20 percent of the men at tango teas were "undesirables." Bold type before the lengthy article's concluding paragraph amplified that statistic, declaring "Most 'Partners' Undesirable." These men, it reported, live by dancing, charging two to five dollars for their services as partners. While in 1911 Maurice Mouvet was depicted as an athletic Horatio Alger of the dance floor, the professional partner was described in 1915 as having found a "not too fatiguing way of making a living."[90]

Journalists began to provide clues about how to distinguish good dancing men from bad. Richard Barry, the writer who introduced his readers to the respectable, middle-class tea dancer in 1913 painted an entirely different portrait two years later. Good men were employed at real jobs during the day. Tango pirates were freed from work by their exploitative relationships with rich young women. Most importantly, even though they may display polished veneers, tango pirates were "ill-born" and heroin users.[91] Readers were warned that the way to tell good men from bad was the color of their spats.

The police complained that they could not arrest men for wearing loud colors and the panic quickly subsided. After reconciling with her mother and admitting that she should not have behaved so badly, Eugenia the heiress reconciled with Al Davis, and married him.[92] Newspaper reports of their activities shrank and returned to the social pages. Eugenia moved to Long Island and gave birth to a daughter who would grow up to be a debutante and inherit her mother's reduced fortune.[93] The police commissioner and mayor resisted the efforts of reformers to goad them into shutting down the profitable tango teas. Two years passed before alarm sounded again regarding men who were free to dance during the day. On March 18, 1917, the headline shouted "ONCE RICH WOMAN SLAIN IN HOTEL; Secret Patron of 'Tango Parlors' Found Strangled and $2,500 in Jewels Missing. MAN COMPANION SOUGHT Had Made a Practice of Dancing in Afternoons While Husband Was at Business."

The crime was linked in the press to the Eugenia Kelly affair and other unspecified "tango cases." With this crime, the popular portrait of the tango pirate gained new details that cast the criminal dancer in ethnic terms. The murder was committed by "a powerful person acquainted with the methods of European garrotters." In a reference that bound staged dance violence to actual violence the murderer was reported to have "display[ed] the skill of a Parisian Apache." The victim had been drugged with red wine. She had been seen a week before the murder with a disreputable Italian. An autopsy revealed that her last meal was spaghetti. Could the pasta be further evidence that the murderer was the Italian?[94]

Five days later, lacking evidence that the Italian was the murderer, the district attorney charged another man, Benny Sternberg, whose surname suggests that he may have been similarly stigmatized as not-quite-white. A witness saw him with her on the day she was murdered. Sternberg's lawyer convinced a judge that his client did not attend tango teas and had him released after a night in jail.[95] The police responded to the murder as they had to the Eugenia Kelly scandal by going to the tango teas and collecting names. They compiled a list of seventy-six men who frequented the teas to have on file "for future reference."

Amid this panic, even the most established good dancers felt vulnerable. Maurice Mouvet, the man who brought the Apache dance to New York, announced that he would refuse to instruct married women unless they carried the written consent of their husbands.[96] He also declared that husbands who came to him unaccompanied for lessons would need letters of permission from their wives. The public was concerned about the stability of marriage, and Mouvet wanted to position his dance lessons as conventional morality's ally rather than its threat. Given the country's xenophobic social climate Mouvet had cause for concern about his reputation and livelihood. In 1917 Congress enacted a law excluding immigrants who failed to demonstrate English literacy. Mouvet's coloring was dark. Though he was born in Brooklyn, dance instruction was so strongly associated with European immigrants that the press frequently described him as foreign-born.[97] Well-born, northern European men, particularly if their origins were British, could be good dancers and reputable, but darker men were easily criminalized.[98] Darker men might gain legitimacy through manly occupations, but could not establish their good character by making money from grace.

At the tango teas the safety of day became the danger of night, classes intermingled, and women's innocence disappeared. The tango tea became a space onto which a series of social anxieties were projected. The lines between masculinity and femininity dissolved and formed anew as men allured women through the performance of grace and sensuality, and women actively and independently sought pleasure with men. Wives and daughters temporarily escaped their dependent relationships with husbands and mothers to dance with men who could not provide them with financial support.

Panics about the intermingling of classes were intensified when they were cast in ethnic terms. The men who became known as tango lizards, tango pirates, tango parasites, and mercenary tangoists were marked by ethnicity and their apparent refusal of honorable male labor. Accused of supporting themselves through the favors of rich women, they violated the line between work and play. Earlier uproars regarding dance halls were led by social workers who described dance halls as places that ruined innocent working-class girls. In those campaigns working girls were often portrayed as victims for whom dance halls offered the only escape from joyless and crowded tenements. In the later scandals we see not ruined, ethnic, working-class girls but rather comparatively privileged, defiant white women. Reports of the scandals described the dire consequences met by women who followed their desires to the tango teas. They squandered fortunes, fell into the hands of the law, developed addictions, or were killed. Yet they garnered little public sympathy. Instead, the reports of scandals and crimes took the form of cautionary tales that attempted to restore hegemonies of race and gender, marking ethnic men as dangerous and unmanly and wayward women as deserving of their fates.

Historians have noted how middle- and upper-class white men were threatened by the image of the dancing man, as he was portrayed in panicked representations as ethnic and lower class. Erenberg argued that middle-class men feared that "women would find lower-class men in the cabaret better able to satisfy their cravings for pleasure."[99] Yet it is important to bear in mind that the majority of dance partners of white middle- and upper-class women were white middle- and upper-class men. The panics regarding tango pirates reinforced the false image that only lower-class, or ethnically and racially marked men, had the capacity to sensuously dance. The white middle-class adult man who danced and danced well was effaced in panics regarding tango pirates. Middle- and upper-class whites who defined themselves in opposition to what they saw as a racialized and class-located sensuality and men invested in images of masculinity as gruffly uncultivated and autonomous placed limits on the way men could move. They disseminated images of masculine dancers as feminized ballroom dancers and priggish instructors, dangerous spielers, or gigolos. These images made it difficult to see that many white middle-class adult men danced and danced well.

THE WORLD OF BOYS AND THE WORLD OF MEN

The criminalization of tango lizards cast a negative shadow on men who danced too much and too well, yet in the same period, there was a category of white middle-class dancing men whose behavior received less public scorn. Many middle-class high school and college students danced at every opportunity, but their respectability was protected by their youth and class. Faddish dance steps became known as "collegiate" dances, an indication that they were viewed by the public as originating in and belonging to college life. There was a protected place for dance as part of age-delimited and therefore harmless youthful frivolities. Adolescence was increasingly being treated as a distinct stage of life, and dance became one of its distinguishing characteristics.

In general, high school boys did not dance in physical education classes. Most schools eliminated dance from boy's physical education before then. For example, at a Des Moines public school, boys and girls received dance instruction from kindergarten through junior high, but in the high school grades dance instruction was only for girls. An end-of-year pageant celebrated the progress of the Des Moines school's children through stages of dance instruction. The final scene for boys in the pageant was the dramatic exit of the junior high school boys who left the stage to go off into "the world of men."[100]

High school boys continued to dance, but the context and meaning of their dancing generally shifted from physical education to romance. In 1910, the students at Oakland High School in California were permitted to hold an informal dance at lunchtime. Students were so pleased with the opportunity to dance that they thanked the teacher who sponsored the dance for her kindness and slipped a plea for more dances into the yearbook: "This is the first time that the girls and boys have been allowed to dance in the gym during the noon hour and it is hoped that this custom will be kept up."[101] In subsequent years noontime dances became customary at the school along with dances organized by graduating classes and dances held to raise funds to cover the cost of medical care for injured football players. Dancing was so popular among high school students that it became difficult to schedule an event. In a review of social life at Oakland High in 1916, the yearbook editors reported,

> Not many dances were given directly under the auspices of the school this term with the exception of a number of noon dances. This is not because Oakland High does not dance. Far from it. Oakland High has the reputation of putting on the best dances in the county. But so many dances were given by Oaklanders and Oakland alumni outside of school that it was impossible to find suitable dates for school dances.

That year at the Junior Dansant "wallflowers were as scarce as polar bears on the Sahara." On the day of the Dansant the football coach gave the players the day off so that they would be fresh for the dance. And again in the yearbook the students asked for more dances.

> These dansants are so popular and so easy to get up that the cry is always for more. If one was given each month a nice sum could be made in the course of a term, and it could be added to some needy fund. Can't we have more of them?

In the early 1920s students who attended Lowell High School in San Francisco danced to a live dance orchestra at several dances each year.[102] Like the Oakland High students, Lowell students sought opportunities to dance beyond those available at school. It is likely that some of them attended Miss Marion B. Wight's dance school, which placed an ad in the school's yearbook. In bold print it announced WHERE TO DANCE. Wight's dance school welcomed high school dancers on Friday evenings from nine to eleven. Miss Wight offered lessons, but as the ad suggests, many students needed to know where to dance, not how. Throughout the 1920s and 1930s dances were important parts of high school social life and were structured around the formation of heterosexual couples. The "first dance" was treated as a milestone within teenaged romances. High school dances were an institutionalized part of school life and contributed to the association of social dance with youth and romance.

The association of dance with youth rather than maturity can be found in *Babbitt*, a novel that became an immediate success when it was published in 1922 and remained high on bestseller lists into 1923.[103] George Babbitt, the conformist businessman created by Sinclair Lewis, struck such a chord that journalists throughout the 1920s and 1930s referred to "Babbitts," "Babbittisms," and "Babbittry."[104] The novel expresses the emerging common sense that adolescence was a unique stage of life.[105] Ted, George Babbitt's son, woefully lacked discipline and serious purpose, but was, nonetheless, an All-American boy and a typical teenager. Ted complained that most of what he was forced to study in college was useless. Proposing to his father that he be allowed to drop out and learn what he needed through correspondence, he said, "Dad, they just teach a lot of old junk that isn't any practical use—except the manual training and typewriting and basketball and dancing—and in these correspondence-courses, gee, you can get all kinds of stuff that would come in handy."[106] Ted then picked up a paper and read the advertisement of a correspondence school course in self-defense. It asked, "CAN YOU PLAY A MAN'S PART?" The answer was not certain. He was not yet a man.

Ted loved to dance. He organized dances at college and imposed upon his parents to host a dancing party for his friends at home. In this novel dancing ability marks the line between adept masculine youth and stumbling, awkward, masculine middle age. In dangerous, adulterous forays away from the safety of home George Babbitt, the father, found himself in situations where he was called upon to dance. At parties the overly aggressive wives of neighbors pressured him to dance. He has an affair and is drawn into dancing at the debauched parties of his paramour's circle of friends, returning home each time full of self-loathing for having made a fool of himself. While traveling for business he dances with a paid escort, "shuffl[ing] along the floor, too bulky to be guided, his steps unrelated to the rhythm of the jungle music, and in his staggering he would have fallen, had she not held him with supple kindly strength."[107] Though fictional characters, the historical record suggests that Ted and George accurately reflect the place of dance in the lives of middle-class whites in the 1920s. In *Middletown*, the classic sociological study of a Midwestern city, Robert and Helen Lynd commented that "dancing holds the position of preëminence with the younger group prior to marriage, while from marriage on the more sedentary [card-playing] predominates. . . . Dancing is today a universal skill among the young; their social life, particularly among the high school group, is increasingly built about it."[108] Dance was one of the most important social activities for high school and college students.[109] In her history of white middle-class youth culture in the 1920s Paula Fass reports that in 1925 alone the University of Wisconsin sponsored hundreds of college and fraternity dances and that fraternity brothers helped each other to master the latest dances in order to maintain their chapter's popularity. According to Fass, "in the twenties young men and women danced whenever the opportunity presented itself."[110] Those who disparaged the wilder popular dances called them animal dances. Others, who viewed them with less hostility, called them the collegiate dances, a name that associated them with youth.

When young men performed the collegiate dances they swung their arms and legs. They bent forward at the waist and shook their shoulders. Jazz music provided them with places to insert improvisational accents within the larger rhythmic structure of the steps. Though student-organized social activities fostered these masculine experiments with movement, opposition to male dancing continued on and off campuses. Opponents to male dancing in the 1920s faulted it for being low class, effeminate, and immoral, categories that often overlapped. Arthur Murray, the successful and entrepreneurial dance instructor, attempted to sever the associations between dance, effeminacy, and lower-class men. In a 1920 profile he explained why he marketed his dance classes to customers as membership in a club. "The club idea was that it attracted many of the manly boys. There is a general impression among them that a dancing school is a place for 'sissies.' But going to a club in an exclusive clubhouse is an entirely different matter."[111] His sales pitch suggests that part of the stigma of masculine effeminacy was that it was associated with lower economic class positions and that the stigma could be lifted within a context that signified wealth.

To some extent colleges in the 1920s functioned as elite clubs. In that decade, only between 2 and 7 percent of eighteen- to twenty-four-year-olds attended college.[112] Yet even on college campuses, men who danced came under attack. Notre Dame football coach Knute Rockne assailed collegiate dancing because it threatened male masculinity.[113] In Rockne's view, "for every woman who smokes . . . we see the male lizard who uses complexion dope; that for every woman who apes man in dress we have the sissie who wears corsets or pinch-back coat, and for every woman who drinks we have that lowest form of degenerate effeminacy, the shimmy hound." To counter the influence of dance on college campuses, Rockne proposed that boxing and football be made mandatory for male students. At least with respect to dancing, Rockne did not carry the day. Young men on college campuses continued to dance in great numbers and in the exuberant kicking of the charleston, which gained popularity after 1923, found a step that was perceived as more masculine than feminine.[114]

Men learned to move in new ways in the 1910s and 1920s but were not seen as new men. The mystery of the missing new man is not solved by finding a corpse. No one killed the new man. He was just ridiculed or marginalized wherever his difference was noticed. The privilege of dancing without stigma was most easily extended to men in college whose respectability was bolstered by their class and who were perceived as being at a unique and short-lived time of life. Dancing was something they would grow out of if they had any sense. According to this logic boys could dance in their youth, until it was time to leave the dance floor to permanently reside in the world of men.

CHAPTER 3

⚭

Dancing in Uniform

The 1929 crash of the stock market signaled the beginning of a long period of business failures and devastatingly high unemployment. Families lacked the financial resources to cover the basic necessities of life, and poverty humiliated men whose claims to authority depended upon their ability to provide. In the years of the Great Depression the slight, graceful, elegantly dressed, and amiable Fred Astaire was the nation's most celebrated dancing man. His lighthearted films provided visions of happiness that were just what some Depression-era audiences wanted to see.[1]

Scholars who look back at Astaire tend to note his masculinity in terms that raise the question they mean to answer. Dance historians Marshall and Jean Stearns claimed that he was "indisputably masculine," while musicologist Todd Decker found Astaire's masculinity "unassailable."[2] If Astaire's masculinity was neither assailed nor disputed, why do historians rush to its defense? Russ Tamblyn, who danced the part of the leader of the Jets in the choreographed rumble in the filmed version of *West Side Story*, said "I think Fred [Astaire]'s greatest contribution to musicals, to movies, and to dancers could be that he was heterosexual."[3] Overlooking Astaire's inventive choreography, his elegant style, and his flawless technique, Tamblyn assessed Astaire's legacy and praised Astaire for making it safe, or perhaps, just a bit safer, for heterosexual-identified men to dance. Historians affirm Astaire's masculinity because questions regarding masculinity hover around Astaire, as they follow any western white man who dances professionally. The questions were answered in Astaire's case by his heterosexuality, his embodiment of upper-class distinction, and the artistic control he exerted over his films. Nonetheless Astaire, the ideal dancing partner, was not the man's man. Cinematic tough guys could more easily claim that title.

Nor was he a great romantic lead. He was famously averse to onscreen kissing. A frequently repeated description of his partnership with Ginger Rogers is "he gives her class, she gives him sex."[4] Fred Astaire was a wonderfully skilled and inventive dancer whose filmed performances were enjoyed by men and women alike. But like Vernon Castle before him, Astaire's exceptional popularity as a dancer did not produce a broad reevaluation of the meaning of masculinity.

Outside of cinematic fantasies, dance, during the 1930s, was more often associated with poverty than prosperity. The public was aware of disreputable halls in large cities where men paid women small change to dance with them.[5] These halls were far from glamorous. The dance marathons of the 1930s even more dramatically linked dance to financial desperation. Some contestants joined the marathons for relatively short periods because sponsors provided meals and shelter to dancers in exchange for their participation in the grueling endurance contests.[6] Others entered with hopes of winning large sums and found themselves struggling to merely stay on their feet and keep moving, week after week, relieved only by fifteen-minute breaks that were too short for sleep.

For most Depression Era men, dance was a leisure activity, not a way to earn money. It helped them to take their minds off their troubles, but it did not solve them. A range of commercial establishments and community organizations provided affordable venues for a night of dancing. Cities organized large free dances for the poor.[7] Whether as participatory event or spectacle, dance provided inexpensive entertainment.

Almost any business struggled in an economy in which people had little discretionary income, and dance schools were no exception. Dance lessons were an easily discarded luxury. The widespread popularity of going out to dance that lasted through the 1920s waned in the 1930s. If trends emerge from high school students, there were signs there that at the end of the twenties and the beginning of the thirties boys were becoming less accustomed to, or interested in, dancing. At Oakland High School, where in the 1910s and 1920s students complained that there were not enough dances, the 1929 yearbook's terse description of a dance held that year was "Too many femmes, not enough gents." Two years later a social dance club began, which suggests that dance was becoming a narrow interest for a small group of students, rather than something all students enjoyed. At the first meeting of the club, each of the small number of boys who attended was assigned a girl partner whose job it was to teach him to dance.

In the early 1930s instructors attempted to protect their livelihoods by organizing the Dancing Teacher's Congress, through which they sought to propagate the view that formal lessons were the only way to acquire social dance skills. The reputation of dance instruction had been tarnished and the value of instructors' services decreased by the ease with which persons could claim expertise and by the euphemistic use of "dance school" by taxi dance halls.[8] Through groups like the Dancing Teacher's Congress the most elite dance teachers worked to distance themselves from the least. A prominent teacher complained that "in the mind of a large portion of the public, the title of DANCING TEACHER is on the same level with TAXI-DANCER and GIGOLO! I maintain that this condition will exist as long as the newspapers refer to a dance hall hostess as a DANCE INSTRUCTRESS!"[9]

The problems surrounding the meaning of dance involved race, gender, sexuality, and class. To elevate the social position of dance, and thereby their own status, dance instructors maligned dance styles that were coded black and American, in order to create a demand for instruction in dance styles coded white and British. The Congress met in New York City in July 1932. The layers of headlines in a report of the meeting capture the organization's attempt to bolster the market for dance lessons by asserting its authority to set standards for popular dancing.[10]

Students Set Pace In Dance Invention:
Their Novelties Are Closely Watched,
Ballroom Teachers Are Told at Meeting Here:
EXTREME STEPS OPPOSED:
But All Will Be Demonstrated at Four Weeks' Session—
British System Is Recommended.

Miss Lucille Stoddart, chairman of the Congress, characterized the origins of popular dances as black and therefore as unacceptable unless modified. "All the popular ballroom dances of the moment, the 'shag,' the 'shuffle,' and the 'Lindy Hop,' are done to fox trot music and are collegiate in style . . . Collegiate dancing is the outgrowth of Negro dancing, just as the popular ballroom music is based primarily on Negro rhythm." She hoped that the Congress would succeed in promoting an alternative to collegiate dancing, which itself was a stultified form of dances which originated in African American communities. The proposed alternative, which was taught at the Congress, was the British system. The concerns the British system addressed were not just about race and class, but about gender as well. The appeal of dance to men and questions of masculine embodiment were central to their efforts to reform dance. Stoddart explained,

All over the British Isles, any place you go now, you will find people dancing alike . . . Their steps may vary, but the fundamentals of their bodily poise are the same. This new British system we are importing as a technique for ballroom dancing whereby people can actually learn to use their bodies well and dance along natural lines. It is all based on the natural movements of the body and in style is extremely masculine.

Though she was describing dances for heterosexual couples, she promoted them on the basis of their masculinity. Her comments suggest that there was no need to sell dance to women. Stoddart advocated a form of masculine embodiment in which masculine dance movement was "natural." Ballroom dance teachers of the 1930s viewed their technique as natural because their reference point was ballet.[11] For example, ballet dancers rotate their legs at the hip when they take steps, producing the characteristic "turned-out" stance. Ballroom dancers under the British system did not rotate their legs when stepping and therefore saw their movement as "natural." The style of their movement, nonetheless, was developed through training. Men had to learn the proper way to move naturally, and the place to learn was a dance school.

Stoddart fought a losing battle when she tried to promote dance on the basis of its masculinity. She headed an organization of a profession from which men had fled. Male dance instructors had once been common, but by the mid-1930s almost all dance teachers were women.[12] Men that remained in the profession were often in prominent positions, the result of the "glass escalator" men frequently ride when in feminized professions.[13] Their prominence, however, did not change the gender-coding of dance.

While the dance teachers were promoting a newly poised and controlled masculinity, other trends were unfolding. In his history of gay New York, George Chauncey argues that a visible gay subculture flourished in the city in the late 1920s and early 1930s.[14] The gay subculture became especially visible to the broader public through a fad for drag shows in Times Square in the early 1930s. The heightened visibility of gay men was met with a backlash of homophobic legislation and police repression. This backlash imposed further constraints on the ways men could move. More and more, the dancing adult man became a sissy.

Dance teachers were pushed into a new defensive mode. Abandoning the effort to establish new forms of masculinity on the dance floor, they retreated to strident defenses of the conventional manliness of dance. *American Dancer* was the leading trade journal of dance instructors and through its pages we can watch dance instructors defend themselves against the popular perception that men who danced too well were sissies. An August 1931 article argued that "It is . . . foolish for a man to dance in a feminine way—as so many men do."[15] The next year *American Dancer* published an article by Louis Chalif, the director of one of New York's largest dance schools, entitled "Men and Boys Should Dance" in which he argued that

> a true man will in his performance avoid daintiness, femininity and affectation as he would sin itself. A man can appear more manly and in the finest sense heroic, through the right kind of dancing than in any other way whatever. Neither slaughtering enemies, nor hunting animals, nor punching an opponent, nor lifting a horse can invest him with such perfect and glorious manhood as can dancing.[16]

Chalif's hyperbolic attempt to claim masculinity for dancers did not succeed. At the beginning of the 1930s, men danced, but rarely took dance lessons. Few men considered dance class a waypoint on the route to perfect and glorious manhood.

DANCE GOES TO WAR

A decade later everything had changed. The United States entered World War II and the jitterbugging white GI became the symbol of the All-American boy.[17] During the war, dancing became perfectly compatible with heroic masculinity. In a magazine for soldiers an article about a coastguardsman who resisted a Nazi bribe and uncovered a spy ring shows him happily jitterbugging.[18] In an entirely flattering portrait of young workers at a defense plant *Life* magazine described tireless youths who went out dancing after midnight. "Ernie worked eight hours before dance but still has lots of pep. He spins Bobbie round and round like great big beautiful top."[19] How did the meaning of dance change so rapidly? A large part of the answer lies in the nature of the jitterbug, which gained widespread popularity among youth in the mid-1930s. The jitterbug was an expansive space-gobbling dance, danced to loud, brassy, driving big-band music. It was a fast, vigorous dance, which boldly departed from more traditional grounded, upright, and slow-paced partner dancing. Though the jitterbug demanded gymnastic skills from women as well as men, the dance's partnering reinforced men's dominance. Men led in all of the era's social dances, but in the jitterbug, leading took spectacular form. Jitterbugging men tossed their partners side to side and lifted them skyward; athletic feats that highlighted differences of strength and size of the men and women dancers (figs. 3.1–3.2).[20]

The dance's athleticism is not the only reason why the jitterbug came to symbolize American manhood. The war provides an answer as well. Wartime

Figure 3.1
Jitterbugging at a juke joint outside Clarksdale, Mississippi, 1939.
Photograph by Marion Post Wolcott. Library of Congress.

government propaganda, censorship, and a generally cooperative press also contributed to the unwavering presentation of soldiers in a favorable light. Historian Allan Bérubé found that during the war, even drag routines were consistently described by the press as "wholesome, patriotic, and masculine" when performed by soldiers in theatrical productions.[21] No one questioned the masculinity of the uniformed man who fought for the nation in a popular war, even when he danced. World War II transformed dance from a signifier of effete foreignness to an emblem of the nation, as the uniformed dancing man became the picture of youthful, white, and ultimately victorious American manliness abroad.

To understand the emergence of the jitterbug as a symbol of American culture it is necessary to follow the shifting ethnic and racial meanings of dance as well as its gendered meanings. In the decade before the war the dancing man was associated with ethnic and racial difference, though as patterns of migration changed, the image of the not-quite-white tango lizard had grown less familiar and the exclusive association of dancing talent with blacks grew. Professional black dancers performing while costumed as either street urchins or servants were common figures in the films of the 1930s. The outstanding tap dancer Bill "Bojangles" Robinson tap danced in

Figure 3.2
Jitterbug contest winners Lona Norman and Chuch Price. Golden Gate International Exhibition, San Francisco, 1939.
Courtesy San Francisco History Center, San Francisco Public Library.

several films in the role of white child-star Shirley Temple's servant. Fred Astaire wore blackface for a "Bojangles of Harlem" number in his 1936 film *Swing Time*. The image of the cheerful dancing black man, performed either by black men or by white men in blackface, was so socially acceptable in the 1930s among whites that it could be included in school curricula. The director of physical education of a Virginia school, addressing a national audience of physical education teachers, wrote, "Any simple clog danced by a couple dressed as Negro children is always popular." An illustration of a dancing couple in blackface labeled "Rastus" accompanied her essay.[22] The dance trade publication *American Dancer* provided an illustrated guide for teachers who wished to incorporate blackface into their recitals. Sketches provided costume details for the "plantation darkey," "Dude Coon," "Colonial type," "Mr. Sambo," "Mistah Bones," and "Interlocutor," and text advised teachers regarding how black to make the face of different characters.[23]

After European immigration was limited by xenophobic laws in the 1910s and 1920s, moral panics regarding the dangers of European immigrants diminished.At the same time an enormous shift in the location of the nation's black population from the rural South to the urban North took place. African Americans fled the brutality and economic deprivation of the southern states to live with relatively greater freedom and economic opportunity in the North.[24] When living in the southern states, African Americans may have lived in proximity to whites but had minimal social contact on any basis of equality with them.[25] Blacks who moved to northern cities in the 1920s and 1930s were drawn to existing black communities. Regardless of their residential preferences, black migrants were excluded by segregation from many neighborhoods. Large black communities formed and within them places to dance, grand and small, were opened by black and white entrepreneurs.

Though dance as a participatory form of amusement transcended demographic categories, most people danced in venues that were segregated by race, ethnicity, class, and sexuality. As historian Chad Heap has demonstrated, middle-class heterosexual whites enjoyed visiting distant neighborhoods for limited forms of contact with lower classes and racial, ethnic, and sexual minorities at places of public amusement. This largely unidirectional and voyeuristic practice had the effect of strengthening racial, class, and sexual boundaries.[26] "Slumming" practices and the accounts that arose from them contributed to a disjuncture between the widespread, diverse participation in dance and its narrower popular representations. Black community venues attracted whites who traveled from white neighborhoods to experience nightlife that appeared more exciting than what they could find closer to home.[27]

Slumming excursions provoked alarm among whites who believed that interracial social contact was inherently depraved. An August 3, 1919, *New York Times* report on riots that occurred in Chicago located the cause of the disturbances in lax city officials who had permitted interracial social contact. Its headline proclaimed "VICE AND POLITICS AS FACTORS IN CHICAGO RIOTS: Negroes and Whites Drank and Danced Together in All Night Cabarets of the Black Belt." According to Heap, "slumming provided a powerful means to naturalize changing notions of racial and sexual difference by 'marking' them into the material culture and physical spaces of U.S. cities."[28] Though residential segregation maintained racially homogenous neighborhoods in northern cities throughout the first half of the twentieth century, slumming meant that whites were frequent witnesses to black nightlife. Whites who traveled to black neighborhoods in the evenings thought these trips gave them insight into black culture. They returned to their communities to spread accounts of extraordinary black dancing.

The lindy hop, which was developed by black dancers in the late 1920s, was renamed the jitterbug and became the most popular and spectacular dance of the 1930s.[29] The lindy hop was not born at Harlem's Savoy

Ballroom, but it was undoubtedly raised there to innovative virtuosity. Opened in 1926 as a dance palace, the Savoy Ballroom had a capacious dance floor and two stages that accommodated two swing bands who alternated playing at opposite ends of the hall. The house band was led by Chick Webb, who paid close attention to dancers whose steps were intimately connected to the music.[30] The Savoy's clientele was predominantly black, though it always attracted smaller numbers of white dancers and spectators. According to historian Joel Dinerstein, "the Savoy was a tourist 'must' in the 1930s."[31] The club's management frequently promoted Battle of the Band nights when Webb's band would challenge visiting bands to contests of swing. Chick Webb battled the leading swing bands of the era including Benny Goodman and Count Basie. In most accounts Webb won the battles.[32]

Radio broadcasts from the Savoy Ballroom and other dance venues helped to spread the energetic sound of swing music nationally. While band battles were special events, informal dance battles happened every night as the most skilled dancers strove to outdo each other on a section of the dance floor reserved for them. Those who viewed these dancers as naturals erased the hard work that the dancers devoted to the perfection of their performances. The best dancers at the Savoy continuously polished their technique, rehearsed their partnering before appearing on the ballroom floor, and invented ever more spectacular steps to bring to the informal competitions. The large majority of dancers among the elite group were black, though occasional highly skilled white dancers were among them.[33]

The jitterbug spread beyond its devoted dancers at the Savoy through a variety of channels. New Yorkers, tourists, and visiting celebrities traveled to the Savoy to see some of the nation's best dancers move to the most famous bands. In 1935 the *New York Daily News* organized the Harvest Moon Ball as a dance competition that attracted large audiences with separate contests for a range of popular dance forms. Dancers from the Savoy won the jitterbug category every year from the beginning through 1942. The most skilled of the Savoy's dancers were organized into a professional performing troupe that was booked at the 1939 New York World's Fair, appeared in films, toured internationally, and spread the jitterbug in its most breathtaking forms to national and international audiences.

In the early 1930s listeners to radio could hear swing music on a variety of programs that were broadcast nationally, but these programs were often aired late at night, in some cases after midnight. Furthermore some radio music directors resisted broadcasting swing band music, even for programs that had dance themes. They favored slower and more melodic dance music, which they viewed as better quality.[34] The resistance of radio programmers to scheduling swing music at prime time slowed but did not halt the broader dissemination of jitterbug dancing. In the second half of the 1930s the popularity of swing music became unstoppable and radio programs featuring dance music played by live swing bands were common.[35]

In 1941 animator Ward Kimball was assigned to depict dancing animals for Disney's forthcoming film *Dumbo*. He traveled from Los Angeles to Harlem's Savoy Ballroom, where he sat at the perimeter of the dance floor to sketch black dancers.[36] After his return to Los Angeles he transformed the sketches into drawings of dancing crows. *Dance* presented images of Savoy dancers and Kimball's crows in adjacent panels with captions explaining their connection.[37] "These two dancing crows at left are the counterparts, in 'Dumbo,' of the two hot stepping patrons of the Savoy Ball Room at the right." "At left" and "at the right" are used as if it were necessary to distinguish the animated animals from the photographed humans. In *Dumbo* and in the *Dance* feature on it, the lindy hop was represented as black, and blackness was rendered as a common and boisterous bird. Seeing no problem in the depiction of black dancers as crows, *Dance* correspondent Robert Baral reported that Savoy Ballroom dancers "should have no difficulty in recognizing themselves" in the crows. Actually the dancing crows in *Dumbo* bore little resemblance to urbane Harlem dancers. The reporter described the Savoy's dancers through stereotypically racialized imagery. "Shoe shine boys in particular, bent on a night's fling, held [Kimball's] attention," explained the *Dance* correspondent. "The flashing teeth, unshackled rhythm . . . fascinated [Kimball] completely." Since it must have been impossible to tell a shoe shine boy from an office worker when both were dressed in their finest dance clothes, "shoe shine boy" served as a euphemism for black men. And completing his depiction of Savoy dancers with imagery familiar to his assumed white readership, the reporter described their flashing teeth, a white representation of blackness that was as old as blackface vaudeville. Beyond revealing the commonplace racism of the 1940s, the article also reveals a turning point in the representation of the lindy hop. Initially perceived as a black dance, the lindy hop was becoming part of a generalized American youth culture. The dances performed with special expertise by black dancers at the Savoy are, the reporter noted, performed throughout the country by young people. The lindy hop was disseminating nationally. Two years after *Dumbo*'s 1941 premiere a pair of white, Italian American dancers took the lindy hop prize at the Harvest Moon Ball.[38] The couple's victory indicates that at least some whites were excellent jitterbuggers, although it must be noted that in 1943 the Savoy's African American dancers were undermined by the ballroom's temporary closure by the city's administration.[39]

The era's most popular dance, the jitterbug had originated with black dancers in the mid-1920s as the lindy hop and had by 1935 disseminated to white dancers who were more likely to call it the jitterbug. The African American origins of the jitterbug move into and out of view in the dance's popular representations. When the dance was presented as characteristic of the nation, its black origins tended to be effaced. The jitterbug was recast from black cultural creation to race-less product of U.S. youth.

Race was obscured in white youthful performance of the jitterbug, but gender difference was highlighted. Men who danced the jitterbug took the lead in a dance in which leading often entailed lifting a partner. Jitterbugging men appeared more athletic than sensual. The erasure of its racial connotations and its compatibility with gender conventions positioned the jitterbug as a dance that could serve the war effort as a symbol of the nation.

MAKING DANCING A PATRIOTIC PASTIME

At the beginning of World War II it was far from inevitable that any dance would become a part of the image of the All-American boy. Arthur Murray, who by 1940 had established a profitable network of dance school franchises, was acutely aware of men's resistance to dancing and worked to overcome it in his advertisements.[40] He used the language of popular psychology in an attempt to overcome the stigma of effeminacy that was attached to dance classes. Murray's ads transformed men's reluctance to enter a dance school into an "inferiority complex" that stood in the way of their business success. The ads promised that if men would just muster the courage to enter an Arthur Murray studio, they would be given the tools for social and business success.

The difficulty of attracting boys and men to dance was such a great problem for dance school owners that the editors of *Educational Dance* devoted the entire February 1941 issue to authors who addressed the problem of masculine dancing and gave the lead article to modern dancer Ted Shawn.[41] Shawn claimed a space for masculine dancing by firmly planting it on the he-man side of the gender binary. This was a view Shawn had advocated in earlier articles and books and through the choreography he created for his company of "man dancers." Shawn's choreography employed muscular and tightly bound movements that referenced hard labor. "Dance," he wrote, was "a full-sized job for a man."[42] The issue's remaining articles suggested strategies for overcoming boys' dislike of dance. Frank Eckl, supervisor of physical education in the Pittsburgh Elementary Schools, advised teachers that they must "Never ask a boy to do anything that he considers sissy." None of the authors questioned the distinction between sissies and he-men. All accepted that divide as real and argued that dance teachers who wished to appeal to boys must avoid teaching feminized movement. The same year dance teacher Paul Mathis wrote to the editors of the largest dance periodical *The American Dancer* about the problem of boys and dance. "Dancing need not be sissy" Mathis wrote, and like Ted Shawn and Franck Eckl he defended dance's masculine potential by reinforcing the belief in the purposeful nature of masculine movement. Dance instruction, he argued, makes boys more masculine because it gives them greater "control and purposefulness" in their motions.[43] These defenses of dance for men were confined to periodicals read by dancers and dance instructors. Their capacity to change the way dance was seen by a broader public was limited.

Dance appeared to be a conspicuously suspect masculine occupation on the eve of World War II. In 1940 as the United States instituted a draft and made preparations for war, dance teachers scrambled to define dance instruction as part of the war effort. Initially some entrepreneurial studio owners openly discussed the potential for profit-making that war provided. In November 1940 in the pages of a dance trade journal, a studio owner urged others to sell dance lessons as a way for men who had not yet been drafted to ready themselves for war. Dance, he declared, was good preparation for marching. Anticipating the role that dances would have in the military's organization of leisure during the war the author wrote that studio business would profit by training women to be competent dance partners. Finally he suggested that studios could find new opportunities for money-making by turning their instructional spaces into small-scale dance halls. Perhaps it was time to bring back the tea dance to fill studios with soldiers on leave who had free time during the day.[44]

A year later John Martin, writing with the confidence of someone who had been the dance critic for the *New York Times* since 1927, contended that dancers should be exempt from military service. Their greatest contribution, he argued, could be made stateside. The troubled relationship between masculinity and dance is evident in his defense of dance's value. He dismissed the oft-repeated charge that men who dance are effeminate, but later argued that these "irrepressible artists" were unfit for battle. In his view dancers were "pretty unstable type[s] liable to go berserk under strain."[45] Within days of the publication of Martin's "On Conscription," Japan bombed Pearl Harbor, making it unlikely that a fit man would escape military service because he had a greater obligation to dance on stage. The United States was at war, and in that context dance as a feminized, frivolous pastime was an expendable luxury. Capezio, a manufacturer of ballet shoes and dancing costumes—products that diverted resources away from boots and parachutes—sought to immediately reframe dance as essential to the war effort and to national identity. Large print declared "THERE WILL ALWAYS BE DANCING IN THE LAND OF THE FREE" in an advertisement that asserted that dance kept Americans fit, raised morale, and was an "indelible part" of U.S. culture.[46] Within two months the message had crystallized into the slogan "Dance for Defense," the name of an alliance between the Office of Civilian Defense and private dance schools.[47] Long suspect as a profession for men, dance on private stages was unjustifiable during wartime if it drew men and resources away from the battle. However dance, when closely allied with the military, could serve the war effort. Civilian men who danced were not celebrated as patriots, but legions of agreeable, attractive, well-trained women could serve their nation as volunteer dance partners for soldiers.

Plans for the provision of recreation for soldiers had begun before the declaration of war. In 1941, a joint Army and Navy committee convened a group of morale officers to identify strategies for disease prevention. The conference issued a summary statement advising that "morale will be fostered and, more specifically, venereal diseases prevented if Service Clubs are staffed, not only by mature and womanly hostesses, but also, under their essential supervision, by a number of personable women of the same age groups as the men themselves."[48] Hoping to protect soldiers from the emotional injury of rejection and the physical injury of venereal disease, the military sought to satisfy soldiers' recreational needs by providing controlled dances with preselected partners. As the nation's young men were mobilized for war, the Army, Navy, the Federal Security Agency, the U.S.O. and countless smaller entities organized to provide recreation for them. Much of this effort was put into organizing dances. In partnership with civilian volunteer organizations, the military appropriated dance spaces to provide for and control servicemen's pleasure. Planners debated how best to control the channeling of sexual desire into supervised heterosexual dancing. An early report recommended that the young women volunteer dance partners wear uniforms, which would visibly communicate their respectability. That view was quickly overturned as dance organizers mandated that volunteer dance partners wear feminine civilian clothing to make them appealing to servicemen.[49]

The Dance for Defense campaign was launched in March 1942 at a time when dances for soldiers were being organized on a massive scale.[50] The campaign attempted to transform the perception of dance instruction from wasteful enterprise to a patriotic effort that required "the cooperation of every dancing teacher in the United States." Dance schools were asked to donate free dance classes to prepare young women to be the dance partners of soldiers on leave. If patriotism was not enough to motivate dance school owners to join the effort, *American Dancer* reminded them of the vulnerability of their profession in wartime. "Dancing, when sponsored by an official source as a patriotic pastime will not run the risk of being relegated to the 'Luxury' category.... Teachers and schools who are willing to cooperate with the Office of Civilian Defense in this campaign to make dancing a patriotic pastime are urgently invited to communicate at once with your local office of the Physical Education Division [of the Office of Civilian Defense]."[51] Dance was promoted as a uniquely restorative pastime for young soldiers because it involved heterosexual contact. In the words of one soldier, who addressed *Dance* magazine readers "To keep 'em flying and keep 'em fighting keep 'em dancing!"[52] Rapidly abandoning the attempt to exempt professional dancers from military service, the dance industry promoted dance as essential for soldiers' morale and, in an assertion that would eventually take hold, a symbol of the nation.

Dances were organized by the military and civilian volunteers on bases and in towns in the United States and abroad. In these dances, the possibility of two men enjoying being partnered was treated as unimaginable or preposterous. In a 1943 cartoon that appeared in the servicemen's magazine *Yank*, a gangly, stunned-looking young man in a private's uniform holds a chubby man at the sergeant's rank on a crowded dance floor. The sergeant quakes with anger. "'Migawd, Sarge,' the private explains, 'I thought I was cutting in on a WAAC!'"[53] The sergeant's anger and the private's mortification tell us that men do not dance together. Perhaps there was an additional implication that mistakes like this would happen when women wore military uniforms. Though women in uniform were welcomed in some dances, such as those sponsored by British Welcome Clubs and the hospitality committees of New York and the District of Columbia, WACS and WAVES were excluded from U.S.O. clubs.[54] The dances were organized to cater to the desires of heterosexual men.

Carefully screened young women were brought in to serve as "junior hostesses," available to play ping-pong with, listen to, and, most of all, dance with servicemen. A former volunteer recalled, "Suddenly, single women were of tremendous importance. It was hammered at us through the newspapers and magazines and on the radio. We were needed at U.S.O., to dance with the soldiers."[55] Older women volunteers were expected to play a different role, monitoring the young hostesses' behavior and being surrogate mothers to the men. The military and the U.S.O. aimed to satisfy men's loneliness and presumed need for physical contact with women by offering chaste, supervised dance as a sex substitute. The junior hostesses' volunteer status was crucial for the respectability of all concerned. Had they been paid dance partners, the U.S.O. would not have been distinguished from a taxi dance hall. As long as women were volunteers, they would not be stigmatized by switching from partner to partner and making every man feel that he was special. They were patriotic young women wearing out their heels for the war effort.

The women volunteers were prohibited from dancing with each other.[56] Through screening, training, and constant supervision, young women were reminded that they were there to satisfy servicemen's desires, not their own. Dances were structured as sites for women's service and men's refreshment. A London notice of a dance sponsored by the Red Cross advertised that hostesses would be provided but that American soldiers may bring girls from the uniformed forces. Presumably uniformed women could not bring themselves or be brought by a civilian.[57]

Dance magazine published rules for hostesses including that volunteers should "consider it a war job and be always pleasant, punctual, reliable and more interested in showing the boys a good time than in having one themselves."[58] A sponsor of dances at the Arcadia Ballroom in New York City presented young women volunteers, called "guest partners" at the Arcadia, with the following rules:

- Guest partners are requested not to wear sweaters.
- Each guest partner is asked to have a small bag to hold her identification card which must always be on her own person. Bags which can be carried on the finger or wrist will prove most satisfactory.
- Guest partners will please meet their girl friends in the lounge and not wait for them in the ballroom.
- Guest partners are asked to be friendly to Service men without introductions, but to avoid discussion of naval or military affairs. When asked to dance by a Service man or introduced to a Service man by a member of the Hospitality Committee guest partners are expected to dance.
- Guest partners are not expected to leave the Arcadia before 10:30 pm.
- Guest partners are earnestly asked to refuse invitations from Service men for entertainment at the conclusion of the Monday evening dances.[59]

Though popular dances ritually displayed men's dominance and women's subordination, dance organizers were seriously concerned about the emotional vulnerability of GIs. While dances were designed to protect men from contracting venereal disease, they were also structured to protect them from social rejection. Selected, trained, and monitored by older, middle-class women, young volunteer dance partners were told how to dress, what to talk about, and most importantly never to refuse a soldier's request for a dance. Obedient, patriotic young women were recruited for dances to be willing listeners and ever-ready partners. Volunteer hostesses were instructed to be assertive enough to invite the shy soldier to dance but always submissive enough to put aside their own preferences. They were brought to the dances to serve the state by serving men on the dance floor.

Dance organizers wanted women to entertain men, but did not want the entertainment to be a prelude to sex. The Arcadia Ballroom's last rule, whose importance is stressed by the author's inclusion of "earnestly," suggests that hostesses were supposed to be fantasy girlfriends for a few hours but were not trusted to spend time with soldiers outside of the strictly monitored ballroom. As explained by the head of the U.S.O. National Women's Committee, organizational policy required that "boys must go directly home after the U.S.O. and are not supposed to see the girls home. Girls must understand this, and make it easy for the boys."[60] Volunteers were often transported to and from dances as a group, and they were prohibited from leaving a dance and returning later in the evening. The U.S.O.'s attempts to contain the behavior of soldiers and volunteers were not always successful. Such slippage was spoofed in a 1945 cartoon that appeared in *Yank*. In a room full of heterosexual dancing couples, one woman's back is stamped "Stolen from U.S.O."[61]

In a history of the U.S.O., Meghan Winchell argued "the job of the junior hostess was sexual at its core."[62] To a degree, yes, but theirs was sexual work designed to exclude sex. It is more precise to say that the job of junior hostess was heterosexual at its core, if heterosexual refers not to a sex act but to a structuring dynamic between men and women. Junior hostesses were at U.S.O. dances to restore men for war by performing cheerful and chaste subordination, not to have sex with them.

Black soldiers and black civilian women were excluded from the majority of venues where soldiers danced in their leisure time. Segregated recreation, including dances in which black women volunteers were brought in to dance with black soldiers, were arranged by the military and ancillary civilian organizations (fig. 3.3). The military and its allied civilian volunteer organizations built segregation into the recreational activities they provided for soldiers. These recreational activities were documented on the pages of servicemen's periodicals, which showed GIs dancing. All of the jitterbugging GIs shown in the pages of the servicemen's periodicals *Stars and Stripes* and *Yank* during World War II were white. In Europe black soldiers danced with white European women. Yet as revealed by historian George

Figure 3.3
Christmas Dance at Negro Service Club. Camp Swift, Texas, 1943.
National Archives.

H. Roeder in his study of wartime censorship, photographs of black soldiers dancing with white women, whether taken by the press for publication or by soldiers for personal use, were banned from publication.[63] As dance became emblematic of American culture, and an activity that was compatible with normative masculinity, black men as well as any men of color were obscured. The All-American jitterbugging boy in military propaganda was white.

On any dance floor actual men were undoubtedly shy and bold, sensual and stiff, graceful and inept. On the pages of servicemen's publications the dancing man existed through a limited array of representations. These representations were selected to serve the war effort. They helped to convey images of happy, vigorous, U.S. soldiers spreading U.S. culture abroad. Photographs of dancing GIs displayed relationships of dominance, between servicemen of different rank, between men and women, and between the United States and other nations. Though the subtle physical pressure involved in leading a dance partner is something that cannot be shown in a still photo, GIs were often shown as informal instructors of foreign women.

While the paid dance teacher had long been the image of an effeminate man, the GI who provided spontaneous jitterbug lessons to Irish, Russian, and Icelandic women managed global relations in his capacity as a charming ambassador of American jitterbug. Typical of these representations was a 1942 photograph published in *Yank* of a uniformed white U.S. soldier gracefully pulling away from the woman with whom he danced in a jitterbug move known as a break. She wears a shiny dark dress, leans back supported by his outstretched arm, and appears to await his next physical cue. The caption locates them in Iceland and explains, "Sgt. Leonard Preyss cutting something of a mean figure with native lass who's willing to learn. Sgt. Preyss is willing to teach."[64]

Photographs often displayed hierarchical relationships between men and women, men of different rank, and people of different nations. In photographs men dominated women, men of higher rank dominated men ranked lower, and Americans dominated all. Cartoons played with these relationships. A May 30, 1942, cartoon published in *Stars and Stripes* shows a matronly woman dancing with a balding, chinless U.S. chaplain. She is fleshier than contemporary depictions of attractive women. Her clothing reveals too much. In the background two trim young couples dance with verve. The background dancers' bodies are crouched, jitterbug style, and circles ring their legs to indicate spinning. The chaplain maintains a staid posture. His stout partner demands more: "I'll show you how to do the 'Pride o' Erin' waltz if you'll teach me the 'Disgrace of the States.'" Racy dancing to jazz music was so associated with GIs that his partner assumed that even an older chaplain would have a provocative dance repertoire.[65]

To produce humor the cartoon reversed the more common representation of the relationship of men to women dancers in military periodicals. Representations of GIs as the ones who taught jitterbugging to the world's women were much more common. GIs in Europe brought U.S. culture to a world depicted as hungry to learn how to be an American hep cat.[66] The jitterbug represented the United States as vigorous, in command, modern, and urban. The August 31, 1945, cover of *Yank* magazine shows a uniformed white U.S. soldier, knees bent and relaxed as he holds and attempts to steer his partner. His partner looks warily upward as she stands stiffly in his arms. She is a young woman with a girlish face and wears the uniform of a Russian WAC. They have met on the dance floor in Berlin. A caption explains, "The mystery of the American dance step is being solved for a hesitant Russian WAC by Pvt. Edmund Kosek of Buffalo, NY." By the end of the war, dance, which had been associated with women generally, with foreign men, and with the perpetual foreignness of blackness, had been transformed into a symbol of the regular guy in the United States. The GI, whose masculinity was secured by his commitment to war, and whose heterosexuality was certified by the woman in his arms, could dance without accusations of effeminacy or indolence. No one would dispute or assail his masculinity. Wartime propaganda, coupled with a dance that easily displayed youthful, athletic vitality and men's dominance, made dancing seem to be the most natural thing for the All-American boy.

The easy alignment between masculinity and dance would not survive after the war ended. The next chapter examines how the stifling 1950s and the tumultuous 1960s created a generation of white men who did not dance.

CHAPTER 4

༄

Sad Sack's Sons

Dancing in the Postwar Years

It was June 1945, just weeks after the Nazi army surrendered, and Sad Sack, the cartoon character who stood for every hapless GI, snoozed on his duffle bag. A dropped newspaper lay at his side, its headline announcing GERMANS FINISHED! Sad Sack smiled as he dreamt of his discharge, his dream revealed in a bubble above his head. He buys a flashy suit, races into the outstretched arms of his sweetheart, takes her dancing, marries at the altar, and two frames on contentedly pushes a baby carriage with his bride.[1] Sad Sack dreamt of a return to normal life, but bad news awaited him. Sarge stood over the sleeping private and held a piece of paper bearing travel orders: "Private Sad Sack will be shipped to the Pacific."

In reality, the war in the Pacific would end in two months and Sad Sack's real counterparts were indeed able to go home. "V.J.!" *Yank* magazine proclaimed, and gave its readers an image of jubilant victory. "A sailor and a WAC tore up the sidewalk on Broadway with a swinging, strutting victory jive."[2] The free-swinging jitterbug that had been a symbol of American culture abroad provided the perfect way to celebrate coming home.

American veterans returned to the United States to live versions of Sad Sack's dream. Large numbers of returning servicemen married and produced a cohort of children so numerous it was soon called the baby boom.[3] Returning veterans passed numerous things onto their sons, but for the most part did not teach them to jitterbug. Many of their sons did not dance at all as young men, or if they did, danced in ways that their fathers could not recognize as good dancing. What was it about the postwar years that made it less and less likely that young men, especially young white men, would learn to dance?

The war and the Swing Era ended together. Dance historians Marshall and Jean Stearns declared that "when the Swing Era faded in the forties, a blackout of about ten years intervened—from 1945 to 1954—with little or no dancing."[4] Several factors contributed to the decline of big band music and the dancing it accompanied.[5] A musician's union strike that halted recordings by big bands between 1942 and 1944 weakened their popularity.[6] Some blame the decline in dancing on the emergence of be-bop music, a cultural change that was perhaps accelerated by the strike. Jazz music shifted from the driving and steady rhythms played by big bands to the complicated, uneven rhythms of be-bop. In 1948 big band leader Woody Herman complained that "even the young people wouldn't know what to do with [be-bop]. When I get even a suggestion of [be-bop] in the music, they stop dancing and look bewildered."[7] Unable to dance to be-bop, jazz audiences became accustomed to enjoying music for its own sake, rather than as an accompaniment to dance. Changes in tax laws made large dance halls and big bands less profitable.[8] In less capacious venues smaller groups of jazz musicians played to audiences who came to remain in their seats and listen.

The generalization that there was "little or no dancing" for a decade at the end of the Swing Era must be qualified by consideration of dancing that continued in African American and Latin American communities. Be-bop was not the only successful postwar jazz form. Small swing bands known as "jump" bands were also popular and continued to provide live dance music for predominantly black audiences. The fast-tempo blues songs they played were precursors to rock and roll.[9] Louis Jordan's Tympany Five played upbeat, danceable, "jump" music and was very successful from the beginning of World War II through the end of the 1940s. When Jordan shouted "Caldonia! Caldonia! What makes your big head so hard?" he solo danced on stage, playfully accenting the end of each line with a kick, as a floor full of couples danced below.

In the 1940s the recording industry's racial segmentation of its markets went through rapid changes of name. Records marketed to blacks were euphemistically ranked on *Billboard's* "Harlem Hit Parade" in the early 1940s. This chart was renamed "Race Records" and then changed again to "Rhythm and Blues," a title which continues today as R & B. The hit songs on these lists always contained dance records, and the consumers of these records, most of whom were black, continued to dance to them in the years characterized by "little or no dancing."

During the same years Cuban and Puerto Rican musicians performed dance music for dancing audiences that were primarily Latino. In the barrios of East Harlem and the South Bronx, Puerto Rican and Cuban couples mamboed to live music at neighborhood clubs.[10] The Palladium, a large ballroom in midtown Manhattan that had formerly featured swing bands and catered to white audiences, began to book Latin bands in 1947 in order to attract Latinos.[11] Fewer white couples were going out to dance in New York, but dancing continued to be popular among Puerto Ricans and other Latino immigrants. When the Palladium began to feature Latin bands, a small number of non-Hispanic white and black dancers joined Latino dancers on its dance floor. The postwar decline in dancing, while real and significant, is a description that applies most accurately, but not exclusively, to white adults. When historians of the United States describe dance booms and the disappearance of dance, they are generally describing the popularity of dance among white young adults. Within that frame of reference, in the postwar years, the place of dance in social life did indeed contract.

HIGH SCHOOL DANCES

Going out to dance had, for the most part, been an activity for the unmarried. During the war and in the immediate postwar years the age at marriage declined, marriage rates increased, and middle-class white families moved to newly constructed suburbs, all factors that decreased the demand for large urban dance halls.[12] Though dance seemed to disappear from adult nightlife in the late 1940s and early 1950s, it continued on in high schools where it had become institutionalized in proms and a host of themed dances that enlivened the school year. On the East Coast, in 1945, WPEN radio station began broadcasting the *950 Club*, a dance music show narrowly targeted to teen audiences. The hosts played danceable records and invited high school students in the studio's audience to dance along. The show's popularity among teens in the Philadelphia market pushed it to the number one afternoon spot in the early 1950s.[13]

Teenagers on the West Coast were similarly enthusiastic about dancing. For example, San Francisco's Lowell High School, a large public college preparatory high school, held at least six dances in the 1950/1951 school year.[14] Students danced at a picnic that opened the school year, and prizes were given to the best dancers that day. There was a "Winter Wonderland" junior prom and a "Blossom Time" dance. A senior prom was held at one of the city's most elegant hotels. In the early 1950s high school students often gave their dances romantic names. The eight dances held at Lowell in the 1952/1953 school year included the "Stairway to Paradise" and the "Snowflake Serenade." Across the San Francisco Bay at Oakland High School students danced at the "Starlight Sonata," "Moonlight and Magnolias," and "Royal Nocturne."[15] At the dances held at Oakland and Lowell, students danced as heterosexual couples to slow tempos in relatively close embrace. At the most formal dances young women wore gowns and young men tuxedos. A Lowell High School yearbook contributor wrote, "soft lights, mellow music, and swaying couples is the best and most accurate description at a Lowell dance."

In the earliest years of the 1950s the Lowell High School Dance Band, a wind and brass group of between ten and twelve players provided the music for dances. They played at the Senior Ball in 1953 and were praised in the yearbook for their danceable "dreamy music." Despite constant turnover of its musicians as classes of students moved through the school, the band had been in continual existence since at least 1922. In 1954, however, the band's place at dances suddenly was less sure. A small group of band members formed a jazz combo to play at a reception in which students listened but did not dance. This perhaps signaled a divergence between the music favored by these band members and the kind of music students wanted to hear at dances. Dance music was rapidly changing in ways that distanced it from jazz. Jazz music was also changing as more players experimented with uneven rhythms that were too challenging for the average dancer. Perhaps the combo attempted to play be-bop, but even if they played selections from the more traditional repertoire, students were more interested in moving to the emerging new sound of rock and roll. In July 1955, for the first time, a rock and roll recording, Bill Haley's "Rock Around the Clock" became the country's bestselling record.[16] Small rock and roll bands using electrified instruments produced the music teenagers wanted to hear. That year, a new paid advertisement appeared in the Oakland High yearbook. "Hot off the juke boxes," it called out to Lowell's students. "29 cents for any used 45 4 for a buck. Come on down we have everything." Students were buying records, and they considered it more fun to dance to recorded hits than to less current dance music played by a live band.

By the late 1950s most teenagers learned the latest dances by watching other teenagers, who were far from their high schools, perform on television.[17] Though *American Bandstand*, which began airing nationally in 1957, was the most enduring show that featured adolescents dancing to the latest music, it was not the first to televise youths dancing. Locally produced televised dance shows preceded nationally broadcast programs.[18] Before national broadcasts of *American Bandstand* began, ABC television experimented with a national broadcast of a similar program, *The Big Beat*, which was originally planned to air for thirteen weeks in the summer. *The Big Beat* premiered on a Friday night in July 1957, hosted by radio disc jockey Alan Freed. Freed has been credited with being one of the first to promote rock and roll, and in particular, to play recordings by African American artists on stations directed at white audiences.[19] The range of music featured on *The Big Beat* reveals the 1950s as a transitional moment in the country's musical tastes. The July 12 premiere showcased, among others, white country music star Ferlin Huskey, African American doo-wop crooner Billy Williams, and Scottish folk singer Nancy Whiskey.[20]

The following week Freed brought on seven acts including black rock and rollers Chuck Berry and Frankie Lymon, young white teen idol Paul Anka, and the older white pop singer Andy Williams.[21] At the program's conclusion members of the studio audience were invited to dance. Frankie Lymon, the fourteen-year-old leader of the group that recorded a tribute to innocence entitled "I Am Not a Juvenile Delinquent," danced with a young white woman who rose from the audience. The broadcast of a brief moment of friendly interracial, heterosexual connection outraged southern segregationists, who swiftly and effectively applied pressure to ABC to cancel the show. *The Big Beat* ended just weeks after it premiered.[22]

What could have been so incensing about a dance between a fourteen-year-old and another teen? From the perspective of segregationists the dance was a form of intimate social interaction. Even the suggestion of intimacy between black men and white women, or even black and white young teens, was viciously punished in the South. Only two years earlier in 1955, fourteen-year-old Emmett Till was brutally murdered in Mississippi after a brief, flirtatious verbal interaction with a white woman.[23] The vicious response of white segregationists to even hints of physical contact between black men and white women can be traced, at least in part, to longstanding and utterly false beliefs in black men's beastlike sexuality and proclivity to rape. In the segregationist South such beliefs were routinely used to justify vigilante violence.

Northerners, especially those who saw themselves as liberal, distanced themselves from the horrors of southern racism, yet beliefs in the wild, sexual capacity of black men circulated widely in the North as well. In 1957, the year that a dance between a black and a white teen caused *The Big Beat*'s cancellation, the liberal intellectual journal *Dissent* published Norman Mailer's "The White Negro."[24] The essay was Mailer's attempt to explain the behavior of nonconformist young white youth to a broad public. According to Mailer's logic, political nihilism drew white "hipsters" to black sociopathic cultural primitivism. Mailer couched his argument in liberal terms as he explained that black pathology was a product of racism. Despite its sympathetic gestures, the essay dehumanized black men. In his depiction of the undifferentiated category, "The Negro," Mailer associated all black men and black contemporary culture with unrestrained, primal sensuality. "The

Negro . . . could rarely afford the sophisticated inhibitions of civilization, and so he kept for his survival the art of the primitive, he lived in the enormous present, he subsisted for the Saturday night kicks, relinquishing the pleasures of the mind for the more obligatory pleasures of the body . . . ."[25] The essay ultimately turned to jazz music as the cultural expression of blackness that attracted white hipsters. Mailer had nothing to say about the technical skill and cerebral creativity of the black musicians who created jazz. Instead, jazz was an "orgasm." Mailer reduced jazz to mere bodily release.

Though in his "White Negro," Mailer appeared unable to recognize black intellect, a black intellectual, his contemporary James Baldwin, wrote a rejoinder. Baldwin argued that it was Mailer whose sexuality swamped his ability to think. In his "The Black Boy Looks at the White Boy," Baldwin characterized Mailer's essay as an example of the way in which white men of the era reduced black men to sex. "To be an American Negro male," Baldwin wrote, "is to be a kind of walking phallic symbol."[26] Baldwin's critical reading of Mailer can be applied, as well, to the panicked southern response to the moment of interracial dancing on *The Big Beat*. Segregationist viewers of *The Big Beat* could not see fourteen-year-old Frankie Lymon as a harmless young teenager. Hysterically fearful of contact between black men and white women, angry southern white viewers characterized Frankie Lymon's brief dance with a white woman as an intolerable offense.

When they cancelled *The Big Beat*, ABC showed that it was unwilling to stand up to racism. The network nonetheless saw the commercial value of black music and continued to showcase just enough safely contained black culture to appeal to youthful audiences. Almost immediately after cancelling *The Big Beat*, ABC began broadcasting *American Bandstand* nationwide. *American Bandstand* aired on weekdays at just the right time for teenagers to turn it on after school. It featured a room full of teenagers, the vast majority of whom were white, dancing to the latest hit records, including, on occasion, recordings by black entertainers. The show was broadcast from Philadelphia and selected its dancers from schools in the immediate vicinity of the station. Those schools had very few black students.[27]

The day after its national debut *American Bandstand* received a disdainful review in the *New York Times*.[28] The reporter granted that the young men on the show deserved praise for their conservative dress and trim sideburns, but "the quality of the dancing, however, was poor. There was also a shortage of boys. Quite a few girls had to dance with other girls, and some of them looked grim about it." The critic thought the dancing was poor and the music insipid, but *American Bandstand* nevertheless quickly had an audience of millions. The format, which gave prominence to recorded music as the accompaniment to dance, and which featured bands lip-synching to their recordings so that listeners would hear exactly what they expected, signaled the end of the era of dancing to live band music.

Chuck Berry's recording "School Days" was number three on the pop charts in 1957.[29] "Hail! Hail! Rock and roll!" he sang. "Deliver me from the days of old!" That year the Lowell High School Dance band, an institution that had been reconstituted again and again to accompany dances since the early 1920s, disappeared. Live music became the background for sports rather than dancing. In the mid-1950s, the Lowell Band grew fivefold and became a prize-winning marching band. Initially the band, or at least parts of it, continued to play at dances, but in 1957 it performed at basketball and football games but at none of the year's several dances. The absence of a dance band seemed to have no consequence for Lowell's social calendar. Students attended the "Sputnik Sprink," "Abba Dabba Honeymoon," "Ski Spree," and the most popular event of all, the "Twirp Dance," which briefly upended the gender order and "allowed" young women to invite young men to the dance. Students wanted to dance to rock and roll, and it was available on records. They no longer needed, or wanted, a dance band.

Nineteen fifty-eight brought an ending much more significant than the demise of a high school dance band. That year the fixtures of the Savoy, the Harlem dance palace where lindy hoppers brought social dance to spectacular heights of creativity, were auctioned off in preparation for the hall's demolition.[30] Harlem nightlife was not what it used to be. The postwar demand for large-scale housing was greater than the need for a grand venue for dance. To clear the way for a housing project, the building that housed the Savoy was knocked down.[31]

DANCING—A WOMAN'S GAME?

The producers of *American Bandstand* assumed that the audience for the program consisted of teenagers and housewives, and that adult men had outgrown their interest in dance. Married women, they surmised, missed the dancing that had gone out of their lives when courtship ended. The producers were probably correct in their assumptions. For a housewife who responded to a survey in the 1950s, the loss of dancing contributed to her unhappiness with married life.[32] Though she explained that she "always hoped to be just what I am—a wife and a mother," she found married life isolating and dispiriting. "I have desired to learn square dancing and to play cards occasionally with my husband, but he does not agree and I have become resigned." *American Bandstand's* producers saw an audience in unhappy wives like her. Addressing women who watched the program at home during the day, Dick Clark urged them to "roll up the ironing board and join us when you can."[33]

By the late 1950s men who danced well, especially men who were beyond their teenage years, fell under suspicion. It is telling that when *American Bandstand* premiered in 1957, its producers were unable to attract equal numbers of young men and women who were eager to dance on television. The public association of skilled masculine dance with youthful masculine good times, which had been fostered by the wartime press, seemed to have evaporated.

It was in this context that Gene Kelly, the dancing star of Broadway theatre and Hollywood movies, created "Dancing—A Man's Game," an hour and fifty-five minute television program broadcast on December 21, 1958, as part of NBC's *Omnibus* series.[34] Alistair Cooke, the series' host, introduced the program by telling viewers that this evening "we offer you an orgy, a well-disciplined orgy of dancing." The *Omnibus* series was a family show and the "disciplined orgy" it presented that evening was a sexless one. No women were present and the possibility of same-gender love was far outside the boundaries of what was treated as thinkable on television in 1958.

Cooke introduced Kelly as a regular guy whose masculinity was bolstered by his working-class origins. He was "a boy from Pittsburgh, a tumbler fresh out of Penn State. [He worked as] a brick layer, [and] a soda jerk" before becoming a star of theatre and film. Cooke exited and the scene shifted to a group of men in tights at a ballet barre slowly warming up to ponderous piano music. Before viewers could begin to question how such dancing could be a man's game, the camera pulled back to reveal that oddly, the men in tights were in a gymnasium. A gymnast whirled around a horse. Men in shorts and tee shirts tumbled. A baseball player crossed the room wearing a striped uniform and cap. There was a basketball hoop. Two men fenced and a boxer punched a bag held by another man. Sports fans would be able to recognize baseball star Mickey Mantle and tennis player Vick Seixas. The boxer was Sugar Ray Robinson. Johnny Unitas practiced football, Bob Cousy basketball, while Dave Sime leapt over hurdles.

Gene Kelly stood among them wearing dark slacks, a dark tight sweater vest, a white shirt with sleeves rolled up and collar open, and spoke to the audience. Kelly described dance as the practice of contained virility, which viewers were encouraged to see as a particularly masculine form of embodiment. Dancers and sports professionals are alike, he explained, because they each possess the same commanding self-discipline. "All of these men possess skill in physical movement and physical movement in rhythm . . . Each must discipline his body to keep it firmly under his command." Like earlier defenders of men who danced, Kelly attempted to define masculine dance, in fact dance itself, in terms that suggested that foremost it is the exercise of bodily control.

Kelly addressed the sports heroes by their first names, establishing by his familiarity that he was among equals. "Beautiful Vic!" he remarked after Seixas swung his racket. "That's great Bob!" "Sugar Ray, give me a punch . . . no not me!" he chuckled. "Dave you're beautiful to watch." "Thanks a million Mickey!" One by one each athlete entered and demonstrated a typical movement required by his game. Kelly followed by showing how a dancer would exaggerate the same movement to make it more expressive. After having shown the audience how to see sports movement as dance, Kelly brought on a group of men dancers to perform a swinging, sliding sports ballet.

Kelly asked viewers to think for a moment about ordinary men and women who dance. There dance is a man's game, too. "On the dance floor the man leads and the woman follows. And if she doesn't, she's considered a bad dancer and she isn't taken out the next time." Having established the masculine credentials of professional dancers, and the average man's dominant position on the dance floor, he turned to the challenging issue of tights. These are uniforms, worn by men, who like gymnasts and divers will be judged on the basis of the lines they create with their bodies. An athlete who is judged by his form "must wear an outfit that shows his form."

Kelly demonstrated the naturalness and masculinity of ballet positions in which dancers stand at an angle to an audience, by demonstrating ballet's kinship with fencing. He took up a sword, turned his body sideways in relation to the audience, and covered his crotch with his left hand. Turning sideways, he said, makes a man "less of a mark to shoot at." Kelly tap danced with boxer Sugar Ray Robinson, danced with Patrick Adiarte, a young Filipino dancer who was being directed on Broadway by Kelly in a production of *Flower Drum Song*, and tossed a football around with Adiarte after the dance. Toward the end of the program, Kelly explained that there is a sharp distinction between masculine and feminine dance.

> We mustn't let you think that we are implying that because a man is physically stronger he's a better dancer. One is playing the female role the other the male role . . . We need women to play the female parts. We need women to play the part of women. When they try to play the part of a male dancer they make a mistake . . . To try to compete with a man on his own ground is wrong . . . The same thing goes for the male dancer. It is as wrong for a man to try and be graceful in a feminine way.

He suggests that there is a sharp line between masculine and feminine dance, but the boundary he identified was marked primarily by the words feminine, man, woman, female, and male, and the assertion that male dancers will always be stronger. What makes a part female? Its femininity. The program ended with a dance. Kelly joined a group of men who danced a story of young toughs hanging out on a street corner. A man entered carrying a bouquet. He walked a bit too sprightly, even effeminately. Kelly snatched the bouquet, and a choreographed fight ensued. The brawl quickly engaged all of the men. A police officer happened upon the melee and dispersed them. Order was restored. The dance conveyed the message that toughs shall dominate feminine men, but police will dominate toughs. Kelly's "Dancing—A Man's Game" attempted to defend masculine dancing by associating it with the exemplary masculinity represented by sports heroes, drawing a sharp if tautological line between masculine and feminine dance, and concluding with a choreographed celebration of male hierarchies.

It is worth considering why Kelly, and the network that so prominently featured the program, felt the need to prove dance's masculinity. Kelly had been a star of screen and theatre and known for his naturalistic, athletic dancing style ever since he won a starring role in the 1940 Broadway production of *Pal Joey*. But while Kelly's style distinguished him as a remarkably masculine dancer, professional dancing remained stigmatized as feminine. In the television special Kelly was surrounded by men who were athletes and interacted with them as personal friends, certifying the masculinity of dance by association. One by one Kelly addressed characteristics that made dance incompatible with masculinity: its grace, its association with women, and those embarrassing, revealing tights. He did not mention what was perhaps the most stigmatizing of the man dancer's associations: his assumed homosexuality. Same-gender attraction was unmentioned in the program though it was central to the problem of dance's effeminacy. Possibilities for reconfigured sexual and gender relations opened by the wartime formation of networks of gay men and the large-scale employment of women were rapidly closed in the oppressively conservative, homophobic, and paranoid period that followed World War II. Popular magazine articles and books announced a "crisis" of masculinity that stemmed, they claimed, from diminished lines between men's and women's roles.[35] These alarming reports had the effect of redrawing firm boundaries around masculine and feminine behavior.

Historians of the postwar years describe it as an era of social conformity and domestic containment.[36] It was a time in which any form of dissent was suspect. Dance historian Ramsay Burt described the 1950s as the most homophobic period in the history of the nation.[37] Cold War

paranoia and economic prosperity combined to promote a heteronormative, patriarchal, family-centered, suburban life as the American ideal.
Following the deprivations of the Depression and of the war, and subsi-
dized by federal home loan programs, white middle-class couples sought
to fulfill all of their emotional and sexual needs within the confines of
suburban homes.

All sorts of political and personal nonconformity were swept together
during the Cold War, vaguely linked, and punished.[38] Literary critic Elizabeth A. Wheeler described postwar containment culture as a "sensual
force."[39] A public culture and legal environment in which sexual difference
was grounds for the loss of livelihood and even imprisonment imposed a
fear that reached down to the level of embodiment. No wonder the young
men on *American Bandstand* danced poorly. Social constraints left them
little room to move. Gender and sexual conformity took hold of men's
bodies.[40] Dancing could even land a man in jail.

In the late 1950s the bars where gay men and lesbians socialized were
routinely raided by police in search of criminalized behavior. For men, the
mere act of dancing with another man was a criminally indecent offense. In
1956 Hazel Nickola's San Mateo, California, bar became the target of an
undercover investigation by police who were determined to shut it down
because it was popular among gay men.[41] The sheriff's office sent undercover agents to gather incriminating evidence, and an agent even managed
to get hired by the bar during the period of clandestine investigation. The
evidence of "perversion" that they gathered included descriptions of men
kissing and fondling other men, but also accounts of dancing. Descriptions
of dancing, mere dancing, were presented to the court as evidence of criminally perverse behavior. The court learned that "the vast majority of
dancers were men dancing with other men in close and affectionate embrace. Many of the men had their arms wrapped around each other's waists,
or shoulders . . . " and that "several employees of the tavern, while denying
seeing any fondling of private parts, or kissing, admitted that men frequently danced with men in close embrace." Same-gender dancing, even in
the absence of overtly sexual behavior, or gender-nonconforming dress,
marked men as homosexual. In the same period women who danced with
women could also be criminalized. Yet in the cases in which bars lost their
licenses because of women's dancing, women's gender-nonconforming
"mannish" dress was always noted by investigators.[42] The prohibition
against same-gender dancing was applied with much greater force to men.
Recall that when *American Bandstand* debuted, young women danced with
young women and the *New York Times* critic assumed that they partnered
only because there were insufficient numbers of young men. In the 1950s

men could not dance in a closed partner dance with men, regardless of the manliness of their attire.

The harassment of gays and lesbians in the late 1950s was one facet of an era whose crushing conservatism would be overturned in countless way by the social movements of the next decade. Every form of rebellion that burst into the open in the 1960s had its smaller scale antecedents in the 1950s. The rebellions that would grow as a generation of youth were radicalized by the Civil Rights and antiwar movements crisscrossed back and forth across the lines that previously had distinguished personal and the political and would affect how a generation of men moved.

DANCERS DISCONNECT

Nineteen fifty-seven, the year that a *New York Times* reporter dismissed the poor dancing and puerile music of *American Bandstand*, was the peak year of the baby boom. The rapid rise in the number of parents in the postwar period meant that young adults were home raising children. They had less leisure time than before marriage and spent more of it at home in front of the newly available television sets. The location of homes in suburbs drew white middle-class families away from urban centers and further contributed to the decline in urban nightlife. Twelve years after the end of the war, the youth of the Swing Era had become parents, and a wide rift was growing between adult and youth cultures, a divide that would swell as baby boom children reached adolescence in the 1960s.[43] The generational cultural divide was not entirely new. Historian Randy McBee found great differences between youth and adult cultures in the first decades of the twentieth century, and Kelly Schrum demonstrated that the advertising strategies used by manufacturers in the 1930s helped to establish a distinct teen market.[44] Nonetheless the sheer size of the youth generation that emerged in the 1960s and the political circumstances into which it was born proved to be significant.

The dancing of the young men on *American Bandstand*'s 1957 debut may have been as bad as the *New York Times* critic said it was. Or, perhaps their dancing was so different from that which he knew as good dancing that he could not judge its competence. Vernacular forms of dance were changing at the end of the 1950s, and a major part of the change was the spectacle of men using more parts of their bodies when they danced and moving in ways that were deliberately sensual. In the late 1950s this sort of movement was most evident in the performances of Elvis Presley. In 1956 *Time* reported that Elvis Presley swung his hips "sensuously from side to side" and that his movements "suggest, in a word, sex."[45] Crowds of teenaged girls screamed, cried, and swooned at his performances. The national press generally portrayed him as harmless, but some clergymen and law enforcement personnel accused him of undermining the morals of his young audiences.[46] Neither the sound of his music nor his lyrics was what drew adoration and denunciation. It was his movement. Defending himself against the criticism of a Florida judge, Presley declared, "I don't do no dirty body movements."[47] But, of course, he did. Presley swung his hips back and forth, took a wide stance and then pulsed his thighs in and out, and jerked his chest forward in apparently pleasurable contraction. He often rested his hands on his belt as he flitted his fingers over his crotch.

Presley's movement style can be traced to pre–rock and roll dances. Decades earlier, dancers doing the snake hips rapidly twisted their legs in a movement not that different from his slower thigh pulsing. His staggering walk, made with feet wide apart, was one of the ways lindy hoppers of the Swing Era might follow a partner off the dance floor. Though Presley undoubtedly developed a distinctive movement style, many of his contemporaries moved in essentially similar ways. Black rock and roll musician Bo Diddley pulsed his thighs in and out when he performed, and Little Richard, another black early rock and roll performer, wildly flung himself around as he sang. Part of the reason that sensual movement became particularly associated with Elvis Presley during the 1950s was that black rock and roll performers were sometimes compelled to constrain their body movements when performing for white audiences.[48] A frequently repeated anecdote is that Presley was also prevented from appearing sensual on a television screen. The story goes that he was filmed from the waist up when he performed on the family-oriented Ed Sullivan show. It is an apocryphal story.[49] The cultural endurance of the false tale attests to the strength of the association between Presley and sensuous movement, and the belief that his movement style was singular. Sensual physicality became his trademark, though it was a style of moving common in the performing culture of rock and roll. Though other performers sensuously danced, only Elvis was "The Pelvis."

Reporters struggled to find the words with which to describe a man who moved sensuously. The images of sensuality they found referred to women or to boys, but not to men. Presley "wriggle[d] like a peep-show dancer."[50] He was "a male burlesque queen." His movements were "the classic bump and grind of the strip-teaser."[51] For a film reviewer, Presley embodied underdeveloped masculinity. Presley's face was "excessively sensitive, almost effeminate." He "resemble[d] an obscene child, a too sensuous adolescent. He cannot hope to reach . . . manliness."[52]

Presley was introduced to the nation as a "hillbilly" from Tupelo, Mississippi, an identity that meant white, rural, and poor, but little else to urban consumers of his music. The hillbilly identity opened a greater space for Presley to move sensuously than would have been available to a black or urban white man. He was not burdened by the categorical, pathologized sexualization that black men endured. His heterosexuality was certified by endless reports of the effect his performances had on young women, and perhaps also, to some degree, by his rural roots, since homosexuality was associated with cities. Presley could perform eroticism in the late 1950s without being demonized. Critics explained that he got away with his sensuality because he was a simple American boy. "By constantly reminding his teen-age listeners of what he so obviously was—a simple boy from Tupelo who had suddenly become famous—Elvis somehow removed the sting from the sexuality that could have easily terrified them."[53] His black contemporary Frankie Lymon, who recorded "I Am Not a Juvenile Delinquent," was not especially sensual, yet his dance across color lines brought the swift end of a television show. Presley was emphatically sexual and played at being a juvenile delinquent yet was able to maintain sufficient innocence to become an enormously wealthy star. He was sensual but white, and sexy but heterosexual, and so was able to create a normatively masculine public persona. The Presley the public knew was just as likely to join a spontaneous football game as he was to sensuously sway his hips.[54]

Still, as a "hillbilly" Presley was the kind of white man who time and again becomes associated with dance in the public imagination. The label "hillbilly" qualified Presley's whiteness by locating it as regional and low class.[55] To a 1956 *Newsweek* critic of a performance at a Las Vegas nightclub Presley was "a jug of corn liquor at a champagne party." For a national audience beyond the southern states for whom Tupelo, Mississippi, was a distant place, Presley could be both authentically American and exotic.

When Presley gained nationwide recognition in the late 1950s he initially received an array of negative reactions from conservative adults. These ranged from withering dismissals of his performance as the passing fancy of shrieking teenaged girls, to denunciations of what some saw as amoral displays of sensuality. The critics did not diminish his success. If anything, they helped to certify his place as a young rebel and thereby enhanced his popularity among teenagers. As the dance styles of young white teenagers became looser and more sensual, Presley's movement no longer appeared quite as startling as before. In the late 1950s on dance floors heterosexual pairs began to separate as they danced. They danced as couples but did not touch. Separation freed dancers to explore a wider range of movement. The changes that were happening on dance floors became most recognizable by 1960 when a dance craze spread nationwide. Its name was the twist.

The twist was followed by many named dances of the 1960s in which dance partners did not touch. Though generally danced facing a partner, the twist was a solo performance in which an individual twisted his shoulders and arms one way and his hips and knees the other. Most Americans became aware of the twist around 1960 or 1961 following Chubby Checker's hit recording of the song of the same name. The song was first recorded by Hank Ballard in 1959 and described a step that African Americans had danced in clubs in the late 1950s.[56] Though a song like "The Twist" may spread a dance nationwide, it could only do so if dancers had been prepared to assimilate that sort of dance, through experience with other similar ways of moving. The twist was a radical departure from traditions of dance that required men to hold their torsos still. However the swiveling hips of the twist had its antecedents in some of the improvisations of jitterbugging. As a man pulled away from his jitterbug partner he might lean against the tension of her grasp and twist side to side. By the time the twist appeared on television screens dancers had learned to dance unattached from their partners if only briefly and incompletely when they pulled away from each other in the breakaway moves of jitterbug and dances like it. Dancers must have had some experience moving their hips before a dance that involved hip swiveling spread across the country on a massive scale. The physical experience of doing the twist caused gossip columnist Hedda Hopper to retract an earlier denunciation of Elvis Presley. "The first night I tried dancing the Twist I suddenly shrieked with laughter. I found myself doing what I'd condemned Elvis for doing. Now I'm devoted to him."[57] Audiences and critics had become accustomed to Presley's movement. With his increasing commercial and financial success, Presley's critics often turned into supporters.

Dances continued to be an important part of adolescent social life in the early 1960s, but the character of the dances rapidly changed. The 1963 Lowell High School yearbook had a two-page photo collage of the year's school dances. Only one photograph captures dancers in the conventional close embrace. Hearts decorate the walls in that photograph, suggesting that it may have been a Valentine's Day dance that called upon students to enact conventional forms of romantic behavior. In every other photograph dancers face each other in couples but do not touch. Boys were on their own in front of girls and had to improvise movement. What did they do?

In the early 1960s they were likely to perform named steps. In 1962 The Contours' "Do You Love Me" hit number three on the *Billboard* Hot 100 and number one on the R & B charts. White and black listeners were converging around a dance tune. In it, a man's love life depends on his ability to dance.

> You broke my heart
> 'Cause I couldn't dance
> You didn't even want me around
> And now I'm back, to let you know
> I can really shake 'em down
> Do you love me? (I can really move)
> Do you love me? (I'm in the groove)
> Ah do you love? (Do you love me)
> Now that I can dance?

"Do You Love Me?" tells men that they must dance and tells them how to dance. It lists two named dances, the mashed potato and the twist. Dancers were separated on the dance floor, but were not left there without re-sources. In the early 1960s named dances with set steps circulated and pro-vided teenagers with a small repertoire of movements. A recording like "Do You Love Me" could be popular because large numbers of teenagers knew the dances, and perhaps more importantly, wanted to know the dances. The early 1960s was a moment when named dances proliferated and pro-vided a transition for dancers learning to dance entirely detached from their partners.

The lyrics of the song may have resonated with young audiences because young women did want men who could dance, but often could not find them. In her history of courtship in the United States, Beth Bailey cites a 1963 *Mademoiselle* survey in which the majority of young women respon-dents included dancing in their description of an ideal date.[58] Though they wanted to dance, in the early 1960s, young white women were likely to have a difficult time finding a white male dance partner who was in the groove. In the Lowell High School yearbooks that were published before the 1960s, particular students had been celebrated as the "best" of certain categories. In 1964, a new category appeared: Best Dancers, with one male and one female winner. Though the school was overwhelmingly white, the winners were Sandra Zabel, a white young woman and William Bell, a black young man, a pattern that conforms to the intersectional race/gender positioning of dance. White women could be superlative dancers at the same time that white men contributed to the assumption that whites could not dance. A smaller poll, conducted the same year, identified two white dancers, a young man and a young woman, as the best among the senior class. Some young white men were learning to dance. In 1965 no students were named

Best Dancer, but when the categories returned in 1966 the race/gender pattern continued. A young white woman and a young Filipino man were named best dancers. In 1967 a young white woman and a young black man were the favored dancers, and in 1968 a young black woman and a young Chinese man. White women were viewed as impressive dancers at Lowell; white men generally were not.

Gender scholar Ann Cvetkovich suggests that in the first discotheques that appeared in the United States at the beginning of the 1960s, go-go dancers helped the public learn the latest dance steps.[59] While relatively small segments of the population were able to go to these early discotheques, by the mid-1960s accomplished go-go dancers were featured in national broadcasts of television programs such as *Shin-Dig* and *Hullabaloo*. In television programs that were geared toward national audiences, and in the mainstream dance clubs that featured them, go-go dancers were women. The 1963 *Mademoiselle* survey found that young women imagined dream dates as evenings in which men took them dancing. The Contours' "Do You Love Me" described a man who learned to dance to win back a woman's love. Even as dance was a popular activity for teenagers, it was construed as a feminized practice, something a young man might do, if he had to, in order to win the heart of a young woman. Cvetkovich describes "a homosocial world of girls practicing dances that tend to be of little interest to boys."[60] Girls of all races practiced dancing, and so it was common for them to step up to the dance floor fully prepared to perform the latest steps. Fewer white boys came to dance floors with such confidence. Their discomfort, and broader prohibitions on the ways in which men could move, may have pulled popular dance forms away from the performance of rehearsed steps and started a progression toward low technique or anti-technique forms of dancing for white youths. Dance that deliberately eschewed technique could even be a way of expressing masculine rebellion.

I interviewed Marvin, a white man who recalled being sent to social dance classes as a youngster in the early 1960s.[61] He rebelled against these classes and enjoyed telling the story of how he offended all the snobs there through his outlandish dancing. Marvin grew up in a middle-class family but went to a racially integrated, mixed-class elementary school. At school he spent time with boys who emulated the kind of attention-grabbing solo dancing performed by African American entertainers such as James Brown (fig. 4.1). Marvin and his friends were familiar with James Brown's movement style from his performances on television programs. What Marvin most admired about James Brown's dance style was his inclusion of athletic elements such as the "split," in which he stretched his legs in opposite directions to sink down to the floor, and then quickly drew them together to rise up again. Marvin's family's middle-class standing granted him an invitation to attend Dart Tinkum's dance club, a somewhat exclusive social dance school for children.

> I was the only kid from [my elementary school] who was asked to join Dart Tinkum's . . . and I got kicked out of Dart Tinkum because I did the splits, and I busted my pants, and I was unrepentant, and I was having a very good time doing it . . . but that was a very formal kind of dance club . . . and when I realized that my upwardly mobile dreams were not only not going to realize themselves or were false and hollow, Dart Tinkum became Fart Stink 'Um.

Marvin was predisposed to dance, but only in the informal, playful way that his schoolmates practiced, in which dance steps were stunts. The staid partnering taught at Dart Tinkum's did not appeal to him, and he still seems proud of having gotten himself expelled. Marvin's parents' attempt to socialize him through dance failed. By the time he reached college age, dance communicated two things for him, sexual desire and smashing convention. He recalled "that was sort of like the beginning of my feeling that

Figure 4.1
James Brown dances with Lloyd Thaxton on the Lloyd Thaxton Show, 1964.
Michael Ochs Archives, Getty Images.

dance was a wonderful form of expression, and it could say not only, "I'd like to fuck you," or, "I'd like to just express myself, but fuck you!" Marvin took delight in watching all of the old social conventions fall away. They had made demands upon him that he had never felt he could satisfy. At formal dances in which he was expected to ask women to dance, he had approached women nervously while thinking, "she'll say no, she'll say no." By the late 1960s he felt released from such social conventions and freed from learning proper form or passing fads in dances. He went to parties and rock concerts where he could dance with a woman without a formal request, and he could dance with abandon. He recalled that the kinds of music his generation listened to expanded and escaped traditional rhythmic and recording formulas.

> '66 turned into '67, and . . . all of a sudden the cuts that were dancing cuts would be longer, and longer, and longer . . . [and disc jockeys on alternative radio programs] were playing cuts that were—instead of three minute cuts, they were ten minute cuts, and they were twelve minute cuts, and they were also cuts that were no longer the 2, 4 beat or whatever it was. All of a sudden it was my man Ravi Shankar's you know sitar raga . . . and people were *still* throwing up their hands and becoming whirling dervishes, and no longer were people trying to do the mashed potatoes, or locomotion, or the twist, or you know the boogaloo or whatever and for *me* that was really exciting.

He could even fling about all by himself. I interviewed other white middle-class men of his generation who similarly described the joy that was released when the rules of propriety gave way. Herb, a Jewish, heterosexual college professor who grew up in an upper middle-class family on the East Coast recalled that he arrived at college in

> September of '68, and the *day* of orientation week that I arrived at Johns Hopkins, which was an all male school, we all had to wear ties and jackets, and the door, you know if you had a girl in the room, the door had to be open. Open door and four [feet] on the floor. And there were all these required courses. That was the first day of orientation week. By the end of orientation week, all those rules had been dropped. All the social rules, and all the required academic requirements, and all hell broke loose.

Hell broke loose and dancing broke loose. As a child Herb had been taught dance conventions by his parents at home and had been sent by them to social dance lessons in his earliest teen years. Signs of his desire to break with social norms were apparent then. His parents imagined a social life for him that involved dance structured by social conventions. At thirteen, he had already moved beyond that:

> I do remember [at the social dance class] moving around the room in a circle, you know, changing partners . . . I went, my friends went, none of us really liked it. . . . We felt similarly the way we felt going to Hebrew school. We didn't really want to do it, but it was what you do . . . it was increasingly common to have dance parties at, you know, the girls and boys of my school. And make-out parties. And we used to go over to somebody's house and we would dance and kiss.

As Herb grew up he continued to dance at house parties and at rock concerts. "I went to Woodstock," he recalled,

> and you get out there dancing with a half a million people . . . Listening to Sly and the Family Stone do "Want to Take You Higher," is one of the highlights of my life, and just dancing in this sea of people on a hillside. And then my friends and I would routinely have dance parties, and not just planned ones; but they would just start . . . There were a whole bunch of us living together, and we would just start dancing, and I became a dancing fool.

In the late 1960s white young men could dance without knowing how to dance. They did not have to lead. They did not have to know steps. In a no-technique dance culture in which he was freed from the need to know steps and from the responsibility of leading, Herb was able to become a dancing fool.

Herb recalls the era as one in which all the social rules had been dropped. Yet in most places, heteronormativity held firm. The romantic pairing of men was commonly treated as a joke, even while a burgeoning gay liberation movement meant that gays and lesbians were more visible. The first homophobic joke that ever appeared in the decades of Lowell High School yearbooks arrived in 1964. Two Asian men are caught in a photograph standing together at a dance. "Look Ma," the caption reads, "I finally got a date for the senior Prom!" This was followed in 1965 by a similar joke. A black young man is dressed in drag for a theatrical performance. "You're my kind of man!" the caption reads. In the 1967 yearbook, white young men perform in drag and a caption says, "Gee Russ, who's your new girl?" In the late 1960s at Lowell High School, at least among the students who produced the yearbook, homosexuality was always presented as a joke. The 1960s brought frequent drag dance performances to the high school, in which boys wore dresses that were tightly stretched over balloon breasts.

Dancing like a girl was mocked in these performances during an era when white boys enjoyed dancing without technique. Teens were dancing, but organized school dances, which only a few years earlier had been frequent and important student events, were perceived as less fun than parties. The 1967 yearbook notes that a dance was held the same night as the "biggest senior party of the year," and as a result only 46 students attended the dance. Parties connoted unstructured sociability; dances, with their formal clothing and slow partnered dancing, were becoming anachronisms. These trends were nearly catastrophic for dance studios as social dance lessons became irrelevant. In the late 1950s Arthur Murray studios attracted one hundred thousand students each year who wished to learn how to conduct themselves on a dance floor. A decade later only a fifth as many students enrolled in Arthur Murray schools.[62]

I was struck by how often white heterosexual-identified men used the word "wild" when talking about dance. Perhaps the reason the advocates of professional male dance never succeeded in recasting dance as masculine is because they attempted to define masculine dancing as controlled. Masculinity, like any social construct, is made of signs whose meanings are unstable. Self-control can signify masculinity, but it may also convey submission to social constraint and the absence of vitality. Sociologist Amy Wilkins wrote that being wild has been given greater value in the context of an economy in which service work demands that we control our emotions.[63] Men in the United States have often sought to restore masculinity through activities associated with the wild.[64] I found that for many white men, wildness, rather than control, was the way that they experienced the pleasure of dance. For example Paul, a fifty-year-old, white, business owner, who grew up working class, described dancing as "just going wild . . . Taking up a lot of room, taking off some of your clothes, getting on the table; somewhat inebriated. You know. There's definitely testosterone in that. . . . You just went wild." Going wild was a way to rebel against the social, political, and embodied containment of the postwar period.

The rebellions of the 1960s sometimes meant a softening of dichotomous gender presentation. Men wore their hair longer. The spectrum of colors worn by young men expanded as did the confines of tailoring. Pant legs widened into bell bottoms. Men wore medallions around their necks and fringe on their jackets. The new sartorial freedom, however, was always aligned with generational rebellion and on that basis could be acceptably masculine. The same was true of white men's dancing. It was dancing as cathartic youthful rebellion, not dancing as controlled grace. Wild dancing could be done while high on drugs. It could be done outdoors.

Men who became accustomed to dancing in this way could not make the switch to styles of dancing and comportment that were expected within the culture of discos. For many men disco music, dance, and style appeared to be a return to the conventional containment of the era against which they had rebelled. This perspective on disco can contribute to an explanation of the intensity of negative feelings that have been directed toward it. Popular musical forms frequently provoke disdain in those who think themselves more cultured or shock in those who see themselves as more moral, but few popular forms are widely hated by youths. Disco stands alone as a popular form that was hated by a portion of its youthful contemporaries. The next section explores why.

DISCO REPRESENTED

How is disco remembered? One image obliterates any other. It is John Travolta in a tight, white, leisure suit, playing Tony Manero, his right arm reaching diagonally upward to expose his arched back, slender hips, and spread thighs. In a frequently reproduced still photograph Manero's partner appears mousy in the shadow of his dazzling, white, grandeur. She watches him, but he stares directly at the camera. That is how disco is recalled and ridiculed. Dance scholar Katrina Hazzard-Donald scornfully described "the apolitical, slick dance and music called disco [which] gave voice to a newly empowered economic strata, the yuppie, and the midlevel service worker."[65] Opposing it to a more authentic and political black music and dance, she dismissed disco as a shallow product marketed to middle-class whites. Even though Hazzard-Donald dismissed disco as bland and vacuous white middle-class culture, I found that middle-class white men were at least as critical of disco as Hazzard-Donald. Heterosexual white men I interviewed who were old enough to remember disco recalled it with outsized negative emotion. Marvin was a young political radical when he became aware of disco as a form of music with an associated dance culture. He hated what he saw as its preening self-involvement. "It's John Travolta . . . dancing by himself. I mean. That's really what it is. I mean he's not dancing. I mean, he has a partner, but he's you know, he's walking down the street with the Bee Gees . . . so it's *him*." Men despised disco for being commercial and apolitical or detested rhythms that they characterized as mechanical. Some rejected disco as an elitist urban scene, but others because it was the lowbrow culture of working-class suburbs.

I was a participant observer in Dance 101, a college-level survey course designed to introduce dance techniques to physical education majors. As a student in Dance 101, I had to work with four young students to produce a group project on disco. It was their misfortune to have to work with me. Every student was required to work as part of a group to develop a demonstration of and lesson on a dance form. I conducted fieldwork in this course while working full-time as a professor. I often forgot to bring my Dance 101 textbook to the evening classes. When the instructor was late I hoped the class would be cancelled so that I could get home earlier. I was a mediocre student and thus share culpability for a hastily assembled group project. A few weeks into the course, the instructor divided us into groups and wrote suggested topics for group projects on the blackboard. A student who performed belly dance at nightclubs on the weekends quickly volunteered her group to present a project on her dance form. My group stared at the board glumly without expressing preferences. Finally Dennis, a young Chinese American man, said "I don't want to do tap." We agreed not to do tap. As more energetic groups picked dance forms from the board, the category "dances from the 1970s and 1980s" remained unclaimed, and by default became ours. I silently worried. The 1970s and 1980s were the time in my life when I danced the most at clubs, and I did not think of it as a period in which there were teachable dances. Dancers improvised at clubs, we did not perform named, repeatable dances. Ryan, a twenty-six-year-old student of Filipino, Mexican, and white ancestry volunteered to be our group leader. I was relieved and forgot about the project until the following week.

The next week Ryan was absent. We were given class time to plan our project and divide the work. We were adrift and very little was said. Time passed. Finally, I broke the silence to suggest that we could watch *Saturday Night Fever* and do something from it about disco. The concrete idea raised their energy. Emily, a young white student, said we could talk about the history of the period like peace signs and the war. Purnima, a young South Asian woman, volunteered to get a video clip from *Saturday Night Fever* to show to the class. Dennis would research the names of specific dances. I offered to bring costumes. The following week our teacher was absent. Our group gathered around a laptop to watch a four minute clip of John Travolta. Having found and watched the clip we decided we had what we needed for the time being and left early.

Weeks passed and various circumstances left us unprepared on the day of our presentation. We arranged to meet an hour before class. Everyone had gathered information on disco via the Internet and we quickly compiled the images and words into a single PowerPoint display. We watched the four minute clip of John Travolta again and tried to extract teachable movements. Ryan volunteered to teach one of Travolta's movements along with the electric slide, a group line dance with which he and others were familiar. Purnima did not want to dance and offered to turn the light switch on and off to create a strobe effect.

The instructor arrived and asked the two groups presenting to turn in their group bibliographies and individual typed paragraphs explaining each person's contribution. No one in either group had these things. Students offered ways to make it up. Could we email it to her? Could we write something now? Things were not going well. We clustered in our groups. Purnima and Ryan asked about how we were supposed to submit this information. Did Ryan, the "captain," have to gather it from us? Did we have to staple it together? They grasped onto these details to try to redeem themselves. Purnima said quietly to me that her contribution had been small. I said you are working the disco lights. Reassured, she said "oh yeah, that's something."

We turned down the lights to project the PowerPoint onto a screen at the back of the room. Reading in dim lights from index cards, we gave our historical overview. Purnima's survey of the 1970s ranged from Nixon's fall to pet rocks. Ryan spoke about dances of the period, including something new to me, the "chicken dance." We showed the four minute clip from *Saturday Night Fever*. Then we raised the lights and asked the students to rise and face the mirror. Ryan stood in front of them to teach a sequence of Travolta's choreography and the electric slide. Emily and I demonstrated behind him. His delivery was confident and relaxed but when he taught John Travolta's classic ceiling pointing gesture, he incorrectly pushed his hip out in the same direction as the upward point. After the lesson, sections of the class attempted to perform the electric slide to the song "You Should Be Dancing" from the film's soundtrack. Purnima rapidly turned on and off the lights. Once the final group performed we called everyone up for one last round together. It was fun and celebratory. Purnima even abandoned the lights and joined in. Things had gone well after all.

All that remained for our presentation was a brief question an answer period. The instructor turned to me and asked "who was Van McCoy?" I did not know. Could she hold me responsible for knowing everything? "He recorded "The Hustle." I can't believe in your research that none of you learned about Van McCoy." She was right; our research had been quick and shallow. She asked Dennis about the origins of the dances we performed He waited a long time and then said "you mean like where?" She responded to explain that almost all popular dances in the United States came from black people who have been written out of history. For example, she explained, Ric Silver, the choreographer who claimed to choreograph the electric slide, did not invent the electric slide or anything else. He only "codified" it and took credit for it. Emily asked, "you mean he stole it?!"

With my suggestion that we watch the film, I had led to my group's downfall by making *Saturday Night Fever* stand in for disco. But what was disco, and which groups can claim it as their cultural heritage? Jane Desmond asks, "how did John Travolta's white, straight character become the heartthrob of *Saturday Night Fever*? In what ways did disco's origins permeate the mainstreamed, commodified style that emerged, ultimately shaping the white heterosexuality of the Travolta character and the disco rage spawned by the movie?"[66] Desmond's question is important, though *Saturday Night Fever* did not generate the disco rage. It frequently stood, however, as the symbolic focus of the rage against disco.

Discos and disco music preceded the 1977 film. *Billboard* used the term disco-hit in 1973.[67] African American singer Barry White's instrumental dance record "Love's Theme," which was a popular among dancers at discos, was a number one hit on the pop charts in 1974. Van McCoy's "The Hustle" was number one on both the *Billboard* Hot 100 and the Hot Soul Singles charts in 1975. In the same year record labels began to issue longer versions of dance tunes geared to the disco market.[68] In 1976, all over the country young people who were old enough to get into dance clubs danced sensuously but separately to the pulsing beat and breathy singing of African American Donna Summer's erotic "Love to Love You Baby." *Saturday Night Fever* was based upon a 1976 story published in *New York* magazine. *New York* commissioned Nik Cohn's "Tribal Rites of the New Saturday Night" because of its interest in a preexisting phenomenon.

"Tribal Rites" follows a well-established pattern of descriptions of the dancing man. The anthropological resonance of the title and the author's claim that "everything described in this article is factual" alerted readers that they were about to peer into an exotic and primitive world. As if returning to the social mapping of the early twentieth century, in which Italians were not yet white, Cohn's account reads like an "I was the only white there" boast, written about the not-quite-whites for a fully white, middle-class, Manhattan-based readership. In the article, white ethnic Brooklyn is depicted as an unfamiliar and dangerous locale where Italian and Puerto Rican men repeatedly clash in near lethal brawls.

"Vincent" is an unparalleled dancer, and like earlier accounts by reformers and journalists of not-quite-white men who danced, "Tribal Rites" portrays Vincent as a social menace. In the space of nine pages readers learn that he is obsessed with fantasies of killing and uses women for casual sex or props to display his dance-floor finesse. He is a "quarterback" of the dance floor who effortlessly controls the foul-mouthed "troops" of less dominant males who accompany him to the disco. His ethnic otherness is marked, by among other things, a crucifix around his neck, the size of his troubled family, and his devotion to his mother. He is a dandy who spends an inordinate amount of time grooming his hair and wears tight pants, bright shiny shirts, and platform shoes. Cohn's article became the basis for the film *Saturday Night Fever*. Though "Vincent" was renamed Tony Manero, the film is faithful to Cohn's original characterization. Many years after the article appeared, Cohn acknowledged that Vincent was a fictional character.[69]

"Tribal Rites" is not history or sociology. We cannot look to it to tell us about working-class discos in the 1970s. It does, however, provide an important example of a middle-class perspective on discos and the men who danced in them. It was not a unique representation. Best-selling author Richard Price provides a strikingly similar account of working-class Italian American men who in his depiction spend their leisure fighting and going to discos. Price often places the characters of his 1976 novel *Blood Brothers* in discos, where they dance to the hit recordings of the 1970s. Al Green's steadily rhythmic but smooth and sensual "Love and Happiness" is played in one disco scene as an angry, white, working-class character, Butler, leaves the dance floor, "his silky flowered shirt sopping wet."[70] Like the men in "Tribal Rites," the white working-class men in *Blood Brothers* dress up to go to discos to spend time with men friends, dance, and have sexually charged antagonistic encounters with women on and around the dance floor. They speak in incomplete, profanity-filled sentences. In a scene Stony criticizes his girlfriend's appearance. She turns to walk away from him but he stops her by grabbing her arm. "'Where you think you goin'?' 'I wanna dance, you mind?' 'Then dance with me.' He pushed her to the dance floor. They both danced in a rage, out of rhythm, stiff."[71] The popular memory of disco was in part established by these fictional representations of white working-class men rendered as exotic and violent for middle-class readers and moviegoers.

The film *Saturday Night Fever* reached a much broader audience than either Nik Cohn's essay or Price's novel. These representations were propelled on an already existing disco wave and so cannot be said to have given birth to the disco phenomenon. They were nonetheless of consequence. The narrative of *Saturday Night Fever* and similar fictions contributed to the establishment of an image of disco as white, working class, and heterosexual. As actual discos were replaced by subsequent trends in nightlife, the images supplied by *Saturday Night Fever* had more power to define what disco had been. The static image of John Travolta's pose exists as the epitome of a disparaged white working-class man's narcissism. When he dances in the film, Travolta is captivatingly sensual, but in the endlessly reproduced and mimicked still photograph, his dance is reduced to a static image of ludicrous masculine vanity.

WHAT WAS DISCO?

The disco audience was a complex conglomeration that included blacks and whites from a range of socioeconomic classes and gay men: groups that danced to the same music at different clubs.[72] According to music historians Larry Starr and Christopher Waterman "disco dancing offered millions of working-class and middle-class Americans, from the most varied of cultural and economic backgrounds, access to glamour that hadn't been experienced widely since the days of the grand ballrooms."[73] Working-class African Americans went to neighborhood dance clubs and danced to music that they were likely to think of as soul music. Working-class white men listened to some of the same music in dance clubs and thought of it as disco. These men were rarely as dazzling, nor as violent, as their fictional and cinematic representations. Bars with dance floors, which in the 1970s played disco music, were profoundly important institutions for gay men. Neighborhood dance clubs that built audiences for disco music preceded the opening of the socially exclusive discos of the late 1970s. In the spring of 1977, Studio 54 opened and immediately attracted the glamorous partiers of New York City. The club was notorious for its doormen who opened the rope and stanchion at the club's door to admit a select few while leaving those deemed ordinary to languish on the sidewalk. Owner Steve Rubell told a reporter that he liked to admit "some guys with guys because it makes the dance floor hot, you know?"[74] Rubell treated gay sexuality as the right kind of difference in a club that generally excluded all but wealthy white patrons who met the standards of beauty and style held by Studio 54's gatekeepers. Though Studio 54 was exclusive and attracted many celebrities, the large number of discos found in urban and suburban areas throughout the country were not, and could not, be as exclusionary.

Disco was the music of gay dance clubs that proliferated in the less oppressively homophobic 1970s. Gay men provided an enthusiastic audience for disco records, and these recordings often featured the voices of black women. In an essay on disco, cultural critic Richard Dyer distinguishes the phallic character of rock music from the more diffuse eroticism of disco. Others have dismissed disco for its insistent beat, but Dyer characterized disco music as growing out of a tradition of black popular music that encouraged "expressive, sinuous movement . . . not just that mixture of awkwardness and thrust so dismally characteristic of dancing to rock."[75] Disco provided the music to which gay men danced with what Dyer described as "whole body eroticism," a form of embodification that defied the stiff and contained carriage expected of white men.

Gay discos were more than a place to party. They were important institutions for the building of gay community. For theatre scholar David Román gay dance clubs provided an "entry point to other forms of queer connection: friendship, sex, employment." Bars where gay men danced were transformational because of the experience of dancing. Gay clubs provided a space for men to move in public in playful, expressive, sensual ways as they danced with other men. They facilitated celebration of the end of the criminalization of men who danced in close embrace. Román argues that public dancing enabled "social configurations of same sex bodies not imaginable elsewhere. . . . dance was . . . the temporal reality that queer people had made for themselves through prior years of political struggle."[76] Queer people had fought for the right to dance, and gay discos were the place for an endless victory party.

The disco culture wars were and are fought not only by those who hated the music, but also by those who loved it, danced to it, came out in it, and who want to own it as the music of the formative years of their lives. African Americans, working-class whites, gay men, and glamorous elites were the dancing consumers and creators of disco culture. Generally they danced at separate clubs, though the categories were never mutually exclusive. A few glamorous black gay men were admitted to Studio 54. Drawing on the African American origins of many disco dances and much of disco music, the Dance 101 instructor claimed disco as an African American cultural product. Gay men, while recognizing the importance of black women musicians as creators of disco music, often claim disco as queer culture. Jeremy, a thirty-five-year-old gay man whose father is white and mother Japanese said he felt "cheated that I pretty much missed it . . . And now it's like, "I'm gay and I don't know disco! I don't know all the words to, 'Dancing Queen.' I could just go 'Fernando' and that's it." The songs that typify disco for him were recorded by the white Swedish group, Abba. Gil, a twenty-nine-year-old Mexican gay man expressed similarly romantic views regarding disco, when he said "To live in that era, to be able to go to those clubs, to do that kind of dancing, to see it where everyone's in it, where it's not just an anomaly anymore, that must've been a beautiful space of time." I asked Gil to describe the image he had of disco. He extended his arm diagonally towards the ceiling to strike John Travolta's Tony Manero pose.

Quinn is a twenty-six-year-old black queer-identified man, who appreciates disco music but resents what he views as its misappropriation by white pop musicians. By chance, as I began our interview in a café, the *Saturday Night Fever* soundtrack began to play. He responded with annoyance. Disco, he explained,

> was like this genre of music that was being produced by mainly black people, like black women were at the forefront of it . . . And now the only memories people have of disco are shit like this . . . This is not disco. This is like at the beginning where pop music got really bad and started to become a commodity.

Quinn valued disco music as black music, not as a racially neutral gay culture. Other gay men I interviewed, particularly young men who knew the genre through available retrospective representations, did not share his view. The desire to claim disco as queer culture is present in historical accounts of the reaction against disco. In these accounts hatred of disco is explained as homophobia.[77] Intense dislike of disco, however, has roots as complex as the communities that loved and love it.

DISCO'S ENEMIES

The emergence of rock and roll in the late 1950s led to a brief convergence of the musical tastes of youthful listeners as teenagers of all races began to listen and dance to black musicians. This convergence did not last long, and despite the broad appeal of rock and roll recordings, never corresponded to a uniform youth culture that transcended race, ethnicity, or class.[78] By the mid-1970s musical markets were again fragmented by race. A large segment of young white men listened to bands defined as hard rock or album-oriented rock. The hardness of hard rock suggested to its listeners that it was masculine and that it existed in opposition to music for older listeners, women, or other softer categories of persons. Dance music was never easily categorized on a scale of durability. It was neither hard nor soft, but nonetheless, in the minds of hard rock fans, it lacked a seriousness that adhered to rock music. The belief that dance music is inferior to music intended for unmoving listeners draws on the enduring dichotomizing of mind and body in western culture. An early hint of the anti-dance sentiment in music that appealed to white youth in the 1960s appeared in the 1962 liner notes of an album of the folk group Peter, Paul, and Mary.[79] It read, "The Truth is on the record. It deserves your exclusive attention. No dancing, please." Great stylistic differences separate the gentle, and often politically left, folk music of Peter, Paul, and Mary from hard rock. What they had in common was that their listeners saw them as authentic and noncommercial. Neither form was meant for dancing.

With large numbers of young white heterosexual men listening to hard rock while African American, Latino, and gay youth continued to listen to music oriented toward dance, the public image and the practical experience of dance became fragmented by race, gender, and sexuality.[80] In 1970 *Soul Train* began its thirty-five-year run as a show in which stylishly dressed African American dancers demonstrated the latest steps for a national audience. Across the country African American youths tuned in to *Soul Train* on Saturdays during the day to learn the latest dance trends. Each week a highlight was the moment when couples on the dance floor divided to form a pathway and dancers took their turns flaunting their finest steps in loosely coupled, strutting solos that moved down the line.

By the 1970s, the notion that white men could not dance began to be common sense and affected the way men experienced their racial identities. Mark was white and heterosexual and grew up in the 1950s in a household in which no one danced. He never gained any confidence as a dancer. His awareness of the stereotypes about white men's awkwardness contributed to his discomfort moving in public. He recalled that as a young man in the 1970s, "I think part of the reason I didn't want to dance is that I knew I would look white . . . We'd go to parties, there'd be some black people there. It was black music. It suggested black dancing . . . and I was very conscious of not being up to that." Mark's refusal to dance carried a measure of shame. He would have loved to have been able to move well, but felt that he could not. The "black music" played at the party may have been categorized by some as disco music. It is not how he experienced it at the time. Unlike his remorse regarding his inability to dance, his dislike of disco had no trace of regret. He was smug about what he perceived as the fraudulence of disco:

> I felt it was about replacing the counterculture with an acceptable form of pseudo-rebellion. Or not even rebellion. It was the seventies version of the prom. . . . That's what it was about. People who wanted to think they were some-how cool, but they were real estate salesmen during the day and disco at night. And I despised it.

His contemporary Norman was similarly unequivocal in his polarized description of rock versus disco. He recalled that when more and more radio programs began airing disco,

> I turned off the radio and stopped dancing . . . To me, rock music had meaning and was a social—a force for social change. And so, you know, my favorite bands and artists were Bob Dylan and Paul Simon and Crosby, Stills and Nash and, you know, people who were sort of making a political statement as well as playing music. And disco was *entirely* fluff. This was, like, let's go out and dance and have a fun time. So to me, when that became the rage, it seemed to me a betrayal of what I thought music was for . . . I think it was the fact that I had always looked at popular music, rock music as being a social instrument, as well as being enter-tainment. And when it completely went away from that and disco really was completely going away from that, I was angry.

MAXINE: Angry?
NORMAN: Yeah, angry that it had sort of betrayed its roots, or betrayed its function.

Thus one of the critiques of disco was that it was shallow, commercial, and apolitical music. The level of passion in their recollections of disco is notable. They did not merely dislike disco, they despised it. Disco angered them. It betrayed their generation. The strength of these reactions suggests the intensity with which men of their generation identified with popular music. Yet in these recollections the divide between political rock and apolitical disco is exaggerated. Some rock expressed political sentiment, but certainly not all of it, and, as Dyer and Román have argued, disco was the music of the defiant political practice of same-sex dancing.

Some of the men who hated disco directed their animosity toward the music. Others who hated disco were provoked by discos as institutions and the behavior of men in them. These critiques are essentially harsh assessments of unacceptable masculine performances. They are scathing descriptions of men who do not properly adhere to the gender binary. What is striking about the descriptions is that they are condemnations of the wrong kind of heterosexual performance. For example Paul described his discomfort when he accompanied coworkers to a disco in the 1970s:

> I'd have jobs, "come on, we're going out." I hated it. Hated the whole thing . . . It was a scene where everybody looked at each other, and um everybody was sizing up what you looked like, no one really talked to you, on anything that was important . . . There was no political talk. You couldn't talk esoterically at all, you couldn't talk anything that was more than what are you wearing or where'd you get that and that kind of thing . . . Everybody had this who was the better dancer and doing the John Travolta thing, and I just, oh, this is so stupid. I just couldn't do it. So I would find a way not to go out to those places. It was a horrible scene. Come dressed in the disco clothes, you know with the medallions and the boots. I just did not fit on the scene. I was definitely more, how shall I say, hippy, I guess. I was definitely more funky . . . It was a t-shirt, pair of jeans, that's all I wore.

He detested discos because they were places where presumably heterosexual men were expected to dance and dress well. He felt that he would be judged on the basis of his appearance and the style with which he moved. These were contests he was not prepared to win. In the disco his ability to talk esoterically counted for nothing. His erudition would have been inaudible.

Previous accounts of the reaction against disco have centered their analysis on a notorious event, the "Disco Sucks" riot that interrupted a baseball game in Chicago's Comisky Park in 1979. Stephen Dahl, a rock radio disc jockey, organized a "Disco Demolition Night" in which baseball fans who were enemies of disco were invited to bring a disco record to throw into a dumpster for destruction in a grand explosion at halftime.[81]

The unruly, drunken crowd almost immediately violated the rules laid down for the event. They chanted "Disco Sucks" and hurled records onto the field during the first half of a planned double-header. Outside of the stadium someone burned an effigy of John Travolta.[82] Albums collected for the dumpster were exploded on the field after the first game, but then the organizer's plans for contained fury went completely awry. Disco's enemies charged onto the field, and a raucous melee ensued. According to sociologist Joshua Gamson, "that 'sucks' was the word chosen to denigrate disco is no accident."[83] Yes, and yet what does the increasingly commonplace vulgarism connote? It denigrates anyone in a sexually receptive position. It is a homophobic term, but also a misogynist one. John Travolta's image was burned that day as the wrong kind of heterosexual man, one too concerned with appearance. He danced too well. He danced as if dancing were a man's game.

In the postwar years few white heterosexual men acquired the dancer's habitus. Their fathers may have been adept jitterbuggers, but few of them found a way to pass that onto their sons. The sons grew up in a culture in which partners danced together without being attached. To some extent, that made every dance a solo, but boys who spent their teen years listening to rock music and developing in environments in which dancing too well was suspect had little incentive to become proficient dance soloists.

Who was Sad Sack's son? He was the stoned guy flailing at Woodstock. He was a young white man who found community every weekend at a gay bar. He was a young black man who felt unwelcome at that bar but happily found another bar and danced with men of color there. He was a middle-class white man who hated discos. He was that guy's white coworker who danced well and thought discos were the best place to meet women. He was a black man whose neighborhood dance club started calling itself a disco. He was a Latino dancing to live salsa music in a ballroom whose events were advertised on Spanish radio stations. He was the guy in flannel shirt and jeans taking up a lot of room on the dance floor at a blues bar once he had had enough to drink. None of them danced like the men of their fathers' generation. The ones who danced drew on pieces of the vernacular dance repertoire available to men in the 1960s and 1970s. They learned and performed the pieces of that repertoire that seemed to fit their bodies. And in learning and performing they made their bodies through practice.

To this point this book has provided historical perspectives on the uneasy relationship between masculinity and dance in the United States. The remaining chapters address the place of dance in the lives of contemporary men. They will focus, in turn, on dance's relationship to sex, how men become dancers or non-dancers, and the racial meanings attached to dance.

CHAPTER 5

꧁

Sex or "Just Dancing"

I mean, she started dancing with me, and to me it's just dancing.
—Charles

Sex draws men to dance floors, but it also keeps them away. Dance can provide young men their first opportunities to feel the pleasure of sustained erotic contact with another's body. Yet the association of dance with sex can make dancing awkward, anxiety producing, or, for some, unbearable. Looking back at himself as a youth, first experiencing sexual desire, Mark, at age fifty-nine, still recalls the terrible unease he felt when slow dancing with women. "I didn't know how much I could touch," he said, or "how close I could get. I didn't know where that line was. It was a very scary line." Dance would be complicated enough for men if it were only a sex act, but as performance studies scholar Jane Desmond wrote, dance is connected to "sex, sexiness, and sexuality."[1] On paper tidy definitional boundaries may be drawn between sex (either erotic acts or biological categories), sexiness (allure), and sexuality (identities). In everyday life, these terms, and the identities and experiences they imply, melt into and assume one another. The uncertainty regarding whether dance communicates sex, sexiness, or sexuality makes public dance performance risky for men. If seen as a means to obtain heterosexual sex, dancing can boost a young man's status. Yet dance's connection to sexiness can place a man in the position of being an erotic object, an extremely uncomfortable position for many heterosexual men. The sexuality with which men's dancing is most stereotypically associated is homosexuality, a connection that inhibits the ways homophobic men move.

How can we know what dance communicates? The question is usually easier to answer when thinking about dance on stage, where intention is clearer. According to dance historian Ramsay Burt, "ballet is a discourse of power that subjects the dancing body and inscribes meaning on it."[2] Ballet trains male dancers to embody a distant tradition of courtly heterosexuality that has been preserved in an artistic technique. Within that tradition audiences witness romances in which princes help princesses to maintain their balance. Dance scholar Cynthia Bull noted that experienced ballet audiences know how to interpret the staged "intention of touching."[3] She distinguishes between staged interactional movement, meant to be viewed as a heterosexual social encounter, and a male ballet dancer's "physical manipulation of the ballerina (his hands on her back, waist, armpits, hips, pelvis, and thighs)," which knowledgeable audiences view as dancing that is free of interactional meaning. Citing Bull's work, dance scholar Helen Thomas described the latter as "just 'dancing',," a phrase I will employ.[4] In choreography, a dancer may face away from her partner and fold her torso into his so that her buttocks rest on his crotch. When performed in a de-eroticized context on a concert stage, such choreography may have no relational significance. It is just dancing.[5] The same coupling has the potential for entirely different signification when performed at the senior prom. Some of the time when nonprofessionals connect their bodies, it is also just dancing, but there is no certainty in those off-stage performances of a shared understanding of the intention of touch.

When is dance sex, and when is it just dancing? Movement that appears sexy may not feel sexy at all. Rapid pelvic-thrusting may stir a viewer, but merely tire the one who moves.[6] Nor is "sex" the best way to describe every collectively induced physical pleasure that dance avails. Some of the time, the joy of dance is the feeling of dissolution of interpersonal boundaries derived from participation in a communal response to rhythm. Ask these dancers what they are doing and "sex" would not be the answer. They would say "just dancing."

On stage and off, movement appears to tell stories. Someone moves, others watch and think that the movement they witness is indicatory of something essential about the mover. This commonplace assumption was elevated to artistic axiom by modern dance choreographer Martha Graham, when she wrote "movement never lies."[7] Her words suggest that the moving body is at all times a trustworthy communicator. Pop singers Shakira and Wyclef Jean reiterated the sentiment in their 2006 hit song "Hips Don't Lie." In the accompanying video, Shakira performs an erotic dance for no one in particular. The semiotic confusion of her Orientalist belly dance set in a staged Caribbean carnival undermines the title's claim. Her hips may not lie, but what they say is far from clear. I interviewed men who worried that their hips might indeed tell damaging lies about them. The untruths they feared usually implicated gender and sexuality. In dance studios the discourse of ballet systematically disciplines bodies. In everyday life men are subject to amorphous discourses of power, which less systematically discipline their bodies, and inconsistently prepare their informal audiences to interpret what they see.

Sociologist C. J. Pascoe used the phrase "compulsive heterosexuality" to describe the obligation felt by adolescent boys to reenact verbal and physical dominance throughout each school day to bolster their perpetually insecure personal claims to heterosexual masculinity.[8] Pascoe gave greatest attention to the ways in which boys used homophobic slurs to dominate other boys and aggressive and uninvited physical contact to dominate girls, but also noted that "dancing was [a] practice that put a boy at risk of being labeled a fag."[9] Compulsive heterosexuality requires continuous bodily self-surveillance, and dance, when interpreted as a feminized practice, can undermine a boy's reputation.

Dance's sexual meaning shifts according to the kind of dance, the setting, the dancer's identity, and the identity of his partner. Dance can be masculinized when it is executed as athletic stunts or when it is treated as foreplay. When performed as dance alone, dance done for beauty's sake, it is most commonly feminized. In the contemporary United States, boys are steered away from ballet by fathers who consider interest in ballet a troubling indication of gender nonconformity.[10]

THE PROBLEM OF BEING SEXY

The risk that dance poses for men arises from its perceived delicacy and eroticism. Dancing may be experienced as engaging in sex, yet in order to dance sexually, a man may have to appear sexy. In the contemporary United States, white middle-class heterosexual men are expected to desire sex but not to be publicly sexy, because being sexy could indicate that they appear so to other men. Many middle-class white heterosexual men are uncomfortable being watched and are particularly uneasy being watched by an eroticizing gaze. I asked a nineteen-year-old white heterosexual young man, Zachary, if he thought women found him attractive when he danced. He treated the question as somewhat difficult to comprehend.

MAXINE: Do you think women would find you attractive when you dance?

ZACHARY: Excuse me?

MAXINE: Do you think women would find you attractive when you dance?

ZACHARY: I have no idea. Um—I don't know. I just—yeah. I don't—that's definitely not what I'm thinking about. [*chuckle*] I'm just in the moment, you know.

The adage "dance as if no one is looking" provides cover for men unaccustomed to being broadly perceived as sexual objects. Perhaps as a result of wishful thinking twenty-year-old heterosexual Tyler, who is of Chinese and white ancestry, described male sexiness as something that a man's dance partner could perceive but that could not be seen by other spectators. "[A guy] can be sexy, like getting very close to her and being sexy toward *her* maybe . . . I wouldn't really say sexy like—I wouldn't say 'Oh he's dancing like sexy.' *She* would only think that, I think. Not like anybody watching."

By contrast gay-identified men I interviewed, regardless of race or ethnicity, had no problem with the thought of appearing sexy, even as they aged. Asked if they looked sexy when dancing Landon, who is gay, forty-three, and black, said, "yeah I hope I do" and Milton, who is gay, thirty-eight, and black, responded with a degree of modesty, "for the most part, yes." Patrick is white, fifty, and regularly goes to a gay country/western dance where he enjoys "shadow dancing," a couple dance where the leader stands behind the follower and steers from the back with his hands on his partner's belt buckle. He said he felt sexy when shadow dancing and imagined that he looked sexy too.

Heterosexual-identified women get to be sexy without being seen as gender variant. In fact many young women feel compelled to appear sexy and as a result become accustomed to and can derive pleasure from looking sexy while dancing. Journalist Michael Ventura described watching middle-class white young women "with faces floating as unconcerned as the moon over bodies that undulated, rippled and bumped."[11] Young women who flaunt sexiness on the dance floor may derive pleasure from taking up a socially validated position, from demonstrating competence in a current dance style, and from the inherent satisfaction provided by moving with others in sync with music. It is a pleasure that frequently turns to discomfort when it leads to unwanted sexual demands from men. Women who dance in clubs often wish to separate the appearance of sexiness from the desire to engage in sexual acts. In a study of British women who attend raves Maria Pini found that "many stress that although they *do* (or sometimes do) enjoy a certain to-be-looked-at-ness within these events . . . many emphasize the point that they do not want such 'performance' to be so unproblematically associated with sexual 'come on'."[12] They wish to cleave sexiness from sex so that they can dance without being exposed to men's sexual demands.

Van, a twenty-four-year-old, gay, Vietnamese American man, sensed that heterosexual men are unwilling to be the object of desire in public and are especially uncomfortable appearing desirable to other men. It made him cautious. I asked him what it was like to watch straight men dance. He took time to formulate his answer. "They uh, hmmm. Well, some of them are sexy while they're dancing. Uh and, and what else? Sometimes I worry that they might be . . . uh . . . looking at me looking at them." I asked Leo, an affluent, Latino, heterosexual, middle-aged, non-dancing man about the possibility that he appeared sexy when he danced. He responded by articulating what might go through his mind at such a moment. "Do I look like a fool in front of, you know, for mostly the opposite sex, and even other men?" He equated looking sexy with looking like a fool in the eyes of the opposite sex, and "even other men." If, as sociologist Michael Kimmel argues, "masculinity is largely a homosocial enactment," and men perform masculinity primarily to establish credibility for other men, they must avoid looking sexy, not "even," but especially in the eyes of other men.[13] Men like Leo feel foolish being sexy because they have not practiced being publicly sexy, because sexiness is a feminine attribute, and because appearing sexy to other men calls their heterosexual identities in question. They perceive that sexiness is bound to the female sex category and to gay sexual identities. When Leo imagined himself being sexy he saw a fool. Male sexiness is the stuff of parody for white middle- and upper-class heterosexual men.

A belief in some degree of gender difference is fundamental to the structure of gender relations within the United States. Yet that gender order is complex and takes different forms in local contexts, which vary in the extent to which masculinity and femininity are viewed as polar opposites.[14] When and where masculinity is represented as opposite and superior to femininity, what may be called femiphobia, or fear of performing feminine activities, especially activities associated with the body, arises. When expressive movement is defined as feminine, boys learn to avoid it. The association of movement with sensuality, and sensuality with women, stifles boys' range of movement. Boys learn that parts of their bodies, most notably their hips, are potentially feminizing and must not be moved. Furthermore, within homophobic contexts, to the extent that boys view dance as a sexual activity, it is impossible for them to practice it among themselves.[15] Normative masculinity in the United States is often limited in its public intimacy.[16] Many men will only touch others or engage in physically interactive improvisation when playing sports. Even athletics, as a form of public, interactive, physical play, are for most men abandoned in adult life. Thus femiphobia and homophobia combine to make boys avoid dance.

DANCE AS SEX

Though many come to the dance floor just to dance, it can also be a place to engage in acts that belong somewhere on the continuum of all that may be considered sex. In an interview at age fifty-eight, white, heterosexual Marvin looked back at his youth and recalled "a couple of evenings of supreme happiness, dancing . . . and on a couple of occasions, having enormously wonderful sexual interactions that the foreplay was the dancing."

Popular fiction provides a window into the meanings attached to dancing men's bodies. A novel's popularity suggests that it expresses something that resonates broadly with the reading public. Philip Roth's *The Human Stain* is the fictional tale of Coleman, a light-complexioned, black professor who hid his black origins to live as a white man. He is disgraced for, of all things, having uttered a racially insensitive quip about "spooks" in a class. Roth depicts Coleman dancing. In the scene, Coleman, the black man who passes as white, is listening to the radio at home when his white male neighbor visits him. Frank Sinatra croons, and Coleman must dance, and asks his neighbor if he will dance with him. Before the dance begins, the text digresses to an account of a steamy heterosexual affair from Coleman's youth. Coleman reads aloud a letter he received from a woman, a description that reaffirms for readers Coleman's heterosexuality before the neighbor acquiesces to Coleman's invitation and they dance in close embrace. Coleman takes the lead. Roth tells readers "there was nothing overtly carnal in it" but nonetheless something intimately physical was there.[17] As he dances, the neighbor thinks about the feel of his hand on his partner's bare back. When they separate they toss back and forth jokes about the sexuality of what they have just done, and in their jokes take up feminine or masculine positions. Humor is a recuperative device common among heterosexual men after circumstances have led them to hug or kiss or dance.[18] Such jokes are payments made toward the demand for heteronormativity and restore the sexual order. Yet in the novel, order is not entirely restored. Later that night the neighbor is restless in bed as he recalls the dance. "My having danced around like a harmless eunuch with this still vital, potent participant in the frenzy struck me now as anything but charming." The sleepless neighbor regretted having been a harmless, asexual and therefore emasculated eunuch as he danced. Roth shows us the white man tossing in bed, mourning the absence of sex in his life, a potency he imagined still possessed by his aging neighbor who cannot listen to music without dancing.

The scene, written by a Pulitzer Prize–winning American author, expresses the common sexualization of dance, of black men, and of black dancing men. The passage imagines dance as a sexual act, and shows us a black man as a sexually dominant man who cannot avoid dancing when he hears music. Dance is imagined in this passage as inevitably connected to, if not synonymous with, sex. The association between dance and sex is why dance has been such a regulated and fraught activity, and also contributes to an explanation of why so many men refuse to dance. Most men, we may assume, want sex, but they do not want to be caught in public performing it badly, or performing it so well that they are sexy, or to find themselves in the wrong passive, objectified position in the sexual dance.

Within recent years high school dance chaperones have been provoked by the dance style known as "freaking." When performed in heterosexual couples, a woman stands in front of her partner and rhythmically moves her buttocks in front of his crotch. As described by young men, men move little in the freak dance couple. White, nineteen-year-old Zachary explained that "freak dancing is really easy for a guy. For a girl, you have to move around a lot more." Likewise white, twenty-one-year-old Aaron said guys "sway slightly in time to the music while the girl sort of goes crazy and does all sorts of things, and the guy can just, you know, raise his hands up high, or something like this, and just be like, yeah . . . look at her . . . anybody can do what the fellows do . . . but, I have respect for the skill that it takes to move like the girls." The dance was described to me many times as a low-technique style that any young man could do because it was just like having sex with your clothes on. Of course, not everyone can have sex with their clothes on in public. Even the low-technique style of masculine freaking requires knowledge of the expected posture and the customary interactional response to the woman's performance, familiarity with the rhythms of contemporary music and an ability to move in time with them, and most of all, lack of inhibitions regarding public intimacy. What is not required of a man is as much ability to articulate his torso and hips as is required of women. Such movement is so feminized that Gil, a twenty-nine-year-old Chicano gay man, said that a man performing it would be understood to be enacting a campy parody.

Using your butt as an object, sexual object, to display that sort of thing. That's something that a man is not typically taught to do. . . . That I would consider more of a feminine move. That's not very masculine, what's going on there . . . And so, those are types of moves I would say definitely have to do more on the campy, more on the fun,—it's sexual, but it's playing with sex . . . they feminize themselves a little bit.

While the capacity to move hips and torso is human, hip and torso movement are gendered, sexualized, and racialized in the United States.

Allen recalled his childhood growing up as an effeminate white boy in the 1960s when he was "teased for being queer or sissy before I knew really what the words meant." Dance gave him pleasure and a feeling of competence, yet his talent lowered his standing among other young boys. At summer camp

> life was often miserable . . . and the dancing certainly didn't help, because I would be the one who might enjoy dancing, and the girls are the ones dancing, and so it wasn't like I was cool cause I got to dance with the girls, it was at the age where girls were, "Ooh, icky."

In his neighborhood, during the school year, boys taunted him. They saw something appallingly wrong about his everyday way of moving. Their comments made him wish to die. He asked himself, "what am I doing, how am I holding myself, carrying myself that is causing that to happen?" He internalized the belief that it had something to do with his hips and at fifty-nine, even after coming out and living as a gay man for decades, he remains vigilant about removing traces of femininity from his body.

> If I'm dancing freestyle . . . sometimes that comes into my mind about how I'm moving in terms of whether I'm doing a movement that's looking feminine or not . . . . I am conscious, like sometimes I'll catch myself. If I put my hand on my hip, taking my hand off my hip in certain settings, thinking—well even if I'm by myself sometimes, 'cause I don't want it to get to be a habit.

For Allen learning masculine embodiment meant learning to minimize the visibility and mobility of his hips.

Though hegemonic masculinity is defined by, among other things, heterosexuality, being the object of heterosexual desire does not necessarily protect a man from being seen as inadequately masculine. While women may appreciate and desire a man whose embodied sensuality allows him to dance well, women are not the arbiters of masculinity within heteronormative contexts.[19] Professional dancing men, from Rudolph Valentino to Vernon Castle to John Travolta, who were adored by female fans, were ridiculed by men. The sensuality that may make a man appealing to women is often just the quality that marks him as the wrong kind of man to homophobic men.

Yet as I write "wrong kind of man" the inadequacy of the unmodified word "man" reveals itself. The sentence holds true if "man" refers to a white man, but does not if it refers to men of color. Men of color can perform sensuality and still be recognized as masculine by other men. For Ralph, a twenty-five-year-old heterosexual Latino, being sexy was not a problem. When asked if he looked sexy when he danced he first responded, "I don't know," but then continued. "I try.... girls, in general, have always been like, 'Oh, that guy can dance, that's sexy'... Like hopefully, maybe I am." Victor, a twenty-seven-year-old multiracial Filipino, easily declared, "the girls are sexy. *I'm* sexy," placing emphasis on "I'm." Forty-nine-year-old, heterosexual, African American Alphonse enthusiastically responded, "Oh yeah!" and said he hoped he had not lost his "swagger." The meaning of dance bends like light passing from one substance to another according to the body that performs it. Race is a refractory device for the meaning of men's movement.

Queer theorist Judith Halberstam argues that masculinity presents itself as "anti-performative. The masculinity Halberstam describes as anti-performative is actually white middle-class masculinity.[20] Masculinity, for men of color, often requires what Alphonse called his "swagger" and what cultural critic Michael Eric Dyson described as the African American aesthetic of the "stylization of the performed self."[21] Dyson described this aesthetic in the context of professional performances, but I would argue that stylized performance as expressed through fluid, rhythmic, and expressive movement is an essential part of the everyday embodied aesthetic of men of color. The ability to move well is essential, not in the sense of having biological origins, but rather is socially essential to men who wish to be recognized as adequately embodying racial or ethnic group membership. Young white men who discover that they cannot dance can still see themselves as sufficiently masculine and unproblematically white. In fact their inability to dance aligns with social expectations and may contribute to sustaining heterosexual identifications. Young men of color whose peers and relatives tell them that they cannot dance are being told that they lack something culturally valued and are more likely to work to improve their dancing.

Many men, regardless of race or ethnicity, are awkward in junior high. At that stage, Quinn discovered that his schoolmates thought something was wrong with his walk. Quinn grew up in a black community in Detroit in the 1980s and 1990s and knew from an early age that he was attracted to boys. When he said he was teased for his walk, I assumed that the teasing was because of his sexuality. No, he explained, "somebody said I walked like a white person." Still thinking that he was teased for effeminacy I asked if

walking white meant an effeminate walk. He made a sharp distinction between the two. He was "checked" for "being rigid."

> It wasn't effeminate, I think it was more stiff. I think I wasn't more fluid or com-
> fortable with my body at a younger age. I had to grow into that . . . white culture
> is just more about being rigid, whereas black culture is more like being more
> expressive with your body. So I had to learn how to walk like a black man, you
> know, kind of like not proper walking, you know, more like the swag.

Ralph, who was twenty-five and Latino, recalled that around fourth grade
he worked to develop

> a certain way of walking that you think is cool and I thought was cool. It was like
> a swagger. . . . You kind of walk with your arms looking like—not like a fight
> stance, but not like they're completely relaxed . . . And you kind of like have a
> little lean going on every now and then.

Young men of color whose torsos lack movement, who lack the ability to
move in sync with a beat, or whose movements are deemed awkward are
likely to hear from siblings and playmates that they move like whites. That
comment prompts many of them to develop new styles of moving.

In a study of high school proms sociologist Amy Best found that within
"white middle-class communities, dance is coded primarily as a gender
activity—it's something *girls* do," while for African-American youths
dance expresses racial membership regardless of gender.[22] While this is an
important insight, I wish to complicate it by emphasizing that just as race
and gender matter in the production of white men as non-dancers, race
and gender matter in the production of African American men as particular kinds of dancers. Dance scholar Brenda Dixon Gottschild argues that
whites interpret "overt use of the separate parts of the torso . . . as sexually
suggestive," while in black diasporan culture, using the torso is not mainly
or necessarily a sexual come-on, but an aesthetic value based on whole-
body dancing." Children who are taught these dances by adults "are not
being trained by their elders to lead a life of promiscuity, but to carry on a
tradition of polycentric, polyrhythmic body fluency."[23] Gottschild's insight
explains the separation of sensuality from sexiness and sex within at least
some contexts within African American culture, and it may explain the
greater space available for black and Latino men to acquire the ability to
move. Gottschild's focus is on race without considering how it intersects
with gender or sexuality. The examples she gives of children learning

whole-body dancing are descriptions of girls. Young black girls develop a racialized and gendered capacity to move their hips and torso. When moving this way they are displaying cultural competency, and when performing as young girls, it is understood that they are not inviting sexual attention.

Black and Latino boys are also expected to become competent dancers. Poor dance performance will be judged as a failed racial or ethnic performance. The ability to fluidly move hips and torso is expected of Latino dancers regardless of gender, and such sensual movement is not stigmatizing for men in Latino communities. However, even though the capacity to articulate movement through the trunk is valued for both men and women, gender difference continues to be perpetuated through the production of embodied difference in communities of color.[24] Within black and Latino communities, dancing well, including the capacity to appear sexy, can signify a man's racial or ethnic membership and is recognized as necessary for heterosexual courtship. Ernest is twenty-nine, black and Filipino, heterosexual, and a school teacher. He explained that other men recognized that dancing well was part of his allure. "Hey, that's his game and that's how he does it." However, even though Ernest and the women with whom he dances both move their hips and torsos, they do not dance in the same manner. Dance is used to signify gender difference based on a logic in which women move more than men.

This differential applies even in the spiritual context of movement within church. As a child and teenager Landon attended a black Baptist church in the South where worshippers who felt themselves filled with spirituality during a service would express it through their bodies. Landon recalled that "when a man would catch the spirit the movement was much more restrained. There wasn't this kind of exclamation in the same way that women did . . . There's an expectation that even though you had the spirit you were going to be more controlled about it." Thus even within a context in which an unrestrained physical response was expected and even valued as a signifier of holiness, social expectations for black masculine embodiment limited men's movement.

Sociologist Margaret Hunter analyzed popular African American rap music videos and described a pattern in which women performed sensuality for comparatively still male partners.[25] Young African American Andre described the limits as he felt them in the secular context of a dance club: "Men can grind up on women," but when separated from a partner, "you can move your feet a little bit. Don't arch your back either. Don't stick your booty out . . . So doing the butterfly—it's like no, no. So no tootsie rolls.[26]

White middle-class heterosexual masculinity is equated with a stolid, self-contained, non-sexualized, minimally expressive body. It is a body characterized by goal-oriented use of arms and legs that are attached to unmoving hips and torso. This form of embodiment occupies a position of dominance, which rests on a claim of normalcy, because of its distance from physically expressive and sensual gay men, women, and men of color. To say that a form of embodiment is associated with the position of white middle-class heterosexual male dominance is not to say that it is characteristic of all white middle-class heterosexual men or that it can only be embodied by them. A stolid, self-contained, non-sexualized, and minimally expressive stance may be taken up by women, men of color, and gay men. This is the dominant form of embodiment of the dominant race and gender, and so to some extent it is a stance that can confer some safety and elevated status on anyone. Douglas, a twenty-three-year-old African American man who danced exuberantly in high school, said he felt inhibited dancing at clubs now that he is older because social norms dictated that "you post up, you chill and you don't expose yourself in any way dancing because you'd look like a fool if you did so." A white gay man complained that his husband's distaste for close contact with others kept him off the dance floor. "He's not a real touchy-feely kind of person . . . He doesn't like close contact with strangers." Avery, a twenty-seven-year-old queer-identified black man whose parents were immigrants from Haiti, recalled that as a young man he went through a period in which he tried to constrain his movement in order to appear more "American."

> Some of my earlier memories are me trying to be American, and trying to integrate into American culture . . . I knew my parents were foreigners and that they didn't speak English, and that the things that they did or said were like a little bit off and weird to my friends . . . so I felt like there were all these things to make me more American . . . there's a difference between the way Haitians dance and the way Americans dance. . . . the television I was watching was very white . . . I had all these white influences, and in looking at how white people dance and white people interacted with each other, there was a little bit for me, it seemed a reservation.

Queer men described what they experienced as homophobic cultures within gay bars in which men who moved in feminized ways were deemed less attractive. In a gender order in which the feminine and the racialized are devalued, women, gay men, and men of color may find some advantage gained in adopting the stolid stance of social dominance.

RANGE OF MOVEMENT

The range of movement available to men who take up dominant forms of masculine embodiment is restricted, but not eliminated. Some forms of movement are safe because they are closely aligned with physical dominance. At hard-core music events, the danger of the mosh pit makes it a safe for male dancing. Moshing, according to Aaron, a white young man,

> . . . is like when you jump up and down and make a big fool of yourself and just run into people, and [is] kind of fun, like get your testosterone up . . . That was something you know I felt comfortable doing is jumping up and down and hitting my friends. . . . I wouldn't do that with a girl, no. I mean, you would hurt somebody, you could . . . you wouldn't want to hurt a girl, but you don't care if you hurt a guy.

The pleasure of smashing into other men is age-delimited as described by Mark, who was led unknowingly to a hard-core club in his thirties.

> I was hiding in the corner praying that I wouldn't die . . . It was fucking hell . . . everybody was jumping up and down to music that was unbelievably loud and they were drinking huge amounts of alcohol . . . I was just fucking stunned . . . I was terrified. I mean I think if I'd have got out on the street I might have just started crying.

The dangerous mayhem that terrified Mark attracts younger men to the mosh pit. They are also drawn by the pleasure of joining in a collective physical response to driving music. Victor enjoyed the mosh pit as a place "to let off steam" in a crowd of men. "In the mosh pit," he explained, "everyone's just a target. . . . [and at] a couple of concerts that I've been to . . . someone wanted to go body surfing. So, you know pass the bodies around. . . . But it's still fun. It's aggressive." Within a homosocial context in which everyone understands that they are engaging in aggression, men can use their hands, sometimes with great care to avoid causing injury, to pass a man's body through the crowd. Moshing's danger, and its accompaniment by forceful, rebellious, and roughly performed music, makes it a safe place for compulsively heterosexual men to move in sync to music and even to support each other's weight. The masculinity, if not the collar bones, of men who willingly enter mosh pits is safe.

Among the variety of dance styles that are performed to hip-hop music, the athletic and improvisational form known as "b-boying," or "breakdancing" has led to a contemporary resurgence of young men's dancing. Masculinity infuses the language of b-boying.[27] Dancers are organized into "squads" or "crews." They meet to "battle." According to ethnographer Joseph Schloss, "battling is the best venue for b-boy style, and the best b-boy style is most suited for battling."[28] B-boying's appearance of distortion, dislocation, and sudden and briefly held freezes clearly distinguish it from other more lyrical and fluid feminized forms of stage dance. B-boying and related hip-hop forms are seen as masculine even when performed by women. In a study of non-black hip-hop dance instructors and students Ghandnoosh found that women instructors believed that proficiency in the form came more easily to men.[29]

Many white middle-class heterosexual boys and men find dancing more comfortable in costumes that serve to protect the normalcy of the man underneath. Sometimes the costume is transvestite drag, worn by heterosexual men in parodies that provide a cover for the feminizing act of dancing. Dancing men in dresses are a timeless source of amusement in high school auditoriums and male homosocial venues. The joke never seems to expire. White men also dance in racial disguise, a form of corporeal drag that only sometimes requires special costume or makeup for its effect. In the first part of the twentieth century boys learned "Indian" dances as acceptably masculine ways to move. Addressing physical education teachers, Ted Shawn singled out "Indian" dances, along with "cowboy" and "stunt" dances, as the most appropriate for primary school age boys.[30] Dance scholar Danielle Robinson argues that in the 1910s and 1920s, young Jewish immigrants in New York City adopted black dance styles in order to assimilate into a racially unmarked whiteness.[31] When performing sensual couple dances that were recognizably black, these dancers demonstrated their difference from their parents and thus used dance to solidify their claims to white American identities. The anxiety of defying gender norms is eased when the performer simultaneously transgresses racial categories.[32] Contemporary competitive ballroom dancers routinely wear bronzing cosmetics when they perform Latin dances, the group of dances that are perceived as the most sensual and least structured in the ballroom repertoire.[33]

FORBIDDEN PARTNERS

Moshing and b-boying are physically daring and therefore emotionally safe forms of dance for men who align themselves with hegemonic masculinity. The forms are highly interactive and so constitute departures from the masculine embodied aesthetic of self-containment, but the interactions are aggressive and competitive, and the movements nonsexual. Though women are sometimes in the room when men gather to mosh or b-boy, these dance forms are primarily ways of moving that men perform with other men.

Heterosexual men may hurl their bodies at other men in mosh pits or attempt to demonstrate superior b-boy technique, strength, daring, and agility in front of a crowd of men, but the taboo against male partner dancing in the United States is long-standing, transcends racial and ethnic boundaries, and stands in stark contrast to the ease with which women may dance together. In a foundational text of queer theory, literary critic Eve Kosofsky Sedgwick argued that heteronormativity compels men to deny the possibility that erotic desire underlies their friendships.[34] Heterosexual men's compulsion to deny any hint of mutual attraction has made it impossible for them to dance as partners. In the post–World War II period this psychic prohibition was enforced by law. While the legal consequences of male partner dancing have ended, social prohibitions continue.

When men dance as partners, regardless of the degree of intimacy they exhibit, they signify gay sexual identity in a way that two women dancing do not. Asked if boys at the prep school he attended in the 1960s ever danced together, Herb responded negatively. "The fear of homosexuality was strong, and in fact, that was part of the problem there. And one of my teachers got fired for being gay." His answer equates homosexuality and male couple dancing. When recalling the dances he went to as a youth, Kevin, a white middle-class heterosexual man ten years his junior, similarly assumed that male couple dancing signified gay identity. "I do remember the girls would dance with each other . . . if they weren't dancing with boys, girls that weren't being asked to dance or whatever. I don't remember if guys ever danced together. . . . Um . . . It was pretty straight crowd." He attaches completely different significance to same-gender dancing depending on whether it was performed by boys or girls, assuming that boys who dance as partners are gay, but not considering the possibility that mutual attraction would cause two girls to partner.[35] Describing his current social life Ernest, a black and Filipino twenty-nine-year-old, explained that his men friends will only go dancing if the objective is to meet women.

> Girls can always go to a club, dance in a group, go home . . . [and] have a good time. While guys could never say like, "Let's go dancing. We're going to go *dancing* tonight . . . I just I don't think my friends would be comfortable doing that . . . My friends . . . we're obviously wanting to go a club to meet women, and even when we were dancing, we couldn't dance near each other because it would be too weird. . . . We're just moving around the edge. We're all venturing away

and then when we find each other, we're like, "Oh, that's not cool" . . . Once in a while, we would hear like a song that we'd like and like, and we'd start dancing to it together for a second and then we move away.

Heterosexual men may comfortably dance together in groups of three or more, but what is absolutely taboo for heterosexual men is dancing in an embrace or dancing with a man without touching but moving in a suggestive manner. Charles, who is thirty-two, African American and Filipino, said he would sometimes dance with men friends, but insisted, "mind you, we're not going to face each other and start holding each other." Twenty-year-old Tyler, whose mother is Chinese and father is white, thought it was alright for men to dance together if they emphatically avoided sensuality. Men who danced together had to "go dumb" through non-erotic clowning. "It'd never just be like freaking with another guy like you see girls doing. Girl on girl . . . You would never see any guys doing that. Like hardly ever. Unless like you're at a gay club or a gay bar you wouldn't see that just at school." "Girl on girl" freaking is acceptable because it is seen as a display of sexiness for the men in the room who are presumed to be ogling women. Cultural assumptions about women's sexual passivity, about the presumed ultimate heterosexuality of women even when they derive pleasure from other women, and about the importance of visual stimulation for men but not for women, structure the different meanings attached to men's and women's same-gender partner dancing. When men dance as partners, they are not assumed to be dancing to arouse women but to arouse each other. Two men dancing together who are not deliberately acting goofy, or aggressive, or attempting to best one another through stunts, are assumed to be gay.

DANCE AS A PRELUDE

The vast majority of commercial and educational venues where people dance assume a dance culture in which single people dance as part of courtship or seduction. Dance studios that train amateurs and professionals in dance techniques are the largest exception, but boys and men are uncommon participants in studio dance classes. Walter, a white heterosexual sixty-five-year-old mathematician, recalled that in his youth in the 1960s school dances were "the way to meet girls." Dance allows for the closest sustained embrace commonly permitted in public, and perhaps the only way in which strangers may meet and quickly have fairly intimate physical contact. Rick, a forty-six-year-old heterosexual white man recalled that holding women on the dance floor as a youth was "both tantalizing and risky, and scary, and exciting. The whole jumble."

I asked Warren, a sixty-year-old white man, if as a youth he was uneasy about knowing what the boundaries of propriety were when he slow-danced with a woman. "Are you kidding?" he exclaimed, "My goal was to violate, [laughter] and see how untoward I could get." He may have been posturing to impress me as he described his much younger self. Nonetheless, he wanted me to know that he recalled the dance floor as a place to have access to sexual experiences. Walter, the sixty-five-year-old mathematician, recalled junior high school dances vividly as ways to explore sexual contact with girls and to report back to male friends.

> So we would put on . . . *Earth Angel*. . . . And we would just play it over and over again and then we would slow dance with whoever we were, you know, trying to make it with, right? So the idea was to dance, to hold the girl as tight as you could . . . When you had an erection that was an issue. Whether you wanted her to know you had an erection you had to be incredibly self-confident to let her know that. . . . and talking about it, right—when the boys were together, we would talk about that . . . Like she could feel me, she could feel me, was something that somebody would say . . . You would try to press against the girls so that their breasts were pressing against your chest, and then the talk would be about whether their nipples were hard or not. . . . So we used to talk about that too.

When I asked young men why they went to dance clubs, many explained that the purpose was to meet women. Gerald, a twenty-one-year-old Chinese man, said that at the end of a night out at a club, "me and my friends would be like, 'How many did you dance with?' Or, 'Did you see me dancing with that girl?'" The assumption that couple dancing is sex, or is a prelude to sex, is the basis for fights that erupt at dance clubs. Dancing can quite literally be dangerous when a man dances with a woman claimed by another.

The association between dance and sex is so strong for some men that they treat dance with great seriousness and only wish to dance with women they love. Other men described abandoning the awkwardness of dance as they grew older because it was no longer the only way to have physical contact with women. As men found their way into stable heterosexual relationships, they stopped dancing. As Marvin put it, "it was . . . [like the] Curtis Mayfield [song] 'Trying to get over,' . . . but at a certain point I was no longer trying to get over, and if I'm no longer trying to get over, well . . . what am I going to do with this behavior?" Phil is white, thirty-one, married, and unwilling to go to clubs where people dance. His explanation is full of stops and starts as he concedes that his wife wants to dance.

I'm not single anymore. I'm just not comfortable with the whole being out. It's just different. Everyone's out for one thing, I think. I think it's just about sex personally out there. You know it's like, it's just everyone's all—I just get the impression that they're all out there to meet each other and get each other's numbers and that kind of thing. And I've been out of that scene for a while. So now, you know I'm married and my wife and I, and for her it's all just about she wants to dance and . . . and I don't want to um—I just don't want to be part of it, you know? So. Yeah. It's like I don't have a reason to be there.

He does not explore the contradiction between his wife's enjoyment of dance and his assumption that everyone at a dance club is "out for one thing." After noting her desire to dance, he returns to his own disinterest in dancing and his characterization of dance as nothing but a prelude to sex. Similarly Gerald stopped going to clubs once he found a girlfriend. "I didn't really care about dancing any more," he said. "If [my girlfriend] goes to the club, it's kind of like a headache. I don't want other guys like looking at [her] dancing." Once they are in relationships, men refuse to dance with the girlfriends and wives they courted through dance.

The assumption that public dancing is sex, or a way to get sex, also contributes to the stigmatization of older people in dance clubs. Older people are supposed to have already settled with partners and so are seen as perverse if they continue to visit the sexually charged space of youthful flirtation. Ralph, who is twenty-five and Latino, explained, "I don't want people to be like 'who is that guy, like he's ten years older than everyone in here' or twenty years older than everyone in here." Carter, a black thirty-three-year-old, used almost identical language when he told me that he has become conscious of his increasing age at clubs. He did not want to become "that guy," a figure he described as a lecherous older man who prowls at dance clubs. Men felt conspicuously old at relatively young ages when in clubs where people dance. Though he was certainly describing a different guy, twenty-one-year-old Gerald also described "that guy":

There's this one guy. He kind of club hops. And he's like real old. He's probably like 50-something. Like kind of old. Not really old. But he always just watch people and I guess just some girls would dance with him because he's old and they probably think it's funny or something but that's kind of weird.

Milton is black and gay and at thirty-eight feels he is too old for many gay dance clubs.

It is interesting that I do see how age is playing into my further and further isolation from going out to dance, because for the most part clubs are geared toward young people and so all of my friends my age we're still interested in going out to dance. We're not dead. . . . but we all kind of lament that there's no spaces for us to really go and dance. A lot of times we find ourselves putting ourselves in environments that are mostly geared toward young people and come away feeling not as fulfilled spiritually or just physically because we're ready to dance. We are ready to kind of experience and share music, but it's just different.

As people move beyond their twenties more serious work and family commitments preclude late-night excursions to dance clubs. Yet it seems that some men in their thirties give up dancing because they do not want to appear to be "that guy." Others, who were awkward dancers and only endured dancing in order to meet women, abandon dance clubs when they have found partners. The act of dancing may be construed as a flashy way of being a man that feels especially ridiculous for older men. Marvin, who stopped dancing because he was no longer "trying to get over," also described a shift that had taken place in the way he could be in his body. "I wasn't a player anymore, and that wasn't part of my display, right? You know I mean dancing is a display . . . All kinds of creatures display themselves before they get down and say, 'I'm agile in this way. I have orange ears.'" As a married man with children he felt that the time in his life that called for bodily display had passed.

Many of my interviews confirmed the paradoxical common sense that though white middle-class heterosexual men do not dance willingly or well, their white middle-class heterosexual wives and girlfriends have deep and mainly unfulfilled desires to dance. I asked white, fifty-nine-year-old Mark, a statistician who never dances, if the women with whom he has been in relationships ever wanted to dance. "Oh yeah," he responded. "I think pretty much all the women." "Okay. And so . . ." I prompted. "So what would happen?" he filled in. "Often I wouldn't go to the parties." Mark's solution to the mismatch between his desires and those of his girlfriends was to refuse to go to parties where he could have been expected to dance.

Neil, who is fifty-four, white, and a lifelong non-dancer, accompanied girlfriends to parties and described them as occasions for inevitable conflicts. "It was really kind of, 'No, you're *gonna* get up and dance, because *I* want to dance. And I'm *not* gonna do it by myself!'" He married a woman who has stopped trying to get him to dance, even though she would be much happier if he danced. Neil acknowledged his wife's continued interest, and her resignation, but finds dancing unbearable. She has "given up on it to a large extent. She likes to dance. She really does." "At weddings," he told me, "People say, 'Well why aren't you two out there dancing?'" and he does not have an answer. At thirty-one, Phil is younger than Neil or

Mark and more accommodating. He dances with his wife to make her happy, but dancing is not something he enjoys.

> I tell my wife I only dance at weddings [*laughs*] . . . She always wants me to go dancing . . . 'cause she loves to dance. But as far as me like just saying, "Hey let's go out dancing." That doesn't happen . . . It's not what I want to do, but it makes her happy so I'll go do it for a little while.

Describing an occasion when he was called upon to dance with her as a time when he "ended up having to dance," he views dance as a concession or a kindness he is willing to offer to his wife. Likewise Leo expected his wife to be grateful when he recently surprised her by asking her to dance after many years of refusing to take her to a dance floor.

> I knew she wanted to dance, so I wanted to, you know, please her and make her happy, so I did that. . . . I think she was pleasantly surprised. We did a couple— two or three, I think. Yeah, we went up and then danced. And we stayed up for a couple dances and then we were done . . . that was it. I tried.

These men know that they have harmed their relationships through their reluctance to dance. The statistician, Mark, felt that not dancing made him inadequate as a partner, and he went on to say that it had implications for him that went beyond partnering at a dance. "It's more serious than that," he said "because it's almost a sort of sexual inadequacy." He saw his inability to dance as one manifestation of his general discomfort with physical intimacy and with being observed. Mark will not dance in public, but sometimes he dances when no one watches. "Now I will tell you," he said, "that there are times, there are *rare* times when I'm actually sort of happy, and I'm alone in the house, and I have some music on and I sort of like move to it. I mean I do something that might be called dance." Being alone and unwatched provides him with the safety to dance as long as he can refrain from watching himself. Such moments, however, have always been brief for him. "I'll get embarrassed in front of myself," he explained. His self-consciousness while moving to music is so relentless that it can rise up to stop his dancing even when he is alone.

DANCING DOMINANCE

If dance is akin to sex at junior high school dances and a prelude to sex in adult night clubs, heteronormative codes script interactions on the dance floor. For most of the twentieth century, dance floor couple formation began when a man asked a woman to dance. Though men faced the possibility of rejection when they approached women, their risk was mitigated, in many settings, by women's need for a man's invitation before they could enter the dance floor. Women were potential wallflowers, a gendered category that has no male equivalent, because extending an invitation to dance in a heterosexual couple was a male privilege.

Throughout the twentieth century women could dance in same-gender couples, and often did, without raising suspicion regarding their sexual identities. At working-class dances early in the twentieth century, typically two young women would dance together until they were approached by two men who would "cut-in" to finish the dance with them in heterosexual pairs.[36] Middle-class reformers disparaged the custom as one in which young women could not refuse dances with unsavory men.[37] In some circumstances, when men were present, women who danced together were treated as unescorted women, a category that placed them somewhere on a continuum with prostitutes. During the Great Depression, the city of New York organized, and regulated, huge open-air dances in Central Park. At a dance the city sponsored in 1936 children under the age of eighteen were not allowed to attend, nor were two women permitted to dance together, and men were forbidden to cut-in.[38] The possibility that two men would dance together in the park was so taboo that it was not explicitly forbidden.

Despite the enormity of changes in social mores and style of dance during the past century, male prerogative to initiate a dance in heterosexual contexts endures, especially among strangers. Men who recalled asking women to dance did not see themselves in a powerful position as they selected dance partners, but rather recalled feelings of insecurity. They felt vulnerable rather than privileged. Remembering his early teen years, white sixty-five-year-old Brian recalled the walk across a junior high school dance floor to approach a potential dance partner as "the longest walk of your entire world." Will, a shy thirty-year-old Filipino man, said that in his twenties, he would go to dances, stand around uncomfortably for a short time, and then leave. "It was miserable, I, I can't do it. I lack the confidence, and I just don't like to go up to people that I don't know. It's just really awkward." I asked if he had ever been turned down. "That's the thing, I never asked." Will, like many of the young men I interviewed, prefers to go to clubs with a group, including women with whom he will dance. Douglas, a black twenty-three-year-old, uses a different strategy. He goes with other men. When asked how he approaches women on the dance floor his response suggested a brave veneer that overlays a fear of rejection.

DOUGLAS: Never ask to dance, man . . . Because if you ask to dance girls will shiii. . . . You don't ask to dance man.

MAXINE: Has anybody ever turned you down?

DOUGLAS: The boy? [referring to himself]

MAXINE: The boy.

DOUGLAS: Only after I—see I don't have to ask girls to dance because I'm so immaculate that girls will just gravitate. . . . I mean—how can I say this? I'm a really shy dude whatever . . . I'll wait for a girl to come to *me* because that's a whole power thing. Because if you approach the girl it's like she's up there and then she's going to be in a position of power.

Douglas' account quickly swings from his boast of his magnetic appeal to women to an admission of his insecurity. He claims that he waits for the women to gravitate towards him, and that they do. What can he be describing under a continuing gender regime that stigmatizes women who approach men? The ritual of men asking women to dance has transformed into a process of modern day cutting-in that no longer requires spoken requests. Twenty-six-year-old Ryan explained that [you] "find somebody dancing . . . and you go dance next to them. If they move away, then you go find somebody else [*laughs*]." Twenty-one-year-old Gerald explained that pairs of young women would dance near a group of men and "and like if a guy comes up behind the girl and then like they start dancing."[39] According to twenty-nine-year-old Ernest,

> At the clubs you would just dance and you dance near people and, I mean, if they wanted to dance with you, then they would turn around and start dancing with you . . . and then they would see me dance and then they'd make an assessment as to whether or not they wanted to dance with me. And if they didn't, they would just kind of move away from me without ever saying anything. It was a much easier way for them, as well as I, to communicate . . . That's kind of how I've always done it, because I feel like it's a much more respectful . . . it gives them an out.

In the new etiquette of dance clubs, requests and refusals are wordlessly expressed. Without the use of language male prerogative to initiate a dance is less visible. Men presume that women who dance together at heterosexual dance clubs are waiting for men to approach them. Without spoken requests the new etiquette reproduces gender conventions in which women have only the right of refusal.

More traditional forms of initiating a dance between strangers continue in venues where dancing is structured through partnered dance forms such as salsa, swing, two-step, cajun, and tango. Within these forms, dancing dominance also means that men control the style and direction of the dance by leading women partners. Though often less confident, experienced, or comfortable than the women with whom they dance, men take command as the "lead." Under the tradition of male leading, women dancers who attempt to take an active role are bad dancers. In a study of contemporary ballroom dancers, sociologists Allison Leib and Robert Bulman found that avowed feminist men and women left their politics at the door of the ballroom to consistently assume their respective active and passive roles in the dance.[40] Within a dance form that required hierarchical partnering, feminist dancers accommodated the demand to conform to traditional patterns of gendered interaction by treating it as "just dancing."

Contra dancing is a traditional Anglo/American form of dance in which a large group of dancers follow set patterns that require them to couple with a series of partners in succession as the dance progresses. Typically, when the couple forms, the man and woman immediately position their arms and hands to facilitate male leading. The man places his right palm on the woman's upper back so that he can steer her around the room while she rests her left hand on his shoulder. Problems arise at heterosexual contra dances in the rare instances when heterosexual men find themselves briefly thrown into a couple with another man. Ossie is a twenty-seven-year-old white gay man who goes to both heterosexual and gay contra dances. At gay contra dances men choose to be leaders or followers. Ossie is an experienced contra dancer who is generally a follower. At the heterosexual dances, Ossie complained, men

> will always try to get me to do this symmetrical hold, instead of the ballroom hold, which I really don't like at all . . . 'Cause it makes it less clear which one's leading. 'Cause once you break away from the close-together figure, you have to both go in the right spot if you're doing the male role, or the female role, and it's more confusing.

Ossie's unhappiness with men who will not lead when he lands in their arms at heterosexual contra dances provides an example of how gender is reinforced through processes of interaction. Failure to do gender appropriately throws everyone's performance into question, expands the behavioral possibilities, and slows interaction. If a logic of dominance and passivity is built into a structure, as it is in contra dance, the dance will proceed smoothly among strangers when the participants' roles are clear. When Ossie goes to heterosexual contra dances men who are momentarily his partner attempt to escape gendered performance entirely. Not wishing to take a dominant position with another man in the sexually coded context of a partner dance, they reach for a symmetrical hold. The dance however relies on a pair of choreographically differentiated roles. When the partners do not differentiate, the smooth, fast interactions that allow rapidly formed couples to proceed through complex chorographic figures break down. The heterosexual men who reach for a symmetrical hold when dancing with a man are not gender visionaries adopting post-gender embodiments. On the contrary, they refuse to do dominance in order to avoid the erotic implications of leading a man.

THE GREAT PLAYGROUND

After years of avoiding dance because all the settings available to him in his youth were heteronormative, Ossie became an avid dancer in his mid-twenties. He usually attends two gay contra dances every week even though his husband does not dance. His husband understands that at the contra dances, Ossie is just dancing. Ossie recalled nervously going alone to his first gay contra dance months after learning of its existence. Once there he found a welcoming group of dancers who were willing to help a beginner. He can still vividly recall the night and the men with whom he danced. Gay dance spaces have been crucially important institutions for queer-identified men. Performance studies scholar David Román explained that for him dance "was a way for me to begin choreographing my own movements through the world as an openly gay man. . . . it gave me a way to be in my body."[41] Patrick, a fifty-year-old, gay white man described the powerful effect of "seeing two men actually doing real couples dancing" during his first visit to a gay country/western bar. The first time Landon, a gay black man went to a gay bar, he had not yet come out to the group of heterosexual-identifying friends who ventured there with him. Landon was thrilled to be there as he watched men dance and thought, "Oh my gosh, he's gay. He's gay . . . That's less about dance and more about the space that dance kind of created for us." Gay dance clubs were transformative spaces because they were public places where gay-identified men could move as they wished and hold other men in their arms. Landon said,

> I think one of the things we as members of Generation X who are gay inherited
> from the generation before us who are called the Stonewall Generation, the first
> real generation of out gay men . . . was this fabulous mess on the dance floor and
> being able to kick and being able to twirl and being able to sashay on the dance
> floor and having that be part of our culture of black gay men. And I love that.

I love, love, love that freedom. When I think about the times when as a man and a dancer that I've been the happiest, that is among them. Just having the freedom to move however I wanted to move and the music was supporting it and the people were supporting it and the people say, "work!"

Milton, a thirty-eight-year-old black gay man, found community in the gay black house music dance scene in Chicago. "I knew that I was finding this connection to other gay men in this club scene and in this new world, and so it was just kind of like this great playground in a lot of ways." Landon and Milton speak of a culture they recognized as specifically black and gay. Landon felt that in clubs where men of color were a small minority, more stringent codes of masculinity prevailed. Avery, a younger gay man, saw it the same way:

I just felt like even at gay clubs, masculine was still really important, like you really had to be really butch, and I wasn't really butch . . . I think that it wasn't until I went to a Latin gay club in New York called Escolita that I really felt like loose and comfortable to dance. I feel like at the other predominantly white, really butch gay clubs, it was like my dancing was really limited.

Thus while gay dance clubs provide spaces where queer-identified men can enjoy same-gender dancing and a greater range of movement, they do not exist beyond the reach of gender conventions.

Nonetheless, one of the pleasures dance provides anywhere to any man is the possibility to transcend rules of everyday embodiment. Michael Gard interviewed professional dancers and found that "theatrical dance offered these men what they saw as opportunities to transcend the 'normal' ways they, as men, were expected to use their bodies . . . dance offered them the chance to 'be someone else' and to experience their bodies in new ways."[42] Dance, in nonprofessional settings, also provides men an opportunity to transcend the normal ways they move. In his daily life Norman, a middle-aged white heterosexual man, is a self-described "klutz." For most of his adult life, however, on one or two nights a week, he rehearsed or performed folk dancing, and he was a very good dancer. "I knock things over all the time, and it's a joke in our family." His friends tell him,

"You don't walk like a dancer. You don't look like a dancer. You don't act like a dancer. You don't move like a dancer. You couldn't possibly be a dancer." So it's sort of like I transform when I become a dancer, from, like, this geeky, klutzy guy to somebody who's—who can move well. It doesn't show up in my day to day life. I mean, if you saw me walking down the street, no, you wouldn't assume I'm a dancer who's been doing it for forty years.

Twenty-nine-year-old Ernest recognizes the dance floor as a place where he can break the rules of everyday comportment. Dance provides "the only opportunity in which you go on a floor and wiggle your body around and it's accepted . . . There's no other place you can do that . . . That's fun for an adult. That's like playing for an adult. Yeah, so why not do that whenever you get the chance?" Why not? Sex, sexuality, and sexiness. For many men dance requires transcending codes of masculine embodiment, appears to misrepresent their sexual intentions, and forces them to see themselves as fools. Dance is a form of fooling around, and public fooling requires either confidence or conditions that lower the fool's risk.

JUST DANCING

One of the ways men make dancing just dancing is by keeping the sex out of it. I learned this when listening to Walter, a sixty-five-year-old white man who has not danced for many years, and for whom dancing was always tightly connected to sex. He vividly remembered when as a teenager, he had the unusual experience of being in a black person's house. He had been brought there by a white friend, David. Three young men—Walter, David, and Vincent, whose home it was—sat in the living room listening to a black radio station's music. A particularly good dance song came on and Vincent's younger sister appeared from another room and asked her brother to dance.

> And then they're dancing and me and David are sitting and watching, right, because they're sensational dancers, right? And I remember, I mean this *really* affected me. I mean this was like a big moment in my life because I said to myself Jesus Christ, this guy's dancing with his *sister*, you know? . . . Is there a sexual thing going on between them? You know? When you dance with somebody it's always sex. Right? You know. Like my mind was like firing on all eight cylinders around this event, you know? But mostly the *main feeling* I had was envy, you know what I mean? Both because they were such good dancers and also because they had this thing that they could do right at home. You know. Like it was like there all the time, what a great thing, you know?

Though for a minute he wondered if there was a "sexual thing going on" between Vincent and his sister, he ultimately realized that there wasn't. He got a glimpse into dancing as just dancing, something a guy could do with his sister. The movements performed by Vincent and his sister may have appeared to be sexual but they were not foreplay, not meant to allure, and not nasty. They were a different kind of pleasurable interaction. Through dance they expressed their mutual connection to the music and their adept ability to respond to the other's improvisation. This kind of dancing is often most available between dancers when, because of the number dancers involved or other circumstances, it is clear that no genuine flirtation is intended. Justin, who is twenty and loves to dance, described parties where everyone dances but avoids pairing off. "I wouldn't describe it as couple dancing. Mostly it's kind of an individual thing. Something you do as a group." The seeming contradiction of the individual thing done in a group highlights the importance of removing intimacy from the dance to open a space for play.

Moshing and b-boying are individual things done in a group and both are accepted as masculine forms of dance. The same-gender physical intimacy that they involve is tolerable to heterosexual men because it occurs in the context of risk, athleticism, competition, or aggression. Yet I encountered many men, gay and straight, white, black, Asian, and Latino, usually but not always young, who can transcend the constraints required by hegemonic masculinity to have fun dancing in less competitive or aggressive forms. What links these men is their ability to experience dancing as just dancing rather than as sex or a prelude to sex. They dance with friends in clusters at clubs, in non-erotic couples at family celebrations, or at folk dance evenings. Wallace, who is sixty-six, white, and heterosexual, enjoys dancing at West Coast swing events where "you [don't] see this 'I got to hide from this guy because I went home with him last week and it didn't work out.'" In an ethnography of gay dances in Sydney, Australia, performance studies scholar Jonathan Bollen found that dancers distinguished between "having fun" and "cruising" while on the dance floor. Men could dance in a more effeminate style when having fun, but not when they wished to attract other men. When men sought to attract other men they adhered to codes of masculinity, and masculinity cramped their style.[43]

I will conclude with Patrick, a gay-identified white man who at fifty still dances regularly even though his life partner does not. He loves country/western-style partner dance. He describes its pleasures in terms that are intimately physical, and even sexy, but still are not a prelude to sex.

> It's fun to sort of feel a body for three minutes. And if you didn't like the feel, you don't have to keep feeling it. If you do like the feel you can always ask that person to dance again. So you know that when you just click with someone, it's just like magic. . . . And, you know it really varies . . . There's one guy who I just love dancing with . . . we're just about the right size. You know we're pretty close in height and weight. And our rhythm is just great on certain kind of fast to moderately fast songs. . . . On the other hand, there's a guy I love dancing with who

is probably I would guess at least 6 inches taller than I am, and quite stout . . .
And because he's so much taller than I am, and he loves to spin people, he gets
me spinning . . . I mean last night we danced one of the very fastest songs that
they play. And he was spinning me just like a top . . . Then there's another guy
who is actually I think maybe an inch or two shorter than I am and quite stout.
And it's really fun to dance with *him* because he goes both directions and, what's
amazing is when he does the other direction he virtually lifts me off my feet.

I asked him if his partner, with whom he has lived for years, is bothered by
Patrick's dancing life. "Nm mm," he said. "I've been going for six years. No, he
doesn't worry. I tell him, 'It's just dancing, even though it's sexy dancing.' . . .
I have a partner. And so when I ask people to dance I don't really want anything from anyone except a dance. And three minutes of fun with that person, just three minutes of playtime really." Patrick can separate sexiness
from sex, and so is able to enjoy dance as a form of play. He is not embarrassed by the thought that other men find him sexy, and at fifty believes he
retains at least a little allure. Country/western dancers wear a costume of
sorts. He invited me to attend his regular dance, where I saw a room full of
men most of whom were dressed in tight blue jeans, button down shirts, and
boots. The costumes make the men, many of whom were drawn to settle in
San Francisco from around the country, appear more homogenous than they
are. Patrick dances in a form that is structured by a gendered code that requires one to lead and the other follow, but he is happy to lead or follow depending on the relative height of the men in his arms. Another man who
attends the gay country/western dance said that people joke that a man's
preference regarding leading or following corresponds to his preference to be
an active "top" or passive "bottom" in bed. It is just a joke, he said, because
dancing, is just dancing.

Within the contemporary United States dance is a way to meet a sexual
partner, but it is not only that. Dancing can provide sensual pleasure. It can
be used to flirt, or to signal an identity. Or sometimes, as Charles suggests
in the epigraph, it is just dancing. Men who dance the most and who dance
as they get older are men who experience dance that way, as a transcendent
form of play.

CHAPTER 6

❧

Home Schooling

Maxine: So how is playing [basketball] different from dancing?

Mark: It's for me totally different. I don't have to care at all about looking good. You have to care about your offensive and defensive effectiveness. . . . It felt like the opposite. *Dancing* felt like *always* having to worry about what you looked like. And the rules were not exactly defined and effectiveness was not even defined . . . I just didn't know what to do and I felt totally awkward and confused.

How did Mark become an adept basketball player but a non-dancer? As he suggests, the experience of being looked at provides a clue. In most situations where people dance, someone watches. It "takes three to tango" wrote dance scholar Marta E. Savigliano, two to dance, and at least one to watch.[1] To dance in public is to allow oneself to be a watched, yet being the object of attention can be a feminizing experience, and preparing the body to be looked at is a central component of doing feminized gender.[2] Basketball is also a public performance, but in the game, as Mark explained, effectiveness, not appearance, matters.

Film scholar Laura Mulvey observed that women on screen connote the quality of "to-be-looked-at-ness" and that within films women are objects of the gaze and men bearers of the look.[3] My interviews with non-dancing men suggest that Mulvey's analysis of cinematic representational conventions may be extended to explain men's lived experiences. These men associated dancing with paralyzing levels of embarrassment. They were not prepared to be looked at. Their self-consciousness is a gendered experience, arising from boyhoods in which they learned lessons about masculine embodiment. They learned to hold their bodies apart from others, associate most forms of physical intimacy with sex, and listen to music without moving. Where others might dance, they stood apart and watched.

In her sweeping study of the disappearance of collective dancing in the West, Barbara Ehrenreich laments dance's decline as the loss of an important experience of human fellowship. "The loss of ecstatic pleasure, of the kind once routinely generated by rituals involving dancing, music, and so on, deserves the same attention accorded to community, and to be equally mourned."[4] Spanning the thousands of years from Roman suppression of Dionysian cults to the contemporary organization of entertainment as spectacle, Ehrenreich paints a history of dance suppression with a broad brush. She describes European colonizers as "horrified witnesses" of African dancers. The colonizers defined "the Western mind, and particularly the Western male, upper-class mind, [by] its ability to resist the contagious rhythm of the drums, to wall itself up in a fortress of ego and rationality against the seductive wildness of the world."[5]

Happily, dancing has not been completely eliminated from public life in the West. Even within the narrower scope of the United States it continues in home parties, crowded nightclubs, Filipino American cotillions, chaperoned proms, gay country/western bars, and countless other venues. In part dancing continues because the activities of social life are not determined by the desires of white upper-class men. Yet as the historical record and my interviews document, plenty of well-to-do white men love to dance and have danced well. At certain historical moments dancing ability was a defining feature of white upper-class masculinity. Recall Elisha Dyer, whose 1917 obituary memorialized his social position as the best dancer in Newport society. Rather than naturalizing white upper-class masculinity as rational and unmoving and correspondingly naturalizing men of color and presumably all women as connected to the rhythm of the drums, the aim of this chapter is to identify how physical and social connections that are essential to dance are formed and disconnects established.

"Natural" dancers are produced through practice, yet a man who rehearses engages in the potentially feminizing practice of preparing to be looked at. Sociologist Michael Kimmel has argued that masculinity is a performance men enact largely for each other.[6] Men watch each other and are aware that they are being watched, yet all of the gazing and preparation for being watched depends on men's denial that it is going on. The gender dilemma of being watched, and the ways in which men solve it, provide a window into processes of masculine embodification.

Though many men cringe at the thought of dancing, drink heavily to attempt it, or simply refuse to do it, others enjoy that gaze and even perform for it. They employ strategies to manage the gaze. Men who dance, and who wish to align themselves with conventional understandings of masculinity, may mask or deny their rehearsals, display unconcern, play the fool, or deflect attention by disappearing into conventional movement.[7] Some men find ways of dancing that reduce the likelihood of being watched, while others have found ways of being a spectacle that will be perceived as markedly masculine. Sociologist Pierre Bourdieu developed the concept of the habitus as an embodied feel for the rules of social games and the desire to play them.[8] Consider the way Charles, a heterosexual working-class African American and Filipino young man, plays on the dance floor of a nightclub:

> First I would do the little one-two. Just move left, move right, do a one-two step. And then I would watch people to see what dances are out so I could at least stay with the trend, so I wouldn't do . . . something like too old—go out there and do the mashed potato. I mean, I guess that would be fine for like, a second or two, [*chuckle*] but I don't want to be too out of place.

The mashed potato was one of the many named steps that proliferated in the early 1960s. It involves rapidly turning the knees in to face each other and then out again in a motion that one could imagine mashing a pile of cooked potatoes if they were under the feet of the dancer. The motion of the legs causes the dancer's torso to repeatedly dip forward to the beat. Done well, the mashed potato is a rhythmic, full-bodied dance. Its moment of popularity ended well before Charles' adolescence. In his account "mashed potato" is a way of describing any snatch of a bygone dance that he can display on the dance floor for brief flashes of comic playfulness. He inserts it alongside contemporary ways of moving as a retro moment within a skillful performance. The core of his dancing is his ability to move to whatever music is playing, his "little one-two," yet he is prepared to look around, see if others are performing a new step, and immediately imitate it. There are boundaries of right and wrong, but not a fixed set of steps. He could be "out-of-place," but that would consist of failing to respond to what others were doing. Good dancing is being connected to the crowd. He is highly skilled at physical interaction, a capacity that requires watching others as he is being watched. Charles possesses both the desire to dance and a feel for the rules of the dance floor. He has the ability to move in time to music but that is just one element of the dancer's habitus. He has a culturally recognizable repertoire of movements and the ability to imitate others, the capacity for parody, and a feel for the limits of the idiom. He is a "natural."

Gil, a twenty-nine-year-old Chicano gay man, also has the dancer's habitus. At dance clubs "[i]t's very easy," he explained, "for me to anticipate the next move."

> Even when they're blending music, I can hear them starting the next song, and
> I'm ready to go . . . and so when they switch it, boom, I'm ready. I can go for the
> next move . . . And I like doing things that play with the music a little bit. This
> might be the main beat, and I'll do that movement a little bit, but then I'll switch
> it up, and I'm still on that beat, but I basically just double speeded it. And then,
> changing genres—I like doing that too.

These men are comfortable being looked at. They enjoy being seen and play to the gaze of anyone who watches. Mulvey's theorization of the cinematic gaze as masculine is helpful to a point. It is usefully applied to countless Hollywood films and many in the audiences who watch them. It has been criticized as a theorization that accounts for neither the complexity of cinematic representations nor the diversity of film audiences.[9] My extension of Mulvey's analysis, likewise, needs qualification. Confident dancing may be conceptualized as a variety of responses to the problems presented by contemporary constructions of masculinity, responses that were nurtured within families and communities. This chapter investigates the structures and conditions that foster the dancer's habitus, and conversely, how nondancers are made.

WATCHING MEN DANCE

I was a participant observer in two quarters of Dance 101, a college-level survey course that was a requirement for students majoring in physical education. Both quarters, almost all of the enrolled students were physical education majors. The class provided the opportunity to observe men who were confident and adept when using their bodies in sports as they faced the expressive and interactional challenges of dance. To a certain extent, the class created a safe environment in which men could experiment with dance. Unlike a public dance club, where some men may sit at the bar feeling superior to men who potentially make fools of themselves on the dance floor, in Dance 101, no man could sit-out the dance, and therefore no man could be faulted merely for the act of dancing.[10] The men were there because they wanted to be physical education teachers or coaches. Dance in this context could be treated by students as one of those incomprehensible hurdles that college curricula place before students on paths to their degrees. I interviewed six of the ten men who enrolled in one of the two quarters of Dance 101 and an additional forty-four men who were recruited into the study through other means. These interviews, along with my observations of students in Dance 101, form the basis of this chapter.

On the first evening of the course Marcy, the African American woman who was our instructor, asked the assembled group of five men and four women if they were dancers. Frank, a tall, lanky, white, young man, answered, "I dance, but I'm not a dancer." Phil, his friend and fellow physical education major, who was also white, but about a decade older, added, "It's a level question." Dance 101 introduced ballet, jazz, modern, social, and African dance as discrete sets of techniques that corresponded to distinct traditions. The context affirmed Frank's self-assessment. In it, he and most of his classmates became non-dancers because they had not received training in any of the traditions. Though neither claimed to be a dancer, in subsequent classes I observed these two white men dancing. Frank, who earned income as a disk jockey for private parties, added understated, voluntary flourishes to the plainer steps that the instructor introduced as the fundamentals of movement. He used his arms, torso, and head to insert his own percussive accents into the choreography and bent his knees low when executing walking steps to create briefly held crouches.

Phil was flummoxed by choreography and did not improvise, but knew one isolated dance step. He could perform the moonwalk, a step in which a dancer appears to glide backwards, which was popularized by pop star Michael Jackson in the 1980s. Phil taught students this step as part of his final project. He approached moonwalking as a stunt that he had mastered rather than as expressive movement. After he taught a fellow student to moonwalk, he challenged her to a moonwalking race. Phil and Frank demonstrate two approaches to dancing. Frank could be inventive with dance. He entertained himself and others by improvising movement. Phil knew one dance trick, the moonwalk, and with it, transformed dance into sport. Frank had the dancer's habitus; Phil lacked it.

Frank was not the only student who layered popular movements on top of the plainer steps in the curriculum. In a section of Dance 101 taught in a subsequent quarter, there were five men in a class of fourteen students. Justin, an athletic twenty-year-old whose father is Mexican and mother is white, also enjoyed amusing himself and others by dancing. On the night of the second class, students gathered at one end of a rectangular dance studio to watch Marcy demonstrate a movement combination in which she walked forward, backward, and in a circle and then performed a sort of scoot, which ballet dancers call a chassé, in which one foot slides out and then the other catches up with it. She asked us to remove our shoes and socks and then to form single-gender rows to cross the floor in successive waves using the walking and scooting sequence.[11]

The students in Dance 101 grudgingly abandoned their athletic shoes and socks in a corner of the room before taking their places in single-gender rows. For almost all, the scoot step was unfamiliar, awkward, and even painful for those unaccustomed to sliding barefoot, but the walking and directional changes were easily accomplished. All but one of us performed these everyday movements almost as if we were simply using them to get somewhere, though generally without the conviction that someone actually trying to reach a destination would have. Justin added his own dance to it and looked good. He was a confident, adept dancer. In between the assigned steps, Justin inserted a popular form of dancing known as pop-locking. Pop-locking sends a sequential impulse through the body in a series of mechanical-appearing waves. Justin's pop-locking was an improvisation surreptitiously placed between the mandated moves. It was, perhaps, a rebellious gesture performed for the benefit of other students, including his girlfriend who was in the class. Yet the rebellion took the form of dance, the aim of the course, and so perhaps this moment of popular dance inserted into the simple required steps was simultaneously rebellion and overachievement.

HOME BOPPING

In a subsequent interview I asked Justin if he minded getting attention when he danced. He responded with nonchalance. "I do get noticed a lot," he said, "but it's not something I try to do. It's just being myself." "Okay," I responded, "but how does it feel to get noticed?" "Alright, I guess. . . . It's not something I really think about though." How did he develop the ability to easily improvise movement and casually accept being watched? Why did he not wither under the gaze? Justin's Mexican father and white mother loved R & B music, "old school" hip-hop, and a bit of rock. Marvin Gaye, James Brown, and Santana provided background music for daily life. "Everybody danced at home," he said. "When we were doing something, it was like, 'Alright, we're going to put on this music and we're going to clean the house' . . . the dancing just went along with it." At the age of five or six Justin's parents took him to a concert where African American dancing male pop stars MC Hammer and Jodeci shared the bill. He has a vivid memory of darting to the aisle to emulate the men on stage. His favorite part of family celebrations is the opportunity to dance in parties that mix hip-hop and salsa. When his family dances to salsa "it's not all uniform and stuff," he explained. "We just try to get out there and do it." When I asked him about dancing with relatives near his own age he described time spent with a boy cousin. "A lot of times we didn't have anything to do. We'd listen to the radio and we'd tape the songs we liked and we'd just like listen to them all day long." When asked about dancing, he described listening, because he automatically associated dancing with listening. Dance was a casual, spontaneous response to music. It was a normal, easily accessible form of amusement, performed in the company of peers and older relatives. As Justin approached adolescence, he began to associate some forms of dance with sexualized heterosexual intimacy. These meanings were added to but did not supplant his earlier experiences of dance as a way to playfully interact with others. When given an easy combination with which to cross the floor on the second night of a university dance course, he spiced it up with a little pop-locking.

Masculine embodiment is a "physical sense of maleness" as described by sociologist Raewyn Connell, and it is socially produced by boys who transform their bodies through work and play and acquire habits of moving in social contexts through practice.[12] A boy does that in constant interaction with others in the family and beyond whose responses to his routine performances let him know how adequately he fills the male category as they imagine it.[13] Childhood experiences with dance provide insight into the place of the family in the inculcation of bodily dispositions. One issue appears to be crucial for the formation of the dancer's habitus. A boy must feel that his parents approve of the pleasure he derives from dancing.

A parent's view that it is acceptable, admirable, or even necessary for a boy to move well (or on the contrary that it is unacceptable, shameful, or unnecessary for him to dance) can be conveyed through different means.[14] Perhaps the most effective way to produce a man who can move is through home environments like Justin's in which physical responses to music are casually incorporated into the family's everyday life. Gil was described above as having the dancer's habitus. Asked if there was dancing in his childhood home, he began by telling me that there was not. "In my actual house, I won't say there was a lot of dancing." He continued by describing a house in which there was constant casual dancing. "My mom like[d] to turn on music when we'd be cleaning, and we would dance and clean," he recalled. And every weekday, "we would dance to music in the morning while we were getting ready." He and his mother danced without a sense of being part of a dancing couple. Their movement stopped and started as he, his siblings, and his mother attended to household tasks. Early in our interview, he resisted calling it dancing. Perhaps it is better described as bopping around at home. In such an environment the acceptability of a man's eye-catching movement was learned without being taught.

INTERGENERATIONAL FAMILY DANCING

A second way that parental approval was conveyed was through intergenerational family dancing, which took place at social gatherings of extended family or through informal lessons given to children by parents. Milton is thirty-eight, black, and gay. He remembers being taught to dance by his mother during a small party at home.

> I think I was around maybe seven or eight. There was a bunch of people at the house, and people were dancing a little bit and my mother called me over and she taught me how to do the rock—it's basically you just move your hips back and forth to the beat . . . and all the adults around were kind of joining in and encouraging me.

Alberto is a forty-six-year-old gay man whose parents emigrated from Mexico to Arizona where they found employment as farmworkers. During his childhood he learned to dance at multigenerational parties.

> Whenever there was a party of some sort, there was always music and there was obviously, always dance. The holidays were a blast because people's houses were open and so people would go to each other's houses. There was ranchera music for the most part [and] cumbia . . . And then I remember when I started growing up, you know, then you start getting the pull from us [kids]. We wanted to hear English music.

Through radio, school, and church-sponsored youth activities Alberto and his siblings and cousins were exposed to mainstream pop culture. At a certain point his older cousins encouraged their elders to add Michael Jackson and Donny Osmond records to the musical mix at the parties. The adults would placate them by playing a few pop records before returning to rancheras. Even in a relatively homogenous community of farmworkers and extended family, the children lived in complex cultural environments in which an ethnic and dominant pop culture mixed. His musical tastes continued to shift in the direction of mainstream pop music. He recalls a Michael Jackson album and the soundtrack to *Saturday Night Fever* as the records that were the most important to him as a teen. However his basic orientation toward and comfort with dance were shaped at parties where adults and children danced to Mexican and other Central American music.

Ryan is a heterosexual twenty-six-year-old student. His mother is Filipino and Mexican, his father white. As a child he and his four brothers would team up with an uncle to imitate the choreographed routines of the

African American Motown group The Temptations, which they performed for the amusement of their relatives. Their routines were imperfect, but that did not diminish their entertainment value. Everyone laughed and they had a good time. In addition to learning to dance informally at home, Ryan received somewhat more formal instruction as he prepared to escort a young woman to a cotillion. Within contemporary middle-class Filipino-American communities, cotillions are formal, coming-of-age parties given on a young woman's eighteenth birthday. Families often prepare their children for cotillions by organizing dance instruction in the cha-cha, waltz, and other partner dances. Ryan recalled that he and his fellow escorts were not initially capable of dancing any of the formal dances. In the weeks leading up to the cotillion,

> somebody that knew how to dance would try to teach the group a dance, pretty simple stuff. . . . basically friends and family would just teach us the dance steps. . . . A lot of the people that were in the [cotillion] court, we all went to school together, so we'd be at school practicing. . . . It didn't come out looking really nice, but it was fun to learn it.

Within the cotillions and the rehearsals that led up to them, his competent performance of the cha-cha and waltz allowed him to escort a young woman and signaled his maturing masculinity. Ryan practiced dance routines with his brothers and uncles at home for the amusement of his family. That dancing was reinforced by the more formal instruction he received to be a part of a cotillion, rehearsals that involved not only family members but peers at school.

The family pattern of living near extended family and gathering at parties, which included intergenerational dancing, and the experience of bopping at home were more characteristic of African American, Chicano, and Filipino men than the non-Hispanic white men that I interviewed. Justin, Milton, Alberto, Gil, and Ryan grew up in families where children and adults spent time together and lived near relatives who enjoyed dancing at parties. At the parties men and women danced in informal ways. At home it was fun and amusing for boys to imitate the choreographed steps of male entertainers. When they did so, they would fail to replicate a star's brilliant technique, but they would succeed in entertaining themselves and their parents and that was their goal.

Home bopping and intergenerational family dancing rehearse movement capacities that are essential for dance. As they move in time to music boys inscribe in muscle memory the ability to shift their weight in rhythm and direct their bodies' movements. However the dancer's habitus is not just a matter of physical capacity. Men who can rapidly pivot on a basketball court or exquisitely coordinate their movements in a soccer game may freeze when asked to dance. The difference between a sports move and a dance step is the meaning that is attached to the movement and therefore to the bodies of the men who perform. Boys who dance have learned that masculinity is entirely compatible with dance. In familial or community contexts that encouraged and legitimated masculine expressive movement, they developed a dancer's habitus. They want to dance and are psychologically and physically equipped to do it. These boys were given a "generative foundation" that allowed them to enjoy improvising and interacting through dance.[15] They have a set of embodied techniques, a repertoire of ways to move to music, the ability to imitate others, and the capacity to improvise playfully within the limits of a physical idiom.[16]

TEACHING SONS TO DANCE

None of the patterns regarding home dance cultures rigidly follow racial or ethnic lines. The patterns are affected by, among other things, the proximity of family and intervening religious cultures, which may discourage adults from dancing. Still, for white boys who danced, there appeared to have been fewer multigenerational dance parties and less bopping at home. The ones who became dancers nonetheless got the message that dancing was an acceptable and even expected part of manhood. Norman grew up in the 1950s and 1960s in an upper-middle-class Jewish family in Southern California and is now the owner of a small company. He acquired the dancer's habitus in his mothers' arms. His earliest memories of dancing are of his sister standing on her father's toes as his father waltzed her around the room while Norman partnered with his mother. His parents wanted their children to be competent dancers so that they would be able to enjoy themselves at social occasions where dancing was expected. Sometimes when his parents went out, Norman and his sisters were left with baby-sitters, but when they were invited to a wedding or a bar mitzvah, Norman got the chance to see his parents dance in public.

> Whatever kind of social events I went [to] with my parents, I saw them going out and dancing without any fear or shame or anything like that. . . . [When] we went to somebody's wedding or something where it was a family event and we were invited, and . . . they had a band and they were playing swing . . . my parents would always go out and dance.

At these parties Norman saw dance performed as an adult activity for heterosexual couples. His parents prepared him for this part of being a competent adult man by teaching him the basics of social dancing at home and sending him to cotillion classes in the neighborhood. While Norman used the word cotillion to name the lessons he received, he is describing something different from contemporary Filipino-American cotillions. For Norman cotillion was a commercially run neighborhood short course in etiquette for middle-class youths aged eleven to thirteen (fig. 6.1). He recalled a series of lessons in couple dancing and had only dim recollections of a culminating event. He explained that

> [m]iddle-class families in our neighborhood . . . the kids did cotillion . . . So we, I learned how to fox trot, I learned how to waltz, and I learned how to swing when I was twelve, with girls. It was a regular, you know, pipeline of kids our age . . . in this particular middle school and high school district, all the kids went and did this cotillion thing . . . so they were all people that we knew that lived close, that I saw—you know, I played base—you played Little League with . . . and the girls were the ones who sat next to [me] in class.

Norman entered the cotillion class with a bit of preparation from having seen his parents dance and having danced with his mother. The class was

Figure 6.1
Asking for a dance at Shorewood School dancing class, Shorewood Hills, Wisconsin, 1952.
Wisconsin Historical Society.

filled with familiar girls and boys from his school. Being there was as normal as being in Little League.

Patrick is fifty, white, gay, and grew up in an upper middle-class Catholic family in the Midwest. He also received living-room dance lessons in what appears to have been a common pattern in upper middle-class white households in the late 1950s and early 1960s. These were homes in which parents were socializing their children to participate in cultural worlds which the parents imagined as being continuous with their own. As it turned out Norman and Patrick's adulthoods became quite different from what their parents had imagined. Norman's wife does not dance, and Patrick married a man. Neither of their spouses dances. Still, both men live in settled, long-term marriages and both are grateful for the early dance training that has been the foundation for the satisfaction they derive from dance.

From similar beginnings, Norman and Patrick grew up to be avid, albeit very different, types of dancers. Norman primarily dances through international folk dance. Patrick lives in a city where there is a gay country/western dance club where he dances twice a week. Both of them are comfortable moving in public to music and consider dance one of life's great pleasures. They enjoy dance for its own sake and do not view it as a means to meet a sexual partner. Their adult modes of dancing may in part be explained by the opportunities available to them. Norman danced for many years as a member of a folk dance group, a context that was not organized around dating or married couples. Among venues for gay dancing in his area, the country/western dance club is the most welcoming for men older than thirty. Patrick was drawn to the club for its friendliness and within the club became a country/western dancer.

SIBLING DANCING

Several men I interviewed learned to dance from their sisters. Sociologist Barrie Thorne notes that schools, while keeping young girls and boys in the same physical space, tend to separate them by gender into distinct and gendered activities.[17] In less-structured home and neighborhood settings, girls and boys may pay less attention to gender and therefore are more likely to participate in the same activities, including dancing.[18]

Charles, described above as a young man with a dancer's habitus, grew up in an impoverished neighborhood in Southern California in the 1970s. His strict parents kept their seven children indoors, and he spent a good portion of his free time dancing with two sisters who were the siblings closest to his age. They choreographed dance routines that they would perform as "talent shows" for their parents.

Ralph's parents emigrated from Central America to the United States. He was twenty-five when I interviewed him and identifies as heterosexual. As he approached puberty, his sister decided it was time for him to learn how to dance.

> She was like, "You need to learn. You need to be able to go to your school dance." . . .
> When you come in the front door of our old house there was like a little entry way
> and it was kind of like raised up compared to the living room next to it . . . We called
> that our stage. We always did like dumb things on there. So she took me on the
> stage and then she taught me how to dance to hip-hop music.

Paul is fifty, white, heterosexual, and from the Midwest. He recalled dancing with his four older sisters as a regular activity in his 1960s childhood. Paul lived in a white community and attended all-white Catholic schools, but every Sunday his parents drove the family to another neighborhood to attend a predominantly black Catholic church. His parents were not political activists attending a black church to deliberately practice racial integration. He recalls only that his parents chose the church because they were drawn to the preaching style of its minister. After church, in social hours, Paul and his sisters observed black children and teenagers dancing, studied their movements, and practiced them at home. "We danced all the time. We danced constantly . . . We just would clear out the dining room, put on our records, and dance." Charles and Paul were boys in large families with sisters. They did not see their parents dancing but learned to dance with their sisters and faced no opposition from their parents for doing it. Crucially, the boys who recalled learning to dance from older sisters experienced parental approval, or at the very least, no parental disapproval of their enthusiasm for dance. Paul's dance practice increased his popularity when he spent time with white male peers in the yard of his Catholic school. Paul and his school friends tried to imitate the movement style of soul singer James Brown and Paul's approximation was especially good. "We'd all do James Brown . . . We did his little turnaround, we tried his little foot thing. . . . If you can do James Brown, man, you were very cool." The distinction of coolness could be won by competently performing dance steps that were certifiably masculine because they were the steps of masculine stars. Socially structured desires led Paul to work, that is, to play at dance. Paul was disposed to practice dance because within his social world, competent dancing was a way to gain social inclusion.

Boys learn lessons about dance as they respond to social expectations to perform masculinities that are socially defined by, among other things,

race, ethnicity, and class. Sociologist James Messerschmidt argues that
teenagers scrutinize each other for perceived incongruence between sex
category and gender performance.[19] It is important to add that gender performances are also scrutinized in relation to racial and ethnic categories.
Within a nation structured by racial and gender inequalities, boys develop
a physical sense of maleness that is always read through race and a physical
sense of racial category that is always read through gender. Masculine embodiments begin taking shape at an early age in institutional and community settings in which dance is either modeled or absent, praised or
ridiculed, legitimated or proscribed, provided for or precluded. These over-
lapping settings are not necessarily bound by racial and ethnic categories
although they often involve them.

Paul and his friends danced to flaunt physical skill within social worlds
in which dance was accepted as masculine. His world was one in which
white boys looked to black peers and black celebrities as models of masculinity. They saw those forms of embodiment as ones that they could take on
as their own. The next section explores white middle-class environments in
which boys learned not to invest time or energy in learning to dance. Parental reactions to a boy's dancing matter a great deal, but those reactions
are shaped, contextualized, and their consequences modified within
broader neighborhood or school environments in which a boy learns that
he should or should not know how to dance. Beliefs about race and gender
circulate within a society and communicate norms for embodiment that
can thwart parents' efforts to encourage their sons to dance.[20] Parental encouragement is a helpful but not sufficient condition for producing a son
who can dance.

LEARNING NOT TO DANCE

Stan, a white, middle-aged, heterosexual electrician, does not dance. He
grew up in the 1950s and 1960s in a white Christian middle-class suburb
around boys who worked hard at sports, but not at dance. As far as he recalls, none of his peers danced well, none had to, and none wanted to. As a
teenager he was not shy about dancing because he felt no pressure to do it
well. Dances were opportunities to have close contact with young women.
That heteronormative desire was all he needed to display when at a dance.
He recalls attending junior high school dances where physical education
teachers roamed the dance floor warning "no honey-bunching" any time
dancers clung too closely to each other. Having heard men of his age recall
their discomfort in similar situations, I asked Stan if he dreaded these

dances. "No, I enjoyed it . . . Yeah that was all right . . . Being with girls." I asked if he felt that he was a competent dancer. He did not, nor did he feel that he needed to be.

> I think I probably had an early, you know, feeling that following the steps I wasn't good at. . . . But it was okay. I was okay with it . . . Dancing was incidental to what the whole significance of it was . . . At that time, dance was pretty free form. You could just do about anything you wanted and it wasn't—people weren't critical of your dancing ability.

I interviewed Stan in his home. His wife quietly worked in the kitchen as he expounded on his lifelong inability to dance. At one point in the interview he loudly called out to her to help him recall and to serve as witness to his account of being asked by an instructor not to return to an adult school, line-dance class. "There's no doubt about it, I was no good at that," he recalled in a way that sounded closer to a boast than to confession. "The whole group goes left, and right, and stuff like that, and does this and that, and I can't do that. Or maybe at some level I could, but I'm not going to put the energy into doing that." Bodily capacities are built up in just that way, by putting energy into the practice of an activity. Stan gave voice to a kind of masculine disposition in which there is a desire to dance with women in order to have contact with them, but not to do it well. As a young man, Stan never felt that inept dancing would cause him to be judged as a failure. As long as he showed a desire to dance with women, dancing poorly was sufficient.

It is possible that the relative diversity of urban areas created contexts in which white boys such as Norman and Paul were encouraged to dance. Stan's dispositions were formed in a geographical and social location, suburban and homogenously white, and a time, the 1960s, in which skillful dancing was not a component of white suburban middle-class heterosexual masculine embodiment. Historian Elaine Tyler May describes postwar suburbs as "isolated enclaves [which] weakened extended-family ties, promoted homogeneity in neighborhoods, intensified racial segregation, encouraged conformity, and fostered a style of life based on traditional gender roles in the home."[21] Nothing in Stan's homogenous surroundings challenged or complicated his conception of masculinity. The importance of dancing skill in a young man's life is therefore a historical and community-specific variable, producing men with and without a dancer's habitus. Within the white middle-class heteronormative context of Stan's youth, dance was a way to have contact with women. The most visible criterion by which he was judged was the distance he kept from his partner. Stan recalls the dance culture of his youth as one in which dancers could "just do about anything you wanted." Yet dance scholar Helen Thomas argues that it is never the case that "any movement will do" in social dance settings.[22] Stan could do just about anything he wanted, as long as what he wanted was to dance slowly and closely with girls.

Stan never learned to dance but was in an environment where he felt he could succeed socially without that ability. He lacked a skill that appeared to him to have little value. Other men I interviewed were less comfortable as non-dancers. A catalogue of discomfort, of all the ways a man may feel uneasy in his body, emerged from their interviews. Their bodies were strange to them, consisting of parts they could not mobilize or adequately control in situations in which they felt quite exposed. Neil, for example, who grew up as a white middle-class boy in San Francisco, recalled that the first time he needed to dance was in the 1960s when, as an adolescent, he was sent to a social dance class. Unlike Ryan or Norman above who went to social dance classes prepared by home schooling and accompanied by peers, Neil felt unready and alone. Through a series of classes in which he felt he had to accomplish something for which he was unprepared, while intimately interacting with unfamiliar young women, without the support of male friends, and wearing uncomfortably formal clothing, he learned that he could not dance.

> I was sent by my parents . . . to Mr. Mack's dance class. Somehow or other it just never occurred to me that the way to get kids to like dance is to throw them together with a bunch of kids they'd never met before in their lives and tell them they had to do it. It didn't work. No . . . I was with a partner and I was supposed to be leading . . . It was kind of tortured considering as I really didn't know what I was doing and didn't want to be there.

With some, but not overwhelming regret, Neil has accepted being a non-dancer. His wife loves to dance, but he cannot find a way to join her on the dance floor. As a married adult, the occasions when he is reminded that he does not dance are few.

Wallace, a white, heterosexual, sixty-six-year-old owner of a small business, learned to dance as an adult, after decades of not dancing. When he turned fifty, Wallace was single and tried dancing because of the social opportunities he hoped it would provide. He had a desire to dance, but no feel for it, and approached dance as a set of steps and rules for moving that could be learned. In his understanding of dance, even experienced dancers must return to beginner's lessons because their experience leads them to stray from correct form.

When I went to these beginning lessons, I saw some people in these beginning lessons who I knew . . . were very experienced dancers. . . . I've asked them about that and they said well because when you learn, you learn the basic steps and then you . . . you learn the embellishments, and you get better and better and you do it more and more, often what happens is, is somebody points out to you that you're not doing the basic steps properly. *That you've developed your own flare which is out of sync.* And you've got to go back and take a beginning lesson just to get that, to get that down again. Just as very literate people who speak beautiful English sometimes pronounce or use words incorrectly.

His goal was correct usage, not the dance equivalent of "beautiful English." Yet the interactional improvisation enabled by the dancer's habitus is precisely the capacity to play with the rules by occasionally breaking them.

Allen, who is white, middle class, and gay, grew up in the 1950s and 1960s feeling isolated and ashamed. He danced in his room with the door closed because his parents expressed disapproval when they saw him dance. When opportunities arose he joined dance activities at camp and in grade school, but did not dance socially until he was a young adult. Like Wallace, he is most comfortable dancing when he can rely on set steps. "I like learning steps in that they give me more tools." When he must improvise to rock or disco music, he said, "I feel like I sometimes don't know what to do. Like I'm not being creative enough with it or I'll get more self-conscious in that regard, 'cause I feel like I'm not able to do it well enough." Wallace and Allen became social dancers later in life. Wallace did not aspire to improvisation, Allen did not feel up to it. Both found security in codified, predictable dance forms.

EAT, TALK, PASS OUT GIFTS

The teenagers and young adults of the Swing Era became the parents of baby boomers. Some of these post–World War II parents wanted to pass along the fun of dance to their children and prepare them for social lives that they imagined would be like the ones they enjoyed in their own youth. While some middle-aged, middle-class white men described learning to dance from their Swing Era parents, others described a breakdown in the intergenerational transmission of dance. Brian, who is white and sixty-five, earnestly takes to the dance floor out of a devotion to his wife, but feels that he does not quite know what he is doing while there and will only dance with her. He has seen photographs of his father dancing and believes that his father was an excellent dancer. Yet he recalled, "They never danced around my sister and myself . . . Mom and Dad talked about dance, that back east that's what they did was go to the ballrooms, the big ballrooms. And my dad was evidently quite a dancer." The one memory he has of his father dancing is of a brief glimpse down a stairway into a basement party. He thinks that before being hurried off to bed he saw his father dancing.

Neil similarly recalled that his father loved to dance. His parents attempted to introduce him to dance by sending him to Mr. Mack's classes, a plan that, as described above, utterly failed. Neil felt alone and unprepared in the class. He somehow knew that his father was a good dancer, but had never seen him dance.

> My father loved to dance. And when I was young he used to go out with Mom . . . Mine was one of the families where, if the adults were dancing the kids probably got left home . . . we're working on almost fifty years of having the family Christmas party at my parent's house. There's never been any dancing. There's rarely even any music. . . . Sit around and talk. Eat, talk, pass out gifts. My parents occasionally had parties, cocktail or dinner parties. And I'm pretty sure there was never any dancing at any of them. If there was I never saw it. They were late and we probably had gone to bed.

For Walter, a sixty-five-year-old white mathematician, the thought of his parents dancing was an unimaginable primal scene.

> I think a lot of kids grow up in dancing cultures where there's a lot of dancing going on around them. I grew up in the exact opposite. I can't even generate, you know how some people go through this exercise, can you imagine your parents in bed making love, you know? Kids can't do it, right? I can't imagine my parents dancing.[23]

While not all white middle-class, post–World War II families adopted child-rearing practices that excluded children from adult parties and dropped dancing from multi-generational family parties, many did, and these were the conditions under which fathers who danced raised sons who did not.

Leo, who is fifty, heterosexual, Latino, and a corporate executive, has neither the ability to improvise, nor has he found security in steps. He does not dance. Instead he describes a feeling of "uncoordination and really not knowing where to put your hands," which becomes worse if he is not holding a partner. "If you're separated, right . . . What do you do, right?" Leo has become accustomed to containing his enjoyment of music in his head. Music does not diminish the physical boundaries he maintains between himself and others. Like Neil, Leo's father was reputed to have been an excellent dancer. Yet he rarely saw his father dance. His parents left their children at home when they went out to dance. "When my parents went to parties and dancing, it was grownups only." As an adult Leo feels acutely out of place where people dance.

DISCONNECTS

Leo listens to music while he works writing software code. Music gives him energy, he explained, but it does not make him want to dance. I asked him if, when listening to music by himself, he danced, even a little. "No," he said with a short laugh, "I don't think so. No, I'm not—no, no, I don't do that, no," and nervously laughed again. His tastes in music are unexpectedly youthful for a middle-aged executive. "I like rap. I like hip-hop, but I can't quite move in the way I think about it . . . I just cannot get it to work. [*chuckle*] I can't get my body to respond to that. So, there's a disconnect somewhere." Where is the disconnect? He locates it within his self, yet the internal disconnect has consequences for the way he interacts in the world. His wife loves to dance and though he feels a bit sorry for her, he has only danced with her on a few occasions during their lengthy marriage.

Similar to Leo, Neil is passionate about music but does not dance. He has, on rare occasions, accompanied his wife to dance floors, but described those attempts as uncomfortable instances in which he did not know what to do with his body. His response to music, he explained, "is something that largely goes on inside my head, and is sort of divorced from, to a large extent from the rest of my body."

Marvin, a white heterosexual fifty-eight-year-old professor, discussed that feeling of disconnect in detail. As a young man in the 1960s, he enjoyed and regularly participated in the unconstrained dancing of the era. Then he stopped dancing. He linked the end of his dancing to his turn toward radical politics and higher education. Though he could not entirely explain it, he felt that neither change was compatible with dance. It was not just a matter of the time spent in those endeavors; it was, he explained, that engaging his mind required disengaging his body. He said that when he became involved in radical social movements he

> became less frivolous, and as I became less frivolous, dancing seemed more of an indulgence than something that you need to do, and it's no mistake really that uh, for example, in Cuba, you will never hear anybody say that Che Guevara could dance. He couldn't dance. He was known as having two left feet.

To demonstrate the incompatibility of dance and revolution, and to defend his own position as a non-dancer, he pointed to Che Guevara, an idolized revolutionary figure, as an exemplar of the non-dancing, serious man. Marvin continued, explaining that he danced less and less as his formal education increased.

> I went to school again, and going to school again I have attributed a real connection between becoming book smart, being able to do précis, getting my bachelor's degree, getting my master's degree, getting my Ph.D., and really losing the ability to cut it loose. Now I know there's no connection between that organically. I know plenty of people who are very well educated people who can cut the rug well, and I know plenty of people who don't have a formal education who are not dancers, but for me, it had that weird process where I got more uptight.

He knows that it cannot be so, and yet he experiences his mind and body competing for his capacities. As his intellectual training increased he lost his ability to move.

Mark, a fifty-nine-year-old Jewish statistician, is so self-conscious about his body that he does what he can to prevent others from looking at him. He chooses clothes that will not draw attention to his body. "Being invisible," he said, "means sort of being disconnected from your body. It's like you're all up here." How do men like Mark get themselves confined "up there?" What sort of disconnects foreclose movement "down there" in the body?

The process of becoming a non-dancer may be described in negative terms as the result of missed opportunities. Yet it may also be seen as an active inculcation of masculinity as stolid, solitary, static, physically inexpressive in public, and non-sensual. Author Barbara Ehrenreich notes that "the well-behaved audience member—who does not snap her fingers or nod her head in time to the music—is not really at rest; she is performing a kind of work—the silent, internal work of muscular inhibition."[24] A similar work of muscular inhibition holds men back from the experiences of touch, release, response, and publicly visible improvisation that produce dance floor play. Dancing can be thought of as a series of connections. It is almost always performed to music or drums and thus at its most elemental is a way in which a connection is forged between the sounds produced by one or more persons and the movements of another. When people dance with others the connection is extended to a partner or to a wider group in any of a variety of ways, from the choreographed figures of cotillions to unison bouncing of young men at a concert. The non-dancer cannot make those connections because he has learned to hold his body still and apart from others at the wedding, the party, and the bar.

Men learn how to contain their enjoyment of music in their heads in households in which there is no intergenerational bopping or where boys sense adult disapproval for their desire to dance. Several men recalled listening to music with their fathers as an activity that did not include dancing. They provided circumstantial explanations for why their fathers listened to music without dancing. Twenty-five-year-old heterosexual working-class African American student Andre is a reluctant and easily embarrassed dancer. He could only recall listening to music with his father in a car, where, he said, dancing was impossible. Others explained that they lived in small apartments or that the music their fathers enjoyed was "listening" as opposed to dancing music. For Gerald, a Chinese twenty-one-year-old heterosexual working-class student who was born in Vietnam, his father was too proud to dance. "My dad used to always play music . . . Chinese music, Vietnamese music . . . He did play regular music too . . . He'd make his own mix CDs with the tapes . . . He had the big subwoofers. He likes music but he doesn't dance." I asked if he had ever seen his father dance, and he described how even at weddings, when drunk and pressured to go to the dance floor he maintained his dignity by refusing to dance.

> When we go to weddings [and] my dad's kind of drunk or whatever and then like his friends will like pull him to the dance floor he doesn't really dance. He just like stands there and like pulls back. "It's time to go." Because usually at the end of the reception and like he doesn't really—he's been drinking. You would think he would be like more loose but he doesn't like to I guess. . . . [My parents] are kind of shy. They don't want to I guess make a fool of themselves. I've never seen them dance.

When a man dances, he puts himself at risk of being a fool. Listening to music with their fathers, these young men learned how to avoid the possibility of being a fool. They practiced stillness, rehearsed ignoring the beat, and learned to confine the pleasure to their minds. They learned this form of embodiment from parents who silently passed onto their sons practices of physical containment. They learned non-dancing as masculine self-control.

These men are modern day Cartesians, who experience their bodies as poorly operating machines split off from their well-functioning minds. Yet despite what they say, their minds necessarily remain connected to their bodies even when they experience what they describe as a "disconnect." Anxious and embarrassed men, stolid men, and men who fend off others' approaches are men who are minding their bodies.[25] Their bodies are locked in the grip of minds that tell them not to act the fool.

The contained carriage of a man who feels connected to his thoughts but disconnected from his body is what men show that they possess when they confess that they cannot dance. Within the United States self-containment, bodily inexpressiveness, and the maintenance of physical distance have been dominant forms of masculine embodiment. The ability to dance marks individual men and groups of men as different from the norm, and different in a way that almost always diminishes the reputation of the dancer. Men who dance too well have been disparaged as overly or differently sexed. They have been mocked for being low class and narcissistic. The admission of awkwardness is a way to steer clear of those wrong ways of being a man and claim the esteemed position of rationality.

Boys know that their bodies are bearers of meaning, and as a result they work to attain the bodies they feel they ought to have. Boys who grow up immersed in movement cultures learn that awkwardness is unacceptable and abnormal. They work at learning to dance. Other boys learn that they ought to accept their dance floor awkwardness as natural, even as they work very hard to attain the ability to integrate their minds and bodies in the context of athletics. After refusing to dance for many years, men form embodied habits that are very difficult to overcome, and they have produced a truth about themselves. They have contributed their bodies to the accumulation of visually verified common sense. They are men who cannot dance. There are costs associated with compliance with the common sense about men's bodies. A cost for many men has been to have to say, "sorry I don't dance." It is a low price for admission to an esteemed masculine status.

DANCE AS IF SOMEONE IS WATCHING

Some men avoid performing before a judgmental gaze by refusing to dance, others meet the gaze with skilled performances, and others manage it by flaunting their unconcern. Young men can succeed in doing masculinity while dancing by boldly claiming the fool's position. Though capable of dancing well in high school, Douglas, a heterosexual, working class, African American young man, delighted in playing the fool. He excelled at it and won battles of foolishness. One day a popular radio station broadcast music from a stage near his school. Someone called out, "Who wants to battle breakdance this guy?" In front of a large crowd of students Douglas entered a dance battle with another student.

> I felt like a million invisible hands pushing me in. . . . Everyone's all like, "Oh, Douglas is going to do something stupid!" So I tried doing all these moves and

then it was my turn and then it was his turn again. And he did this move where he did a handstand with one hand and grabbed his crotch like Michael Jackson. Upside down. Right in my face . . . And I was like—everyone said, "Oh, Douglas, you going to let him do that to you?" I was like, "All right." I had a plan right? . . . Then I just stood up and then I pulled my pants down and did a handstand and mooned the entire school . . . the whole school was like, "Oh, my God. We just saw Doug's ass!" And I was very happy. I was.

Douglas was a fool, but one with physical prowess. His capacity to play the fool rested on his ability to dance at least as well as his peers. Moreover his fooling took the form of a competition in which he exceeded his opponent's rude gesture with one that had even greater shock value. The masculine problem of preparing to be looked at can be eased or made more difficult depending upon the meanings attached to the movements being per- formed. Michael Jackson's moonwalk, while originally performed by an ambiguously gendered celebrity as part of a larger dance routine, could be rehearsed by boys as an isolated and difficult stunt. Similarly, the daring qualities of breakdancing more than compensate for any feminizing ex- pressiveness that the movements also possess.[26]

Carter is the thirty-three-year-old son of a white father and black mother and identifies as black. He was raised in a middle-class and multiracial neighborhood near a university and fondly recalled practicing, though never mastering, breakdancing. "There was a period when everyone thought it was a good idea to bring cardboard to school and try this at school. And so we all would hack away at it, with some kids being very adept and really good at it and fun to watch." His description of this form of dance perfor- mance differs starkly from his account of a more problematic performance rehearsed and performed at his high school by two young men, one Japanese and the other white. Inspired by the performance style of Color Me Badd, a male pop group whose members dance in unison in their videos, the two young men choreographed and rehearsed a dance routine and performed it at school. "It was actually in fact a pretty rare thing," Carter recalled,

and it got its own fair amount of joshing and clowning because traditionally it was sort of like, you know, the girls that would do these sort of dance routines, cheerleaders and these sort of cliques of girls that practiced them . . . the one group that I can think of that made this whole thing sort of popular was Color Me Badd . . .

And so that's where he got the idea, he was like "guys can do this, we're totally going to do it." I thought this is—it wasn't cool in the same way that you get sort of tandem popping and locking where it really is—it was more like

Janet Jackson-y. I was going to say, I think if I had to take my sort of gut sense, I think I felt like it was sort of an emasculating dance . . . and maybe that's only because the precedent had been set by women doing dance routines prior in my experience.

And it wasn't, um, and maybe that's it too . . . [it] was just the style of dance. It wasn't sort of confrontational like you know some breaking is or some, you know where you just have these break battles. It wasn't kind of like that. It was more like performance and you know, my experience with that at that age was like that's just not cool.

He accepted the athleticism of breakdancing and the contorted robotic movements of popping and locking as self-evidently masculine. Break battles were not "performance," a word he thought more appropriate for his classmates' rehearsed dance routine. Though the pair of young men who performed in his high school was inspired by the men of Color Me Badd, Carter likened their performance to that of Janet Jackson or women cheerleaders. A generation earlier, men who were R & B performers typically moved gracefully in sync in choreographed routines. Their movements had been accepted as masculine performance. Masculinity however is a dynamic construct, and performances that had been acceptable in earlier moments had lost their credibility. Dancing in sync with each other rather than competing, and performing steps that exhibited grace as opposed to daring, left the two young men who performed at Carter's high school open to ridicule.

Enjoying being a spectacle is, in some respects, a game that it is easier for young men to play. Douglas' spectacularly foolish performance required significant strength and agility. Recall that Marvin, introduced in chapter 4, boasted of being expelled from a snobby dance school for performing a split there. He enjoyed being a spectacle of impropriety. Looking back on his youth Marvin said, "there [was] something supremely peacocky about a great dance." As an older man he feels he has lost his swagger. He hopes to regain it. "I needed to get less self-conscious in order to return it again, because I'm never going to be, you know a twenty-one-year-old, you know, cock of the walk."

Many men have never felt that they were the cock of the walk, and dancing is an experience that heightens their self-consciousness. Kevin, a forty-four-year-old, white, heterosexual business owner, is one of several men who said they become embarrassed when they catch themselves dancing a bit, even when alone. They can imagine how foolish they look. Mark, the fifty-nine-year-old statistician who wished to be invisible, contrasted his own inhibition with the confidence of rock stars. They had what he lacked, a fearless capacity to be spectacular.

I envied tremendously the guys who could dance. At that time of course rock and roll heroes were like *the* heroes. Jim Morrison. Bob Dylan. . . . The Rolling Stones. The Beatles and they were all people who you could imagine dancing. Very kinetic. Unafraid of showing themselves.

Walter, the mathematician, has not danced for decades and still holds in his mind the mortification he felt at dances as an adolescent. "I was always afraid that people would look at me and say, 'This guy doesn't know his ass from a hole in the ground.' He doesn't know how to dance." Fear of being seen looking foolish is ironically the reason some men will only dance when drunk. Phil was the student in Dance 101 who could do the moonwalk, but was otherwise a reluctant dancer. "After a few drinks," Phil said, "I'm not seeing myself as that person who might be ridiculous." Neil could not recall the times he had danced because, he said, he was very drunk when they had occurred. Jamar, a thirty-two-year-old, heterosexual, middle-class, African American manager, said his friends know that he will only be persuaded to dance when drunk. Alcohol and dancing were so strongly connected that older men explained that they no longer dance because they no longer drink.

While heterosexual men may seek to gain attention in many ways, bodily display is rarely one of them. Masculine display of the body in the context of competitive sports is an exception. Bodily display in sports is legitimated by its occurrence within a realm of masculine dominance and because conventions of sports spectatorship do not eroticize male players' bodies. Sports like gymnastics, which lean more towards display, are stigmatized as feminine. In the epigraph to this chapter Mark recalled youthful dancing as an unbearably uncomfortable experience. He has not danced since his twenties. Yet Mark is well coordinated and regularly plays pick-up basketball games in neighborhood parks. These games often attract groups of spectators. Phil is self-conscious on the dance floor but enjoys playing football. "Football," he said, "is just, it's more about—I guess I would say I'm less conscious about how I look. Unless you miss a play or something and you get down on yourself or whatever. But as far as like coordination and things like that, you're more conscious of it when you're dancing." Neil explained that on the few occasions that he danced with his wife, his discomfort arose from the experience of being looked at. "Even though I'm also from a more intelligent point of view, fairly confident that on a whole they're not [watching]. But I always feel like they are. Put it that way. I always feel like it's being on display. And I don't really like being on display."

While men were, in a general sense unprepared to be looked at, many were also literally unprepared to dance. Men who felt uncomfortable as visible bodies felt doubly uncomfortable exhibiting physical incompetence while dancing. Masculinity requires bodily competence. Competence in dance, as in any other physical skill, requires practice, yet the families and male peer groups of boys who become non-dancing men provide few safe places to practice.

RULES OF THE GAME

Masculinity is a performance, and one most often directed toward other men. Indeed as sociologist C. J. Pascoe argues, young men feel constant pressure to proclaim and thus defend their masculinity through speech and behavior.[27] Yet while men feel compelled to perform masculinity, successful masculinity has to appear unrehearsed. Normative masculine embodiment requires having a feel for the game of masculinity, knowing what is at stake in the game and having a desire to play it, while under most circumstances denying that a game is being played.

The work involved in masculine embodiment, particularly when it involves acquiring potentially feminizing skills, must be masked. The chapter opened with Justin, who was completely comfortable dancing. Though he has years of informal practice behind him, Justin talks about dancing as something that is unlearned. That was how he described freaking, a popular dance genre in which young dancers place their crotches together and move in sync in what is often described as simulated sex. "It's kind of like, you know, you got to dance with somebody, it's just what you do. So everybody knows it. So it's not like, 'You want to dance?' 'Well, I don't know how to dance,' like that, you know. Because everybody pretty much knows." Like Stan before him, he describes the dancing of his generation as completely without technique. However, the very intimacy of freaking makes demands on the body, demands that can only be answered successfully with experience. Quinn, a twenty-six-year-old gay black man recalled that as a child he saw older students dancing at a school dance and recalled being repulsed by a dance style that seemed "nasty," but also thinking, "I don't know how to do that. I don't know how to use my body like that." Freaking is just like kissing; not everyone knows how to do it. Some may have trouble imagining it, and novices would have a difficult time relaxing enough to perform it in public.

By saying that the dance he performs is something anyone can do, Justin situates freaking within a gendered discourse in which authentic dancing is unrehearsed and authentic masculinity spontaneous. This is the construction of masculinity that Halberstam described as "anti-performative."[28] It poses as the embodiment of naturalness and is formed in opposition to feminine artifice. In the course of interviews some men revealed that they had spent hours practicing, yet often these recollections were accompanied by denials or embarrassment. For young men like Justin, authentic movement, a component of successful masculinity, whether on the dance floor or a soccer field is unrehearsed. Justin spoke about the feeling of performing choreography as part of Dance 101:

> Like in class when we do the choreo[graphy], and I—if I really like the music, sometimes it's hard for me to follow because my body wants to do other things. And I was telling [my girlfriend] like when I play soccer, I never—there's a lot of people that will practice a certain move and I'm going to use it at a certain time. I never do that. It's all freestyle. It's what I feel at the time.

Justin rejects learned steps. He experiences his movements as unrehearsed. The dichotomy he establishes between rehearsal and improvisation, however, is false. Improvisation is only possible because of learned technique. Justin understands and describes his capacity to dance through a discourse that values spontaneity. For Marvin, the act of privately practicing dance seemed so perverse that he likened it to masturbation. He recalled a friend who learned how to dance in advance of most of his peers. Marvin saw Tommy do the twist and wanted to copy him.

> I remember being really interested in that. I thought that was cool and Tommy was also a couple years older than us, and he was sophisticated, or we thought he was sophisticated. Actually, he probably was sophisticated. . . . and I remember practicing that stuff, but it was a solitary activity, so it was like jacking off.

Without practice, men cannot become dancers, yet deliberate dance practice is incompatible with many conceptions of masculinity and becomes increasingly so as boys reach adolescence. Douglas, the young African American man who exposed his buttocks to his schoolmates, derided men who brought steps to the dance floor that they practiced at home. "Those dudes that do that are just posers that want to be dudes. You know what I mean? Like it's like 'dude, get out of here. You learned. You watched them practice it on YouTube, but get out of here.'" Phil, the student in Dance 101 who enjoys playing football, expressed similar disregard for men who rehearsed dancing. He was drawn into watching a television dance competition with his wife and told me that he thought the man who won was deserving of the honor:

> The guy that won, Drew. He was good. He was a really good dancer. He just made it look so effortless. And it just looked so . . . It just didn't look like something

that uh he learned. It just looked so natural . . . You would have thought he was a professional dancer. It was really good.

Drew won Phil's admiration for combining the technique of the profes-sional with the untutored spontaneity of the amateur. This combination is perhaps the fantasized ideal of the masculine dancer who has competence without the stigma of having prepared to be looked at or the dishonor of being a professional in a feminine profession. Drew danced as if for him-self. He undoubtedly practiced, but his practice was well hidden.

Zachary is a nineteen-year-old, white, heterosexual college student who energetically dances with his friends to hip-hop music. I asked him if it was practice that allowed him to become a confident dancer. He answered "I've never—I've never *practiced* per se, but I definitely have danced in my room alone, just because I might have had a lot of energy at the time, and I turned on some music that was good to dance to, and then just couldn't hold my-self back." I asked him if he ever watched himself dance in the mirror, to get a sense of how he was dancing. He chuckled and then said "I guess—I prob-ably have danced in the mirror by myself before, but just—it's not some-thing that I make a habit of doing." The notion of watching himself dance was a bit funny to him. His understanding of dance, like Phil's and Justin's, was of something that should be done unselfconsciously, something that erupts, uncontrollably, from his body.

Some of the men I interviewed expressed disdain tinged with resent-ment toward men who moved easily on dance floors and won women's at-tention. Phil repeatedly called one friend a flirt and said it as if "flirt" was a slur. "I had a friend," he said,

> He was always dancing . . . if there was a party and there was music he was always one of the first to grab. He was kind of a *flirty* guy though. He always, it was more, I think it was more about the girls than the dancing . . . You know he prac-ticed. I could, you can tell that he, somewhere he was practicing. You know, I don't know where. But he was always the first one to try and grab a girl and get them to dance with him. You know. It was more a *flirty* thing . . . you know, he's a *flirt*.

The flirt was comfortable performing and being looked at. Phil suggested that his friend secretly practiced and seemed to hold this against him.

The disparagement of performance and of rehearsal for performance was distinctly heterosexual. For Milton, a gay black man, the need to pre-pare to perform on the dance floor was obvious, and not something he felt the need to mask. He knew that he danced well at clubs because he had watched himself dance at home. He explained that when alone in his apartment, "I would just end up dancing in front of the mirror just so I could kind of see what my body looks like moving, which I think is also really important to do." He wanted to attract attention on the dance floor; he practiced and felt no need to deny it.

Within my interviews, among white heterosexual men who were old enough to remember discos, the disco stood for everything that made them uncomfortable on dance floors. They spoke about disco music, discos, and the people who went to them with contempt. I came to understand this as connected to discomfort being the object of the gaze. The disco was despised as a space of feminized narcissism. Disco music called for the "expressive, sinuous movement" described by cultural studies scholar Richard Dyer that many men were unprepared to perform.[29] Men hated discos because they were "sized up" in them and felt that they fell short. They had no feel for the game they thought was being played at discos. Discos were places for making a spectacle of the body, of its clothes, its appearance, and its movement. They were sites for unabashed parading and watching. Men who hated discos resented men who appeared to thrive in them. They hated them for playing the wrong game too well.

Just as young men practice without revealing their practice to others, young men are cautious about revealing that they watch other men dance. Young men monitor each other's movements and learn to monitor their own. A common theme among men in their twenties and thirties was that male pop performers in the recent past danced, but that the performers they currently watched did not. They associated this with a performance of a hardened masculinity. Phil recalled that dance trends circulated in his high school in the form of named steps:

> The roger rabbit. The running man, that style kind of started fading away about my senior year, and it was more about like Tupac and Dr. Dre and Snoop Dog. They started getting big. And then they were, they're less dancy. . . . They're just more attitude. They're moving but it's less, you know, dancing.

He and others felt that the popularity of these performers established limits on the ways in which they and their peers could dance. A form of embodiment they recognized as "hard" was ascendant, and men who moved beyond the boundaries it established put their masculine standing at risk. The hard stance limited body movement to aggressive walks and belligerent hand gestures.

Douglas was the young black man who developed a reputation in high school as the most outlandish dancer. In our interview he asserted, "I'm the best dancer in the universe. You can tell anybody. Put that in. Make that the title of the book." Sporting a large retro Afro, he found a niche in high school as the one who put on a show for others. His position as the absurd one who intentionally made others laugh gave him room to perform. He has been unable to carve out a similar space in the more anonymous clubs available to him as a young man, and he complains that the current configuration of masculinity is stifling. He no longer enjoys dancing and as a result, at twenty-three, feels old. He lamented,

> Dance that was cool five years ago is not cool now. Like you can't do the macarena . . . Or the cabbage patch. Now people do it mockingly. . . . That's why I'm like if people are too sensitive about dance I'm just going to retire and just dance in my bathroom from now on.

Spoofing one's own physical performance appears to be one of the easiest ways for contemporary young men to find comfort spectacularly dancing in public, but clowning is something more easily accomplished when surrounded by friends or family. Though the popular embodied configuration of masculinity may have shifted to a harder stance during these young men's lives, it is also possible that as they aged and circulated in more anonymous environments, they encountered narrower possibilities for masculine embodiment.

As a young teenager Ryan participated in Filipino cotillions and received dance training to prepare him for those events, and as a result is somewhat comfortable dancing. He is ambivalent about being watched. "They say dance like nobody's watching but there's people watching," he said, and laughed. "And it makes it feel sort of funny." Heterosexual men are aware that they are being watched. Some manage the gaze by playing the fool in front of it in order to avoid the impression that they are taking themselves seriously as dancers. Others move, but not too much. Some were lucky enough to have found or created environments in which they could practice and gain competence. For many, the knowledge that they are being watched prevents them from dancing. Some stay away from the dance floor with feelings of regret. Others justify their absence from the dance floor by disparaging the narcissism of men who feel comfort playing that game. Their awkward incompetence is a gendered production. They traded the opportunity to dance for what appeared to be the more appealing, suitable, and accessible rewards of being a man.

This chapter has touched on the ways in which representations of race and gender interact in the processes through which boys attain a physical sense of masculinity. The following chapter foregrounds race, as it exists in the imagination, as a lived experience, and as an enduring structure of inequality.

CHAPTER 7

cᴧɔ

Stepping On and Across Boundaries

Race. Now you see it, now you don't. Zachary sees race, sometimes. He was born in 1989, too late to directly know the young adult dance cultures of the 1970s or the 1980s, but nonetheless formed his own, largely inaccurate image of those decades, a picture implicitly structured by categories of race and gender. "Even during the '70s and the '80s," he said "when it was not cool for guys to dance, they still had a lot of black men dancing." If a lot of black men were dancing when it was not cool for guys to dance, either black men were not guys, or different rules of coolness applied to them. Within Zachary's race and gender schema both were true. Black men were never just guys. "Guy," unmodified by color, was the position occupied by white men.

When Zachary thought about men dancing, racial categorization came to the fore, and led him to remark that black men danced at a time when dancing was not cool. Vernacular dance has a way of bringing race to mind. It is a practice infused with racial meaning. Still, when thinking about dance, but envisioning white men, Zachary saw only guys. Asked if he was aware of being white when he danced, he hesitated, asked for clarification, and then responded earnestly that whiteness was not something he felt intensely or even consciously. In his racial schema, black men are black, white men are guys, and that made him just a guy.

Race. Now you feel it, now you don't. Race is a sturdy and powerful structure that slips from visibility by, and the consciousness of, those most privileged by it. Ossie is twenty-seven, white, gay, and rarely thinks about race. Asked if he ever feels white, he responded, "It doesn't really occur to me." He dances regularly at queer contra dances, events that are generally all white. Contra is a folk dance form with English roots that developed in

New England and gained popularity throughout the United States. Few people of color attend contra dances. The organizers of the dance he regularly attends have a political commitment to racial diversity and are troubled by the whiteness of the event they sponsor. Ossie is aware of their concerns and said,

> I think that some of the organizers of the contra dance, the queer contra dance, they feel like it is um—I know it concerns them—the demographics. You know they feel like they want it to be more inclusive I guess. Um. But it's just not really something I think about.

Ossie is often made aware of his sexuality, but his surroundings rarely remind him that he is white. Ossie is privileged by race but does not and perhaps cannot see it or feel it most of the time. The minimal presence of race in his perception of the world can be characterized as misrecognition. Pierre Bourdieu developed the concept of misrecognition within the context of his investigations of class reproduction.[1] Systems of inequality work most effectively when the transference of privilege that keep them going is misrecognized as merit, luck, or anything but a social structural advantage.

This chapter examines how men deny, cross, stretch, and solidify boundaries of racialized masculinities as they talk about, imagine, and perform dance in everyday life. Vernacular dance provides a particularly useful perspective on the intersection of race and gender categories. As men dance or avoid dance they participate in everyday spectacles through which racialized masculinities are defined. Men step on and across the boundaries of social categorization when they dance. Though ways of dancing and even the ability to dance at all are popularly associated with particular racial categories, there are many routes to proficiency in popular dance styles. Dance performances that appear racially incongruent are common, yet continue to be perceived as exceptions, surprises, or acts of fraud. The frequent tension between dance performance and perceived race provides a place to examine the relationship between the performing body and stubborn social structure. Race exists in society as a discourse, as a felt basis of identity and community, as a structure of inequality, and in everyday performance. Racialized bodies are popularly imagined as having particular movement capacities such that black men who waltz and white b-boys are seen as anomalies. What do these incongruous pairings of bodies and movements do to popular racial categorization? Does dancing across boundaries transform racial structure, or does it contribute to a process of misrecognition that keeps structures of inequality intact?

Interactional theories of gender suggest that the illusion of naturally opposite and unequal genders is sustained through broad conformity to gender expectations in day-to-day interactions. As men "do dominance" and women "do deference" they support the naturalization of socially constructed gender difference.[2] Conversely when men and women refuse to comply with normative gender expectations they expose and reconfigure gender processes. This chapter looks at men dancing within and across the boundaries of racial categories to test the limits of applying interactional theory to race. Is race dismantled, reconfigured, or exposed as a social construction when men step across racial boundaries?

A man's movement on the dance floor has the potential to affirm or call into question his masculinity. As West and Zimmerman have argued, men are held accountable for behaving in ways that are seen as congruent with their categorization as male.[3] Zachary's conjuring of the 1970s and 1980s suggests something additional. Gender performances are judged in relation to perceived sex category, but not according to consistent criteria. The criteria involved in the assessment of gendered performances shifts according to perceived race category.[4] Perception of race category is salient in the interpretation of gendered behavior. According to Zachary, in the 1970s, cool guys did not dance, except for cool black men, who did.

While the rules of masculine coolness often change, the boundaries of race are resilient. They are more resistant to personal inattention or transgressive performance. Racial categories are rooted in and strengthened by meaningful cultures of solidarity. Racial boundaries are also propped up by enduring residential segregation and patterns of inequality. At the most formal level categories of race are codified in law. Though the legally recognized categories of race have gone through significant change since the establishment of the first U.S. racial codes in the eighteenth century, the pattern of a privileged white category, which is distinguished from racially marked others, has remained. Race is fundamental to the logic of everyday categorization within the United States. It is a complicated logic, however, one that allows Zachary to have only a dim awareness of being white. As a member of the dominant and historical majority race, normal stands in for whiteness, and he feels that he is just a guy.

The concept of race may be elaborated into parts: race category, racial identity, and racial performance.[5] Race category corresponds to the historically variable, socially constructed, popularly and legally recognized races within a society. In the contemporary United States black is a popularly understood and applied category, while quadroon has become obsolete. Persons who had one black and three white grandparents had to be quadroons in the nineteenth century, but there is no socially supported way to be a quadroon today. The category is no longer available. Racial identity is where a person locates him or herself, and is placed by others, within the available racial categories. Racial identity suggests subjectivity, in its dual aspects of being a felt sense of self and the ways in which a person is socially placed by others.[6] Racial performances are ways of behaving, speaking, and appearing that are interpreted as signifiers of racial categories. The symbolic occupation of the unmarked, middle-class position by whites, and historical and contemporary impoverishment of blacks, and geographic concentration in cities means, that broadly speaking, everyday performances perceived as middle class are coded white, or, often as racially unmarked normal, and performances associated with urban poverty are coded black. Within the contemporary United States, the word "ghetto" most often signifies black and poor.[7] The popular racial coding of performance shapes the way embodied masculinities, including everyday performances of dance, will be seen. Authenticity is one of the criteria by which masculine vernacular dance is popularly evaluated, and incongruence between racial identity and racial performance can render a man's dance performance inauthentic.

That dance is learned is something that everybody knows and everybody forgets. On the one hand, dance is treated as a manifestation of innate racial identity; on the other, it functions as an authenticating cultural practice, a learned skill that serves as proof of properly acquired cultural knowledge. This contradiction was present in the words of Malcolm X, when he identified dance as a black instinct but one that can be lost in less than a generation of racial integration. "Whites are correct in thinking that black people are natural dancers. Even little kids are—except for those Negroes today who are so 'integrated' as I had been, that their instincts are inhibited."[8] The quotation suggests that the ability to dance is an innate black racial characteristic and yet also treats it as an indicator of cultural, rather than biological, membership in the community.

The ability to dance and the way in which a man dances have often constituted informal tests of racially authentic performance in the United States. Dance can signify racial group membership because social segregation sustains racially divided movement cultures. When viewed as proof of sustained membership in a community, dance is recognized as a socially acquired ability. Yet dance is often misrecognized as a natural racial capacity. When performed in everyday life dance always has an element of spontaneity as the dancer responds to the music, a partner, the surrounding crowd, and the physical space. Arising in the moment from and through the body, dance is easily naturalized. Seemingly spontaneous and embodied, dance appears to be a natural part of the physical self.

Ernest is black and Filipino, was raised in a middle-class suburb, and was well aware that within a black context his inexperienced dancing would lead others to view him as insufficiently black. With no access to direct involvement with a larger black community, he and his sisters learned what they could from black dancers on television. "It was our glimpse into the city, and I think that's what spoke to us because we lived in the suburbs and we wanted to get out. We always wanted to get out and that was our glimpse in." By the time he went to college he danced well enough to gain some legitimacy among black men. "People were like 'All right, all right, you can get down. All right, that's cool, you know. You're kind of down.'" Similarly Raymond, who identifies as Mexican but does not speak Spanish, felt excluded from Mexican cliques in high school but felt legitimately Mexican when dancing salsa, a dance form that is a part of contemporary Chicano/Latino culture. For Ernest and Raymond, their skin color and features guaranteed that they would be recognized as black and Latino, but their bodies and claims of lineage alone were insufficient for acceptance within the black and Mexican communities in which they sought inclusion. They gained increments of inclusion through dance.

Salsa dance as a contemporary Chicano/Latino dance form with Cuban and Puerto Rican origins has a complicated relationship to identity for Chicanos and Latinos. Though Raymond felt more legitimately Mexican when he danced, neither salsa music, nor the dances that are performed to it, are distinctly Mexican. Ralph was described in the previous chapter as being taught to dance by his sister. Ralph's parents, who immigrated to the United States from Mexico and Nicaragua, did not know how to salsa dance. His sister, who introduced him to dancing by teaching him to dance to hip-hop music, subsequently pressed him to learn salsa. He was less interested in salsa as a young teen, but accepted her instruction. "At the time, I was like, I didn't really care. But in retrospect I'm really thankful that she taught it to me." He became especially appreciative of her efforts when he went away to college in North Carolina and joined a Latin dance team that was associated with a Hispanic student organization. Within the context of a predominantly white university, he learned to claim salsa dance as an important part of his culture.

In part, the racialized boundaries of masculinities and their perceived associations with ways of moving reside in a discursive realm. Associations between sorts of persons, ways of moving, and temperaments circulate in mass media and are broadly recognizable in the United States. These associations define racial authenticity. They position men whose dance abilities or styles are incongruent with their racial or ethnic categorizations as anomalies or imposters. When describing themselves and others, men I interviewed mapped capacities for physical, sexual, and emotional expressiveness to racial categories. They linked racial and ethnic categories to natural abilities and natural constraints. Inhibited men desired embodiments that they imagined naturally belonged to others. Some men were aware of the popular association of dancing ability with racial categories, but resisted such formulations in favor of a conception of dance as a race-neutral, youth culture. Nonetheless all described worlds structured by race, and not by race alone, but by race intersecting with class, gender, sexuality, and age. Some men who saw themselves cast, because of racial categorization, as naturally sensual and rhythmic expressed resentment about the meanings erroneously attached to their bodies. Others used narratives of innate racial or ethnic sensuality to understand their own experiences. Men locate themselves in racial and ethnic categories and are located by others. Their movements are subject to scrutiny for incongruity with their race and ethnicity. They step onto dance floors, or avoid them in bodies that are classified, and perform or avoid movements with an awareness of how they are popularly coded. The social boundaries of masculinities are forged in the interplay between imagination and practice. As men move they perform identities, establish meaning, embody masculinities, and bolster or trouble and thus rearticulate categories of belonging. As an embodied practice, vernacular dance performance has the capacity to naturalize racial and gender boundaries or to transgress them. Practicing at home and performing in public, using insult, disapproval, and praise about ways of moving, rehearsing techniques, or avoiding dance, men stretch or harden social boundaries.

SIZE, SWEAT, AND MONEY: THE DANCING SELF AND THE DANCING OTHER

Jeremy was raised in a white suburb by his Japanese mother and white father. He complained that in high school he was generally misclassified by peers as Chinese. They called him the Chinese Cowboy, a misnomer he acquired after dancing a cowboy role in the school's production of the musical Oklahoma. His classmates were so taken with what they considered the incongruity between his partially Japanese features and his cowboy-costumed dance that the image of the apparent contradiction permanently adhered to him. Jeremy outwardly tolerated but was nonetheless annoyed by their simplistic and incorrect categorization of Japanese as Chinese, and cowboy as unmarked white. While he saw the illogic of simplistic racial schema when they were applied to him, Jeremy nonetheless employed essentialist racial

constructions in his descriptions of others. He is an enthusiastic practi-
tioner of the electronic game Dance Dance Revolution (DDR) in which
players gain points by mimicking steps that scroll on a screen while they
dance on a grid that senses the patterns they make with their feet. Asians,
he said, were built for DDR:

> These little Chinese guys would just get up there, and these Chinese girls, or you
> know maybe they were not Chinese, or some other Asian . . . just had this inner
> rhythm and reflex and ability that was just beyond any other race possible . . . It's
> just part of the stereotype, but there's—I don't know if—you know I always had
> the thought that people who are shorter tend to have better sense of balance
> and gravity because they're lower to the ground. You know I just have this
> theory.

Jeremy held his theory despite his own experience of mastering DDR
through practice. He spent hours and fed many quarters into commercial
DDR machines while practicing and performing in public, and even more
time privately building proficiency with a home system. As an avid practi-
tioner and spectator of DDR he has seen skillful performers who were not
Asian. Just as he was racially marked as the Chinese Cowboy, he marks
difference when he sees accomplished white DDR performance. He recalled a plump white woman's skillful DDR performance in the lobby of a
movie theater. "She was a white girl, you know a little bit on the stockier
side, and she was in flip-flops and she was bouncing up and down, jump-
ing all around in flip-flops, and I just could not believe how skilled this girl
was in flip-flops." Jeremy notes more than one element that made this
performance surprising. Certainly the flip-flops, and probably her weight,
made her skilled performance unlikely. Though it is generally assumed
that women can dance, DDR takes dance into the masculine environment
of video game playing, and so perhaps her gender is also surprising. He
also notes her whiteness, the category that usually goes unsaid, but becomes remarkable in this account because it violates his theory that
Asians excel at DDR. Discursive racial constructions are stubborn. They
resist contradiction.

Popular theories about the racial foundations of the capacity to dance
are common. Charles, who acquired the ability to dance by practicing
with his sisters, felt that because he was black, he received no credit for
his acquired skill.

> There's an expectation as far as African Americans dancing in that people say or
> they expect you just to be able to dance . . . You're born, you pop out, you got

curly hair, and guess what else? You dance. Just comes with the package . . . Maybe I'm just imagining it. [*laughs*] It's like a vibe that I just feel. Like, they see me dancing. It's like, okay, yeah, you dance cool, whatever.

When out dancing with a Chinese friend, Charles felt that his own abilities were seen as innate and therefore unworthy of comment.

> People say, "Oh, yeah, look at that Chinese guy. He dances really cool." So it's like he's not supposed to dance cool? Or he's not supposed to have rhythm? . . . You know, we're doing similar moves, but I'm just, like, on the wayside.

Rather than seeing ways of moving as the acquired habits that they are, regardless of the racial categorization of the dancer, popular theories account for them as spontaneous expressions of innate talent. Such explanations of dance talent would be of little social consequence if all they suggested about the world was who would be most likely to master DDR. Yet associations apparently demonstrated within the harmless field of dance naturalize broader structures of inequality, anchoring chains of signifiers between racialized bodies and moral, emotional, and intellectual capacities. The abilities that Jeremy imagines are the natural gifts of Asians are capacities to move in precise, complicated, and nimble ways. His categorization naturalizes broader representations of contemporary Asians as skilled, competitive, and unemotional. The skilled, exacting Asian performance contrasts sharply with contemporary popular assumptions about the movement capacities, and associated moral, emotional, and intellectual characteristics, of blacks. The black dancer occupies a lot of territory in the public imagination. He is skilled but untutored, cool and sweaty, inventive and primal. His presence makes white men aware of being white.

In the fifth week of my fieldwork as a student in Dance 101, we were introduced to African dance, and the instructor taught a series of kicking and bouncing steps that students would use to travel the length of the dance studio. The men and women of the class found the routine aerobically challenging but determinedly tried to execute the steps in two passes across the dance studio. Before the third time across the floor, when a majority of the class had demonstrated the ability to perform the sequence, albeit with a grim level of concentration, the instructor suggested that we find our own ways to stylize the movements. Students stood in three lines to travel across the floor in groups of three. A young black woman at the head of one line turned to the white young woman who stood behind her in line and said "put some stank in it" before she left to travel across the dance floor. The white young woman turned to another white young woman behind her and said "some white stank." What were they talking about? What was stank and why did she qualify it as white stank? Why was it necessary to name the usually unnamed whiteness? Stank is the addition of sensuality or syncopated rhythm. Sweat links movement and smell, and they all come together in the word "stank." In the white woman's mind, plain, unqualified stank was black.

The representational association between sweat and black dancing bodies recurred in my interviews with black and white speakers. Douglas was black and from an impoverished family. By his estimation, Jalonnel was the guy who danced the best in his high school. I asked Douglas to describe the quality of Jalonnel's movement.

> What made him the best dancer? Um . . . I guess it'd be uninhibited . . . He's freaky. I mean this, well here's the, here's the, it comes out of another racial thing like you know at black parties everyone gets grrrrr . . . the only thing I'd compare him to would be a, like imagine if like back in like the 1800s, like we found a tribal African and everyone's like "Ah!" And they'd be so amazed. "Oh my God!" That's the sort of like image that he had. Even though, you know, that's that aura that I could compare it to . . . He was just really . . . he'd be all stinky and sweaty.

Though Douglas identified Jalonnel as exceptional, he also portrayed him as typical, as expressing through movement, sweat, and freaky sensuality an essential black African character.

Sweat also had a central place in the picture of an ideal black dancer described by Brian, a sixty-five-year-old white man who had been raised in a de facto segregated white community in which most families had more money than his. By age sixty-five, he had unhappily accepted his inability to dance well and expressed what he knew to be an impossible desire to be transformed into another sort of body. When he described the embodiments he desired, Brian alternated between two starkly different bodies, one uncultivated, soaked in sweat, the other cool and dry: sensuous black Baptists versus Fred Astaire. He said,

> I'm essentially a basic inhibited white guy. It's like I would fit in perfectly with Episcopalians . . . One time I was at New Orleans Preservation Hall . . . July; ungodly hot inside the Preservation Hall. We were ankle deep in perspiration and they were playing a funeral dirge and this woman, black woman, felt the call. She was about five or six rows back. She got up and she just belted it out and all the other white people went [and here he mimed a stolid unresponsiveness]. I'm one of those, [unmoving white people], but inside I'm Fred [Astaire].

Later he returned to the contrast between his inhibitions and uninhibited black Baptists. "This idea about everybody watching you when you dance . . . that's a common fear that every Episcopalian white guy has. Oh to be a black Baptist." He is actually neither Baptist nor Episcopalian, but another Protestant denomination, yet for him the Episcopalian church conveyed inhibited, middle-class, dry whiteness.

He cannot actually imagine himself as the black Baptist. His true self, his unrealized "inside," is Fred Astaire, a man whose movies he watched as a child and young adolescent. Astaire did not sweat, nor did he belt it out from the back of an inexpensive music hall. Fred Astaire personified the well-contained dancing man. He embodied cool, graceful elegance. In a top hat and a tails, with absolute control, and no sweat, an "Episcopalian" could dance. Often the storylines of his films were about a man whose dance floor finesse allowed him to win the heart of a higher status woman. They provided fantasies of class mobility that appealed to Brian. Born working class, Brian experienced the upward mobility of whites of his generation, but did not become upper class. He contrasted the image of Fred Astaire to Gene Kelly. "I never associated elegance with [Gene] and with Fred it was always—with Fred for whatever reason the guy always seemed to have a top hat and tails. I never saw Gene Kelly with top hat in tails. It was always a shirt." Though he fantasized about being Fred, Brian has never worn a top hat, or tails. Thinking of himself in a tuxedo led him to recall his feelings of inadequacy at school dances, and these feelings he linked to the injuries of class. "[It] was an outrageously rich town," he said. "It took a little while to overcome the sense that you didn't have station. It was almost British caste."

In his fantasies Brian was Fred Astaire, but when he thought about actual class privilege he recalled his working-class origins. Brian wanted to be a black Baptist, a subject position he imagined as unfettered by puritanical constraint. In relation to the freely moving black woman he saw himself as Episcopalian, class faded from his consciousness, and he experienced his identity as simply white. In that moment whiteness appeared as a bereft position, cut off from sensuality. However, when he thought of himself in relation to upper-class whites, he felt excluded from that category, too. He recalled the shame of having been a young boy who failed to embody white upper-class masculinity. He wanted the bodily freedom of being black, but more than that he wanted the social esteem that accrued to white upper-class masculinity.

Had Brian imagined uninhibited blackness as a man he might have imagined Andre. Andre was raised in the Holiness Church. Church, Andre said, was the only place where, as a child, he saw men dance. Andre, however, was not the uninhibited mover of popular racial imagery. He was a romantic, a bit of a prude, and was self-conscious on the dance floor. At twenty-five he felt out of shape and sluggish, and was mortified if a female dance partner became too sexually expressive. Furthermore the pressures he felt from other black men constrained his ability to move freely. Moving too much would violate the boundaries of black male embodiment.

> Because I am black, I should dance this way. You always have this sense of, like, you're black and it's a hip-hop song and you're around other black people, so let's not dance too much. Let the girl just do her work . . . You think about, you know, where you come from . . . you know, in the ghetto, you know what I'm saying? My next-door neighbor was a crackhead, you know, my good friends were drug dealers.

Andre's perceptions of the narrow range of acceptable dance movement among black men were echoed by Milton, a thirty-eight-year-old gay black man. According to Milton, "men, particularly black men, [are] encouraged to not be expressive, and to have this very kind of stiff masculine, kind of hard image. And so a lot of times, for instance in Oakland, I don't go out dancing in Oakland, because most people don't dance in Oakland." Andre and Milton are not the sweaty, expressive blacks whose image circulates in cultural representations. Andre, in particular, is a wary minimalist on the dance floor, his movements inhibited by what he perceived as the limits of acceptable black masculine embodiment. Brian explained his inability to move in contradictory terms. He lacked the physical confidence he imagined came easily to rich whites and the physical freedom he supposed was the birthright of poor blacks. Andre was poor and black, yet within his community he experienced not a gender-blind freedom to move but rather gender-specific social constraint. The girl may "do her work," but he could not dance too much. Both Brian and Andre held conceptions of embodied masculinity that were fundamentally structured by race, class, and gender. They made sense of their own abilities and limitations by drawing on available discursive constructions.

Andre told me about the crackhead next door to locate himself in intersectional race and class terms as black and poor, a social location that, as he said "always comes into play," but plays in different ways in different situations. On the dance floor it demands a cool, heterosexual pose, expressed as minimalist dance while the woman does her work. In his narrative both his masculinity and his blackness were judged by the way he moved. He felt socially compelled to dance, but also compelled to constrain his movements and not violate what he perceived as boundaries that defined the embodiment of working-class black masculinity.

BOUNDARY CROSSINGS

For a long time in the United States racial boundaries have been reinforced by residential and social segregation. In interviews a type of narrative repeated, which I have termed the "I was the only white there" boast. This is a historically situated narrative. In the 1920s and 1930s earlier generations of middle-class whites regularly traveled in groups to dance in black neighborhoods in "slumming" excursions.[9] Slumming as a popular activity for young whites declined during and immediately after World War II as whites began to perceive urban black neighborhoods as more dangerous than alluring.[10] In the post–World War II–era suburbanization, intensification of the poverty of urban black neighborhoods and the shift from public to home-based leisure activities combined to make white youths fearful of entering black neighborhoods.[11] Domestic dance tourism declined and became an experience rare enough to warrant a boast.

Fred was eighty-six at the time of his interview and served in the Navy during World War II. While on leave in New York during the war, he befriended a black man who took him on a musical tour of the city that ended at the Savoy Ballroom in Harlem.

> The last thing I was told when I left Iowa, which is, you know was white at that time, you know, very few Negroes. I grew up with several, but they were very nice, but anyway, [*chuckle*] you don't want to be caught in Harlem after sundown. . . . [At the Savoy,] there must have been 1,200 to 1,500 people in the middle dancing . . . Ninety-nine percent of them were black. It was just a few, myself, and a few other whites. But there was no way to describe it. Their dancing, when they're in their own area, uninhibited, they've got steps the white boys don't know. But see, that's what I like.

Mark is white and a generation younger than Fred. He recalled being in a black crowd at an R & B concert in Trenton, New Jersey, as a peak experience of his fifty-nine years. "As a white man in a sea of black people? Well, I was *proud* as hell. You know. I was proud as hell . . . I was very proud that I was digging the same stuff. You know. And that all the other stupid white people didn't know about this." Though social, residential, and educational segregation remain common in the United States, younger men I interviewed did not spin boastful narratives of joyful excursions into racially segregated slums for freer forms of pleasure. Intensified poverty and policies of mass incarceration have devastated black communities. The slum, which had sustained alluring nightlife in the 1920s and 1930s, has been replaced with the fear-provoking ghetto, a term currently applied disparagingly to poor black people and the communities in which they live.

There was never a parallel move of groups of youth of color into white spaces in search of freer pleasures. For most of U.S. history, legal, illegal, and de facto segregation made that impossible. In the 1960s Alphonse, who is black, lived in a small Louisiana town that had one Catholic Church, which used times of day and partitions to separate the black and white activities it sponsored:

> We wasn't allowed to go in [to the white dances]. We can see 'em because they
> had the glass doors. They had round and round—what'd they call it, like country
> dancing or something? . . . Yeah, they did a lot of that square dancing. . . . They
> was into their country music, waltzing and stuff like that.

He described seeing whites dance but did not attempt to emulate them. After legal segregation's end, black participation in predominantly white social dance venues has become more common. If blackness is sweat and sensuality when seen by whites, what is whiteness when seen by blacks? It is worth pausing to listen to descriptions of black crossings to white dance floors for the contrast they provide to narratives of slumming and to consider the significance of the absence of "I was the only black there" boasts. Perhaps what lay under the thrill of slumming and the boasts that accompanied it was the unusual experience, for whites, of finding themselves in the minority. Discovering that one is the only black man in the room provides no equivalent thrill. Ernest, the black and Filipino man raised in the suburbs, described being at fraternity parties in college where he was one of the only men of color. His account expressed neither fascination nor pride. He noted only that there was more drinking and less dancing than at black parties. Avery, a twenty-seven-year-old queer black man who found that gay clubs in San Francisco where he lived were generally all white, said,

> I had to learn really quickly that I was I going to be one of the few people who
> were the darkest people in the room . . . That if I wasn't here, this party would be
> exclusively white . . . And how did I experience that? . . . I just had to embrace the
> fact that I was the only person of color there, and almost push it to the back of
> my mind, as if it was something that wasn't important.

Only one account by a black man suggested excitement about entering a predominantly white dance space. Douglas expressed no pride at being the only black man in a techno club; instead he was disdainful of his black friends who refused to go with him. Yet as he told of his willingness to be adventurous he could only imagine an adventurer as white, and unexplored territory as the domains conquered by Europeans.

> I was talking to my friend yesterday. Like, "Dude, you want to go to an electronic club?" "Nah, man." Why? You know what I'm saying? Now it's like now I'm ready. I feel like I'm ready to explore. You know it's one of those things. I feel like I'm about to leave England or whatever, Spain to go in search of the new world. These people are just so like, you know, I don't know if we're going to make it to the other place. What if there are cannibals there? And everyone's making these decisions based on fear rather than courage.

The culturally available narrative of exploratory adventure is about whites crossing into uncharted black territory. It was the only narrative available to him and so he used it to describe his courageous drive as a black man over the bridge to a predominantly white techno club in San Francisco.

Douglas had to drive across the bridge to find a techno club, but racial boundary crossing does not always require travel for contemporary youth. Many urban high schools provide opportunities for cross-racial contact.[12] Furthermore, non-blacks acquire black dance culture in a variety of non-black settings and consequently experience black music and associated dance styles as youth rather than black culture. Without ever leaving their neighborhoods, white and Asian youths learn to love music and accompanying dance styles that originated in African American, African Caribbean and African Latino communities.[13] Though the music and accompanying dance styles still have the capacity to signify blackness, they have become the movement vocabularies of many youth regardless of race. The music and dance belongs to them in the sense that it is the main music they listen to, the only way they can dance, and the taste culture that binds them to their friends.

Justin grew up in the 1980s and 1990s in the primarily white and Latino Central Valley of California. He danced with confidence. When first developing a style of dance Justin modeled himself after black performers. He watched the black dance television program *Soul Train* with his parents. When Justin was a young child his parents took him to a performance of the black singer MC Hammer, and he recalled dancing in the aisle in imitation of MC Hammer's kinetic on-stage dancing. Black musicians performed most of the music that Justin listened to as a young man. Justin however did not see the dances he performed as black. On the contrary Justin thought coding R & B and hip-hop dance styles as black as "ignorant." "People have told me like, 'Why do you dance like that? You're white' . . . But it wasn't something that bothered me because it just—if you're going to be that ignorant then

I don't really care." Their ignorance was double in his view. His father was Mexican, and though Justin was often perceived as white, he valued his Mexican heritage and identified himself racially as "Caucasian and Mexican." Though the dance styles he performed had recent origins in black communities, and he learned to dance by studying images of black performers, he consumed those images and practiced and personalized the ways of moving that he learned through them, within the white and Mexican environment of his home, family, and school. He regularly danced with a male cousin during the hours they spent in childhood listening to recorded black music. His experience led him to claim an array of R & B, rap, and hip-hop music and dance cultures as part of a race- and class-neutral, masculine, youth culture.

Justin had reservations about contemporary rap performers, many of whom have, in his view, forsaken dance. He did not consider the aggressive stances, strutting, and gesturing that comprise their on-stage movement, dance. Justin linked that mode of performing to the increased popularity of a style a rap he described as "harder." He initially said nothing about race as he offered a theory about the transformation in styles of performance:

> I have like a theory about that. . . . Cause like in the '80s, people danced a lot. And then hip-hop rappers danced. . . . in the '90s and the beginning, like earlier 2000s, rappers didn't dance. You don't dance, you just rap. You move. But it's not, it's not, really dancing though. It's just, I don't know, like you could tell like they're trying to be hard. They're trying to be harder.

To attend college Justin moved from a semirural part of California to the San Francisco Bay Area. Once there he discovered an emergent local genre of music and associated dance style called hyphy. Hyphy dancers move in an exaggerated and comic style. "Now it's coming round like for hyphy music and stuff. Rappers will dance. You see them in the video and they're doing like the same thing everybody else is doing." In this description, who is "everybody else"? Perhaps Justin referred to the women who often dance in the videos of hard rappers. Or perhaps, but less likely, "everybody else" referred to non-starring men who dance within the videos. Regardless, his point was that within hyphy videos, the men who rap in the videos, dance. He continued, they "might do it—not do it as much, like to the extent, but they are dancing again." He thought about how these men could dance while maintaining hard personae and that led him to an analysis that brought, in coded form, race and class into his explanation. "It's not like people look at hyphy and like, [say] 'They're not hard.' 'Cause of the *area* that it comes from. It started in Oakland." For a young man from a semirural part of the state, "Oakland" signified black and poor. Thus the energetic, attention-getting, and playful movement of the hyphy style could be "hard" because of its association with a place and its population. The hard gene-alogy of hyphy movement validated its masculinity and by association, the masculinity of anyone who performed it.

Justin's wish to claim hip-hop styles as race- and class-neutral masculine youth culture is grounded in his experience of learning and practicing Afri-can American–derived dance forms within non-black social settings. Victor, a twenty-seven-year-old whose mother is Mexican and father Filipino, de-scribed breakdancing to me as rebellious youth culture. "You know like this is not the norm." Describing it as abnormal might be a way of racially marking it as not white, since as sociologist Amy Wilkins argues "normal" is the identity occupied by the unmarked white middle class.[14] I asked if he thought of breakdancing in racial terms. "Never," he replied, but soon qual-ified that by acknowledging breakdancing's East Coast black and Latino origins and establishing the credibility of the top Asian DJ by noting that he grew up in the racially signifying "inner-city."

> Out here on the West Coast, it's run by Asians. . . . You know the top DJ in
> the world is a Filipino. Grew up right in Daly City. He goes by DJ Q-bert . . .
> But he grew up in the inner city. . . . they went to New York and battled, you
> know they battled the black crews. *Stomped on them.* [chuckle] It's not just a
> black thing anymore. It's very much, you know all cultures getting together.
> You know what I mean? Whites, blacks, Latinos, Asians. You know it doesn't
> matter.

His narrative tells us that it doesn't matter and that it does. The cultures get together, but meet to battle in crews organized by race. The Asian crew established its supremacy by musically stomping on a black crew, the crew whose blackness raised the value of the Asian crew's victory.

Ralph, who identifies as Latino, parsed hip-hop dance into performance styles. In general, he said, it can be performed by anyone. "I hate the stereo-type of only black guys can do it or black girls can do it." As he continued his explanation he began to use his hands to demonstrate gestures, which he called "gangster thug movements" that whites should not do.

> When white people want to imitate black people, they always have those dumb
> movements. They add "yo" at the end of every sentence and things, "Dog and
> what's up? Yo." And you don't have to do that kind of stuff if you want to fit in or
> dance that dance . . . I feel like someone who is not—doesn't have to do that to
> try to imitate it. I don't know how to say it.

Hip-hop. Now it's racialized, now it's not. Race. Now it's speakable, now it's not. Ralph ends his description by confessing to his inability to talk about race and the performance of hip-hop dance. In the sentence that precedes "I don't know how to say it," he is indeed at a loss of words. The clause that begins "I feel like someone who is not" abruptly ends before finding its conclusion in the word "black."

Ralph, like many other young men, experiences hip-hop as a racially neutral youth culture. Yet the appeal of hip-hop and rap, and their ability to signify a performer's masculinity, rests, at least in part, on their continued racial and class coding.[15] Transracial and cross-class embodification entails a form of misrecognition. Diverse youth must forget race and class coding in order to make hip-hop and rap their own and yet, to some extent, the forms' appeal derives from the masculine legitimation provided by their continued race and class coding as black and poor. Sociologist Jason Rodriguez argues "whites who pick up on African American styles and music do not necessarily want to be black; they seek to acquire the characteristics of blackness associated with being cool."[16] The hip-hop and rap music that receives the widest distribution celebrates what may be called outlaw masculinity. Recording companies market outlaw masculinity to young men of all races who are drawn to its angry stance and fantasies of power. These fantasies of power correspond to a reality of black disempowerment, black poverty, and the mass incarceration of black men. Hip-hop and rap can convey masculine cool because of their association with the social alienation of black criminalization.

At national and global levels Asian and Asian American men have been winning b-boy contests. The national diffusion and globalization of b-boying may ultimately change its racial coding, just as the lindy hop's origins as an African American dance practice were obscured as it became American jitterbugging. At this writing I would argue that b-boying's origins in poor African American, African Caribbean, and African Latino communities remain central to its representations. Asian American Studies scholar Sunaina Maira has written about how racial groups located on the periphery of power may obtain "another kind of otherness," one with greater cultural cachet, through the acquisition of cross-racial cultural forms.[17] Adopting a black dance style can facilitate movement within local social structures.

Race does and does not define the lived experience of contemporary dance and associated musical forms. Gendered racial boundaries are erased in multiracial practice but also reinscribed in the same practices. In interviews some men referenced "Lean Back," a popular song that epitomized and promoted minimalist trends in masculine dancing. The 2004 song was the transnational, multiracial production of a Puerto Rican/Cuban,

"Fat Joe," an African American, Remy Ma, and a Jewish Canadian, Scott Storch, and therefore demonstrates how popular musical forms transcend racial boundaries. Yet the song's repeated chorus reinscribes the centrality of black race: "I said my Niggaz don't dance, See we just pull up our pants and, Do the Roc-away. Now lean back, lean back, lean back, lean back." Repeating "Niggaz" over and over again, the lyrics describe the minimalist way to perform cool masculinity and identify it as black.

Andre was one of the young men who quoted this song to me. He and Justin listened to the same music and felt constrained by the same codes of masculinity it promoted. Justin thought of this culture as a race-neutral, masculine, youth culture. When he needed to talk about race, he spoke in geographical code, saying Oakland instead of black. Andre was black and from Oakland and discussed race without code, yet he additionally relied on the same geographical place, Oakland, to attest to his own authentic race and class identity. "I come from Oakland," he says, "you know, in the ghetto." While Justin thinks that any movements originating in Oakland will necessarily be accepted as "hard" Andre knew that there were wrong ways to move. He was expected to dance, but not too much. Racial and gender identity are co-constructed. One of the ways they are constructed is through embodiment, and part of embodiment is movement. Within his own black community, if Andre moved too much and "worked" his body like a girl, he would be both feminized and perform a failed blackness, regardless of the color of his skin or where he lived. An insufficient performance had the potential to stigmatize him within his own community. Outside of his community, his skin color would have greater consequence for how he was perceived. He would be seen as black, regardless of how he moved.

FLUID MOVES AND HARD BOUNDARIES

Despite the widespread sharing of popular dance and music culture, different sets of meanings remain attached to Asian, black, and white men's bodies. Even as hip-hop is performed and consumed by youth who are not black, the hip-hop performer and the rapper remain icons of contemporary black masculinity and contribute to the global representation of black masculinity as fiercely hypermasculine.[18] Meanings established at the end of the nineteenth century with the rise of middle-class office work continue to adhere to white male bodies. The successful white male middle-class body is imagined as a product of self-control. This productive middle-class white male body does not sweat, is not especially muscular, is covered in a suit, and is ready to secure masculinity by earning money indoors.[19]

Representations of black male dancing bodies have a complicated relationship to that normative productive male body. The black dancing man's potentially feminine expressivity has masculine credibility because of the simultaneous presence of signs of toughness. His sensuality has heterosexual certification through the presence of even more sexualized women. Is it toward this image that non-black men move, adopting black dance styles as a way to embody masculinity, as a way to dance? Justin was drawn to that image. The dance styles of black performers helped to form his earliest movement language. These styles provide his movement vocabulary; he has no other. Yet the meanings attached to his body, when driving, when in a classroom, and even when performing dance styles that originated in black communities, are those that adhere to white bodies. He is seen by those who do not know him as a young white man, potentially productive, innocent until proven guilty.

Justin performs what might be called blackbody, the latest incarnation of blackface, the performance of blackness, within the safety of a body not perceived as black. According to political theorist Michael Rogin the fusion of domination and desire has a long history in American mass culture.[20] The nineteenth century's most popular theatrical form was blackface minstrelsy. The blackface tradition was central to the most heralded films of the early American cinema and could be found in attenuated form as late as 1964 in Dick Van Dyke's chimney-sweep dance in the innocent and beloved children's film *Mary Poppins*. Yet as Rogin argues, blackface performance is a masquerade that produces its opposite. It reinforces rather than undermines racial boundaries. Performing blackface was the vehicle by which European ethnic immigrants became white, and therefore distinguished themselves from blacks. Unlike blackface, blackbody does not always ridicule as it imitates. Nonetheless it is a form of desire that depends upon continued black subordination. Blackbody gains masculine credibility from blackness, but in a culture that simultaneously claims color blindness and maintains white privilege it performs blackness unmarked by color. As a performance of outlaw masculinity, blackbody depends upon, because it draws its masculine credibility from, the continued poverty and criminalization of black men.

Dance scholar Linda J. Tomko has written about social dance as a self-making activity.[21] Dance, as an expressive, interactive activity, allows men to make selves, but not exactly as they please. What they do with their bodies will be assessed in the light of what others think they are. Musicologist Susan C. Cook identified gendered constraints to self-making on the dance floor when she wrote "social dance [is a] bounded sphere in which women and men test out what it means to be male and female."[22] In a society structured by race, the limits of what it means to be a man shift according to race. Ernest, the suburban Filipino and black man, knew that and studied black dancers on the televised program *In Living Color* to prepare himself to enter black social life in college. Through a form of distance learning he erased the incongruity between his habitus and his race category, moved into line with codes of black masculine embodiment, and was rewarded with approval when he heard the words "All right, you can get down. All right, that's cool, you know. You're kind of down." Ernest displayed sufficient rhythm and not too much movement and achieved coolness according to the rules that would be applied by black men to his black male self.

An aspect of race as it exists in the United States is its everyday performance. Dance is a practice through which men enact race. Ernest's inexperienced dancing threatened his acceptance within the community of black men at his college. Nonetheless these narratives of dance and race indicate that the performing body can trouble racial categorization but not escape it. Regardless of how they dance, and regardless of the complexity of their ancestry, Ernest, Andre, and Douglas were seen as black while Zachary, Ossie, and Justin were seen as white. Their performances were read and judged in relation to their racial categorization. Transgressive performances, when they occur in sufficient numbers, do shift popular expectations regarding racial embodification over time. Asian hip-hop performers frequently take away the prizes at dance competitions. In some but not all instances, their performances arise from personal histories of transracial experiences beyond the dance floor. The growth of communities in which poor blacks and poor Asians live side by side is shifting the contours of racial embodification. However, new performance has a way of being assimilated into existing understanding. Asian hip-hop performance is popularly fitted into existing meanings attached to Asian bodies. Meanings attached to racially marked and unmarked bodies, meanings supported by ongoing inequalities, endure, push back against bodily transgressions, and stubbornly resist contradiction.

This book has asked readers to pay attention to dance because it is a practice that reveals processes that make gender, sexuality, race, and class. Dance is significant because it signifies. Boys and men know that dance signifies. They know it because beliefs about gender, sexuality, race, class, and dance circulate as common sense. Mindful that common sense will be applied to judge their masculinity as good enough or failed, authentic or fraudulent, boys practice or avoid dance. They practice particular ways of moving and eschew others in order to claim particular places amid inescapable systems of social classification. The final chapter will bring the historical and contemporary portions of the book together by reflecting on the ways in which what everyone knows regarding who can dance and who cannot, has changed over time. It considers what contemporary men gain as individuals when they say "sorry I don't dance." And it considers what we lose as a society by accepting their refusals as inevitable.

CHAPTER 8

How to Solve the Mind/Body Problem

Her life was made up of emotions which were markedly different from his. He went forth with determination to outdo his enemy, and she danced with joy at his success. These emotions and the manner in which the maternal ancestor expressed them are handed down to her of the latest years, and it is no coincidence that the twentieth century girl has the same desire to dance when she is happy. It is the establishment of her racial act—the natural sequence of her racial life—and she is true to every racial instinct when she dances.

—Lillia Belle Otto, "The Demands for the Twentieth Century Girl—Are We Prepared for Them?" *American Physical Education Review* (1916)

It was 1916 and a group of professionalizing physical education teachers gathered in Cincinnati to shape the future of their burgeoning field. Not all of them welcomed dance in their gymnasiums. Few within the field considered dance a worthwhile activity for older boys and some questioned its moral value for girls. Lillia Belle Otto addressed the gathering to make the case for dance as woman's most natural physical activity. Dance, she argued, is in woman's nature. Women dance and men do not because our earliest maternal ancestor joyously danced every time her man returned home from conquering an enemy. It became a habit. Dance entered women's make-up in those early celebrations, and through Lamarckian inheritance, the habit of dancing was passed down to her distant daughters.

When read today, Otto's affirmation of gender difference appears quaint. But strip away the tales about ancient ancestors and the beliefs embedded in her talk lose their dated feel. Contemporary declarations regarding gendered propensities to dance do not resort to imagined prehistory; they rest instead on common sense. In an essay subtitled "What Every White Guy

Like Me Owes to Michael Stipe," a writer thanked Stipe, the lead singer of the rock band R.E.M., for "making our natural awkwardness intentional and cool."[1] The author claimed natural awkwardness for white guys, and the editors of the nation's leading newspaper deemed his thoughts fit to print. At a time when beliefs regarding innate racial differences of talent or character should belong to the distant past, white men still easily, even boldly, confess to an innate, racially explained, inability to dance. This book has asked readers to find that natural awkwardness, and its easy ownership by so many white men, strange and troubling.

THE COMMON SENSE

Why would a man shamelessly confess to dance floor incompetence? It is because the apparent deficiency contains an advantage. Men who claim innate awkwardness concede sensuality and rhythm to women, feminized men, and people of color, while locating themselves on the socially powerful mind side of the mind/body split. The common sense belief in the natural awkwardness of white men is not a harmless notion. It is one point in a larger set of interconnected beliefs about the determinative power of race. It connects, for example, to a comment made in 2006 by Arnold Schwarzenegger, who was then governor of California. Speaking about his colleague California Assemblywoman Bonnie Garcia, Schwarzenegger explained, "she maybe is Puerto Rican or the same thing as Cuban. I mean they are all very hot. They have the, you know, part of the black blood in them and part of the Latino blood in them that together makes it."[2] Schwarzenegger thought his comments harmless and was taken aback when criticized for them. He could not see the problem contained in a casual remark intended as a compliment. He did not understand that his words placed his colleague on the socially disempowering body side of the mind/body divide because of her race.

It is good to be thought innately hot when in bed with a lover, but not in many other circumstances. All of us have bodies and minds. Neither race, nor gender, nor the intersection of the two, should be used to sort us into the passionate and the rational. Therefore the belief that white men cannot dance is not an innocent truism. It is no less harmful than a belief that black and Latino blood is hot. These clichés have everything to do with how we imagine what a governor looks like, whose body welcomes uninvited touch, and who appears to be made for a jail cell.

The preceding chapters have worked to dismantle the common sense regarding race, gender, and dance by tracking its historical shifts. There have been times when there was nothing exceptional about white men dancing. Chapter 2 introduced Elisha Dyer, a man who epitomized the upper-class white men who danced at the beginning of the twentieth century. When elite social life was organized around balls, the ability to dance was a hallmark of cultivation, and upper-class white men were expected to dance well. Those assumptions were made unfamiliar in the 1910s and 1920s as patterns of elite, middle, and working-class social life changed. An array of types of dancing men circulated in popular representations, and these images helped to alter the prevailing common sense regarding race, gender, and bodies. The proliferation of types of dancing men created a complicated new social mapping of dance and bodies. That social mapping was never as simple as the current cliché that white men cannot dance.

In the 1910s and 1920s young people of all classes danced in new full-bodied ways. As upper- and working-class dance styles converged toward informal and improvisational styles, cultivated masculine bearing was more likely to be parodied through the figure of the formal European dance master than to be seen as the look of a man of wealth. While the priggish dancing master was seen as a laughable character, he was not perceived as dangerous. But in the press, and in the campaigns of social reformers, some dancing men were depicted as menacing. These endeavors arose in the context of widespread anti-immigrant sentiment, which characterized southern and eastern European immigrants as dangerous foreigners who were unlikely to assimilate. Though some of the dance hall reformers were Jewish, their campaigns, as taken up by the press, often incorporated popular xenophobia to focus moral panics regarding dance on recent European immigrants. Sensual dances were certainly associated with Africa and blackness, yet segregation severely limited social contact between whites and blacks. Dance hall reform efforts were crusades to protect the purity of white girls from the risks posed by contact with dancing men who, more often than not, were depicted as European but dark.

In the 1910s and 1920s, the image of the dancing gigolo, while powerful enough to affect municipal policies, was not the only one that circulated regarding boys and men who danced. Elementary educators and social reformers advocated for teaching of various kinds of group dances, such as folk dances, to children. Those educators who worked to include dance in the physical education of all children supported the belief that dance was an activity that any boy could and should do. The dances they taught to children were derived from myriad cultural contexts, including some, from Europe and the United States, in which the dances were most likely to have been performed by adult men. Yet folk dance instruction was incorporated into public education at a time when there was great concern about the alleged feminization of boys and masculinization of girls. Divergent physical education curricula for girls and boys became the norm. Boys were frequently excluded from dance instruction and girls from competitive sports. This training and the resulting public displays of competing boys and dancing girls contributed to the belief that non-couple dancing was an activity most appropriate for girls.

In the 1910s and 1920s, the range of prevalent images of dancers included parodies of dancing masters, alarming accounts of gigolos, and endearing images of young girls forming big circles. Another man blithely danced amid these images. He was young, white, well-off, and wore a college sweater. In collegiate contexts, men could be thought of as dancers without jeopardizing their character. The notion of the zany college kid helped to establish the concept of youth as a specific period of life between childhood and maturity. Dance was one of the practices that distinguished youthful men from their sedate elders. In the public mind in the 1910s and 1920s, it was neither surprising nor alarming, that young white men exuberantly danced within the confines of collegiate social life. The connection between youthfulness and dance contributed to the belief that an older man on the dance floor was a fool.

When considering the assortment of images of dancing men that circulated at the beginning of the twentieth century it is important to bear in mind the gap between representations of men and men themselves. The images of dancing men that were created and disseminated by educators, social reformers, journalists, and novelists did not accurately represent the world of dancing men. White working-, middle-, and upper-class women who danced in public were most likely partnered by men who shared their racial identities and class locations. These boyfriends, brothers, and husbands, young and older, many of whom were undoubtedly competent dancers, are effaced by narrower representations of men who danced. Yet behavior and representations are loosely coupled and mutually influencing. The popular images of dancing men were foolish dancing masters, swarthy criminals, and immature college students. As it became difficult to imagine a respectable, mature man moving in time to music, men were more likely to refuse to dance. By the end of the 1920s, it was not that the public believed that mature white men could not dance, but rather, that they should not.

The war years, 1941–1945, shifted the way the nation would think about men and dance. Dance would continue to be considered a youthful activity, but it would begin to have a new national significance within the context of war. The jitterbug began in the 1920s as an energetic, improvisatory couple dance within black communities. It gained popularity among the entire nation's youth. When the United States entered World War II the military and affiliated civilian organizations sponsored dances for soldiers' recreation, and the jitterbugging white GI became the symbol of the All-American boy. In wartime representations, the black origins of the jitterbug were often obscured as it was celebrated as an exuberant product of American culture. It was a dance in which male leadership could be vigorously displayed as men swung and tossed their female partners. For the duration of the war, dance seemed entirely compatible with heroic masculinity.

Change in the way dancing men would be seen arrived again after the war. Young adults raced into marriages, whites fled demographically heterogeneous cities to live in homogenous, newly built suburbs, and these patterns had consequences for the place of dance in everyday life. In the 1950s dances continued to be popular events in high schools but white young adults, sequestered in suburban homes, no longer went out to dance. Changes in popular styles of music increased the improvisational demands made on dancers who, entirely detached from their partners, had to perform solos in front of them. In the broadly conservative and homophobic climate of the late 1950s and early 1960s many young men shied away from that challenge. In the later 1960s and subsequent decades, popular music cultures became fragmented by race. Soul, funk, and salsa continued to be dance music, while much of the music that white youths preferred was less conducive to rhythmic dancing. By the 1970s, the belief that white men could not dance had become common sense.

We have become accustomed to accepting that common sense. Its apparent truthfulness makes it hard to recall the white jitterbugging GI or his father, the zany white college kid who danced in the 1920s, or his grandfather who led cotillion. The new common sense appears to conform to a larger logic of a racial, gender, and sexual order in which the white heterosexual All-American boy should not dance. That boy will grow up to be a man who wants sex with women but is not sexy, a rational man whose public touching of others is limited to firm handshakes and hearty pats on the back. Once different capacities become embodied, socially produced differences appear to have arisen, naturally, from our bodies. They appear to exist timelessly, outside of history.

Common sense shapes practice, and practice shapes our bodies. Practicing some activities and avoiding others, boys remake their bodies. Some men dance and others do not because the ability to dance is learned. The acquisition of the dancer's habitus—a desire to dance and the ability to move in time to music, a culturally recognizable repertoire of steps, the ability to imitate others' movements, a feel for the limits of the idiom, and comfort being observed dancing—requires investment of energy from a relatively early age in the company of others.[3]

Practice, or play that results in practice, is most likely to occur where boys sense social pressure to dance. Many white boys sense just the opposite: that there are reasons to shy away from dance. At the level of cultural representation the most elite forms of dance are disparaged as homosexual. The gender and sexual coding of ballet in the United States powerfully communicates to boys, regardless of race or ethnicity, that certain ways of moving are forbidden. Cultural representations of masculinity and femininity as polarized opposites provide a broad ideological framework for the acquisition of the body's habits. A boy whose body develops under the constraints of femiphobia and homophobia learns not to be too delicate or expressive.

At least as powerful as cultural representations is what boys learn about their bodies by watching and interacting with the boys and men around them. The conditions of production of masculinity are multiple. There is not one ideal of masculinity circulating in a society, but many, always experienced in local circumstances and existing in dialogue with broader national and transnational images. Furthermore, the representations of masculinity a boy sees will be inflected by race and ethnicity, as will the gendered expectations he faces. African American, Latino, and Filipino cultures sustain traditions that connect music to dance. These traditions include the ability to dance as part of being masculine, even as they distinguish between the ways in which men and women move.

For boys who hear that dancing is gay, or for girls, or blacks, or Latinos, or Asians, or men of a different class, but not for them, attempting to dance appears riskier than refusing. A boy growing up under such constraints is likely to direct his energies into becoming an All-American boy who can nimbly kick or toss a ball, but not bounce in time to a beat. He can develop an athletic body, and even the capacity to perform on the playing field before a large crowd of spectators, but not a dancing body. The dancing body is a sensual body, and therefore a potentially feminized body, and that is what he avoids. He will not develop an assertively stylized presentation of self, but rather its opposite, a bearing that proclaims the absence of style. He will learn to practice the perpetual self-surveillance, the body minding, which is demanded by compulsive heterosexuality.[4] As an adult he will feel unable to physically connect to music and strangely disconnected from his body when called upon to dance.

THE MIND/BODY PROBLEM

Historian Gail Bederman describes masculinity as a "process" through which "men claim certain kinds of authority, based upon their particular types of bodies."[5] Bodies are not static entities. They are works in progress, they are used, they move. The support a man's body may offer to his entitlement to a position of authority rests on his body's appearance, its capacities, what he does and can do with it, and also what he apparently cannot and will not do. When men move, they "engage in behavior that is at risk of gender assessment."[6] The possibility of claiming authority through the body also makes the body the site of potential failure. Constructions of masculinity that equate it with dominance make masculine embodiment a problem for men to solve. Solving the problem by rejecting dance is a way to distance oneself from physically passive, incompetent, erotic, emotional, and therefore less authoritative others. When men adopt stolidity and physical reserve as habitual forms of embodiment, they contribute to the disparagement of those who appear born to dance—women in general, racialized others, and gay men.

What do men gain when they confess that they do not dance? They gain the right to claim the position and associated benefits of the normal, rational man. Drawn into accepting their places on the intellectual and unemotional side of a culturally perceived rift, they relinquish identification with and connection to the body to sexualized and racialized others. Social expectations for dominant forms of masculinity often stifle a boy's desire to learn to dance and limit the opportunities where such learning would be possible. Women and people of color are too often reduced to their bodies and disparaged for it. A consequence of that positioning is having more space to experience the pleasures of dance. White middle-class men are rarely reduced to their bodies, and the price many of them have paid for that privilege is dance floor awkwardness.

There is nothing natural about adopting such a form of embodiment. It does not come to white middle-class boys by nature. Anyone who wishes to claim the social position that white middle-class men are generally granted can take up that stance and attempt to make it his or her own. Their success in claiming that neutral position of authority will however be read against the way their bodies are perceived. A black or Latino man's awkwardness may be treated as a surprise, as an embodiment that is out of expected character, or even as a pose. He may be accused of acting white. A woman who cannot dance is likely to be perceived as too cold or masculine, her gracelessness bewildering.

No man ever permanently solves the problem of masculine embodiment. The problem demands perpetual attention and reworking through daily enactment. Avoiding dance is one approach to the problem, and it is especially available to men who are viewed by common sense as innately lacking the talent. There are, however, other available strategies. Men who are uncomfortable dancing find ways to dance through forms that provide particular answers to the stigma of men's performance. For young men b-boying, the athletic, competitive, stunt-filled dance style performed to hip-hop music, is popularly recognized as a notably masculine form. Moshing is another form that is compatible with contemporary formulations of adolescent masculinity. It is dance as aggressive abandon. Both forms are generally performed by groups of men and do not involve partnering, except, in the case of b-boying, of the antagonistic pair of battlers. Current highly sexualized modes of dance popular among adolescents and young adults are performed through codes that stipulate that women will move more, and more erotically, than men, and that within heterosexual contexts men will never dance together.

Older men find comfort in the codified steps and anachronistic gender-defined leading and following built into the array of partnered social dance forms such as ballroom, salsa, East and West Coast swing, country/western and contra. Most of these forms, especially any that require torso or hip movement, specify that men will move less than women as they lead them around the dance floor. Men raised in homes with little or no home bopping may find the demands of any of these forms of dancing too difficult. They see themselves as foolish, feel tense, and experience the instructions as too complicated. If called upon in Latin forms to move their hips or articulate their torsos, they may have trouble even locating the muscles that will move them. Other men build up the capacity to dance in these forms gradually and gain competence and confidence through an expanding repertoire of movement. Some discover that they become "naturals" late in life.

Boys form the habitus of the sitter-out as they develop into men under intersecting gender and racial regimes. To speak of a habitus is to describe deeply inscribed dispositions and physical habits rehearsed incalculable times. Yet old bodies can learn new tricks, when they find contexts that support their learning, and especially if they have a compelling reason to try. Many of the men I interviewed confirmed the paradoxical common sense that though white middle-class heterosexual men cannot and do not want to dance, their white middle-class heterosexual girlfriends and wives can and long to dance. These women rarely get to dance because the way they will spend their leisure time is limited by their partners' interests and comfort level. The pattern reflects enduring gender inequalities within heterosexual couples. Men who wish to be in more egalitarian relationships are doing more housework and childcare than previous generations of men. They should also consider dancing, if it is something their partners wish to do. Saying "sure, let's dance" instead of "sorry I don't dance" would be a step toward creating fairer relationships that could possibly, over time, provide them with a new way to interact in the world and the feeling of greater connection to their own bodies.

A NEW COMMON SENSE

Dance, while fun, is not a trivial thing, and its importance goes well beyond the dynamics of relationships. It is an aspect of culture within the United States that lends support to the false belief that there are naturally occurring racial and sexual differences in the distribution of talent and temperament. Anyone who finds racism and sexism unacceptable should be troubled by truisms about race, gender, and dance.

What would happen if we forgot the prevailing common sense, if we refused to place categories of persons on either the mind or body side of a mind/body divide, and recognized the impossibility of splitting minds from bodies? Let Charles, whose mother is Filipina and father is black, stand as the average guy. Ride with him and his friends as these young men drive to a dance club listening to selections of dance music they've prepared to put them in the mood. "By the time we hit the bridge . . . we're sitting there blasting the music, dancing in the car . . . Woo. Woo. Woo. Woo. Woo. . . . My friend Anthony. He's a good dancer, and my friend Will. He's in there. And my friend Joe. Just getting it going." Charles and his friends arrive at the club, and he spots a woman who is a fantastic dancer.

> She was dancing really, really well, and other dudes were trying to dance with her, but I could almost see in her body language—she was like 'This guy can't keep up.' [*laughs*] . . . So I was like, 'Hey, would you like to dance?' . . . So I was just out there just dancing, dancing, . . . just mixing up moves . . . and she was like, 'Oh!' I could see in her body language, she was shocked, [and she] even stepped up her game, and that was a lot of fun.

Imagine that Charles' ability to keep up is not shocking. At the same time hold in your mind an image of him as a serious intellectual of good character. That would be the basis for a less hierarchical society. It would be a society that was not divided into the dominant and the subordinated, thinkers and shakers, rigid and sensual, sexually normal and deviant, minds and bodies. Lend your body to that new common sense. Be a thinking boogier, an intellectual with a body, a revolutionary mover and shaker. Put those thoughts into practice. Lay down this book, turn on some music, and dance.

Methodological Appendix

To learn about the meaning of dance in contemporary men's lives I conducted in-depth interviews and participant observation. I interviewed fifty men aged eighteen to eighty-six. Some were recruited through announcements in university classes; others began with referrals from personal contacts. I located a couple of the men by going to a gay dance club, approaching men, introducing myself, and explaining the study to them. I asked the men I interviewed if they could refer me to other men and in some cases those referrals led to another interview. All of the interviews were recorded and transcribed. All but two of them were conducted in person. Two were conducted by telephone.

At the end of their interviews, men were given a brief questionnaire, which asked about age, current type of employment, race, ethnicity, sexuality, religious background and current religion, highest level of education, parents' education, country of birth, and parents' and grandparents' country of birth. They were encouraged to use their own words in responses regarding sexual, racial, or ethnic identities and were invited to skip questions that asked about categories that were not meaningful to them.

The ages, races or ethnicities, and sexual identities of the men are listed in a table below. I followed their self-categorizations with regard to race, ethnicity, and sexuality. For example, I only identified a man as multiracial if he identified himself in that way. Within the text I refer to speakers' class origins or class positions. Class is not listed in the table. Though I knew men's current occupations, and individual and parental educational levels, many of their class trajectories were too complicated to characterize with one word in a table. Occupations are listed in the table. The occupations of some interview subjects have been changed to ones of equivalent status to protect subjects' anonymity. All names of persons quoted from interviews conducted for this book are pseudonyms.

In the interviews I asked men to talk about their lifelong experiences with popular forms of dance. Some were avid and regular dancers; others had not danced in decades. The interviews covered men's childhood experiences dancing at home, school, and in neighborhood settings, and in adolescence and adulthood at dances, clubs, non-professional performances, and parties. Interviews were a particularly effective way to capture the place of dance in the imagination, the meaning of dance in men's lives, the emotions dance recalls, and the fantasies it inspires. At a distance from the moment of performance, what remained were the strongest feelings associated with dancing and watching others dance.

I also attended two quarters of Dance 101, a ten-week dance survey course at an urban university in which students were introduced to modern, jazz, ballet, social dancing, and African dance. To protect the anonymity of the instructor and students I have changed the name of the class. As an "activity" rather than a lecture class, students learned the material primarily by attempting to do it. Dance 101 was a requirement for physical education majors who wished to work in educational settings. Students who aspired to be physical education teachers or high school coaches had to take it. Unlike most other university dance classes, Dance 101 regularly enrolled men. The first quarter, five of nine, and in the second quarter, five of fourteen students were men. In addition to observing these men in class, I conducted in-depth interviews with six of them.

During the two quarters in which I participated, nine of the ten men in Dance 101 were physical education majors who were in the class because it was a mandatory course. I participated with the instructor's permission and introduced myself to the class at the first meeting. I explained that I was in the class because I was studying men and dance but that I would also participate in the class. During the first quarter I audited the course, which meant attending the classes and participating in all of the dance activities but not submitting assignments or taking exams. In the second quarter in order to fully experience the class, I enrolled for credit and like any other student, had to complete all assignments and received a letter grade.

DEMOGRAPHICS OF MEN INTERVIEWED

Pseudonym	Age	Race/ Ethnicity	Sexual Identity	Occupation	Additional Information
Aaron	21	white/Jewish	heterosexual	student	
Alberto	46	white	gay	bookkeeper	parents emigrated from Mexico
Allen	59	white/Jewish	gay	attorney	
Alphonse	49	black	heterosexual	teacher's aide	
Andre	25	black	heterosexual	student	
Avery	27	Black/Haitian	queer	student	parents emigrated from Haiti
Bill	47	white	heterosexual	manager	
Brandon	51	Chinese	heterosexual	contractor	
Brian	65	white	heterosexual	library director	
Carter	33	black	heterosexual	college staff	father is white, mother black
Charles	32	multiracial	heterosexual	student	father is black, mother Filipina
Dennis	18	Chinese	bisexual	student	
Douglas	23	black	heterosexual	student	
Ernest	29	Caribbean/ Filipino	heterosexual	teacher	father is black from St. Vincent, mother Filipina
Fred	86	white	heterosexual	scientist (ret.)	
Gerald	21	Chinese	heterosexual	administrative assistant	born in Vietnam to ethnic Chinese parents
Gil	29	multiracial/ Chicano	gay	teacher	
Herb	56	white/Jewish	heterosexual	professor	
Jamar	32	black	heterosexual	city government	
Jed	63	white	heterosexual	professor	
Jeremy	35	multiracial	gay	system administrator	father is white, mother Japanese
Justin	20	Mexican/white	heterosexual	student	father is Mexican, mother white

(*continued*)

DEMOGRAPHICS OF MEN INTERVIEWED

Pseudonym	Age	Race/ Ethnicity	Sexual Identity	Occupation	Additional Information
Kevin	44	white	heterosexual	business owner	
Landon	43	black	gay	non-profit executive	
Leo	50	Latino	heterosexual	corporate executive	
Mark	59	white/Jewish	heterosexual	statistician	
Marvin	58	white	heterosexual	professor	
Milton	38	black	gay	researcher	
Neil	54	white/Jewish	heterosexual	paralegal	
Norman	55	white/Jewish	heterosexual	business owner	
Ossie	27	white	gay	system administrator	
Patrick	50	white	gay	college staff	
Paul	50	white	heterosexual	business owner	
Phil	31	white	heterosexual	warehouse worker	
Quinn	26	black	queer	unemployed	
Ralph	25	Latino	heterosexual	medical student	father is Mexican, mother Nicaraguan
Raymond	24	Chicano	heterosexual	student	
Ren	21	Japanese	gay	student	
Rick	46	white	heterosexual	therapist	
Ryan	26	multi-ethnic	heterosexual	student	father is white, mother Filipina and Mexican
Stan	55	white	heterosexual	electrician	
Timothy	21	white	bisexual	student	
Tyler	20	multiracial	heterosexual	student	father is white, mother Chinese
Van	24	Vietnamese	gay	student	
Victor	27	multiracial	heterosexual	ballroom dance instructor	father is Filipino, mother Mexican
Wallace	66	white	heterosexual	business owner	
Walter	65	white	heterosexual	mathematician	
Warren	60	white	heterosexual	theatre director	
Will	30	Filipino	heterosexual	retail	
Zachary	19	white/Jewish	heterosexual	student	

NOTES

CHAPTER 1

1. A range of interchangeable terms may be used to describe dance as it is practiced in everyday settings. Dance scholars call it "vernacular" dance. I will use that term along with "popular," and "everyday," with the assumption that the reader understands that the tighten up need not be performed every day in order to count as everyday dance. Since it is so often associated with social dance classes, the term "social dance" conjures up images of partners doing the box step. All of the dancing described in this book is social, but I avoid the term "social dance" because of its narrower connotations.

2. For a time in the thirties "stag line" was used to refer to unattached young men at a dance; however, when used, the term's meaning was not consistent. It was applied both to men who were too shy to dance and to men who observed potential female dance partners before approaching them. For examples of these uses, see *Oxford English Dictionary*, online edition, "stag line"; Agnes L. Marsh, "Social Dancing as a Project in Physical Education," 30; and Harold Wentworth & Stuart B. Flexner, *Dictionary of American Slang*, 2nd suppl. ed. (New York: Thomas Y. Crowell, 1975), 515.

3. See Eduardo Bonilla-Silva's "The Linguistics of Color Blind Racism," for theorization of color-blind racism.

4. Brett St. Louis makes a similar argument about the acceptance of beliefs in biologically based talent in the supposedly "innocent play" of competitive sports. See St. Louis "Sport, Genetics and the 'Natural Athlete'," 84.

5. See Juliet McMains' "Dancing Latin/Latin Dancing," 312, for a discussion of popular associations between innate ethnic character and dance.

6. For a brief discussion of the reluctance of heterosexual white young men to dance at proms see Amy Best, *Prom Night*, 95. There are descriptions of dance in C. J. Pascoe's ethnography of masculinity in high school. Pascoe's study includes short descriptions of black young men dancing, of a gender queer, white young man dancing, and of white young men parodying feminized dancing. See Pascoe, *Dude You're a Fag*, especially pp. 63–74.

7. Lewis Erenberg in *Steppin' Out* and Susan Cook in "Tango Lizards and Girlish Men" and "Passionless Dancing and Passionate Reform" are exceptions. Though Cook wrote about stage dancers, she importantly discussed how they may have represented masculinity for ordinary men.

8. Cressey, *Taxi-Dance Hall*, 109–129.

9. See Gail Bederman, *Manliness and Civilization*, John Kasson, *Houdini, Tarzan, and the Perfect Man* and John Pettegrew, *Brutes in Suits* for the importance of Tarzan

in defining masculinity. See Pettegrew, *Brutes in Suits* for the importance of the Western as a genre.

10. Max Brand, *Destry Rides Again*, 233. James M. Cain, *The Postman Always Rings Twice*, 108.

11. For the historical construction of masculinities in the United States see Bederman, *Manliness and Civilization*; Kasson, *Houdini, Tarzan, and the Perfect Man*; Michael Kimmel, *Manhood in America*; E. Anthony Rotundo, *American Manhood*; and Martin Summers, *Manliness and Its Discontents*.

12. Connell uses gender order and gender regime synonymously. See *Gender and Power*, 99.

13. Connell, *Gender and Power*, 84.

14. Connell, *Masculinities*, 122.

15. Messerschmidt, "'Doing Gender,'" 87.

16. Connell, *Gender and Power*, 186. This position has been challenged by Demetrakis Demetriou in "Connell's Concept of Hegemonic Masculinity" and by Eric Anderson in "Inclusive Masculinity in a Fraternal Setting," both of whom describe greater acceptance of gay men within the current structure of hegemonic masculinity. Laura Grindstaff and Emily West, in "Hegemonic Masculinity on the Sidelines of Sport," question Demetriou's and Anderson's critiques and note that styles associated with gay identities may be incorporated into hegemonic masculinity in societies that continue to stigmatize homosexual sex.

17. Pascoe, *Dude You're a Fag*, 54.

18. Ramsay Burt, *Male Dancer*, 11.

19. Ibid., 24.

20. Michael Messner, "Masculinity of the Governator," 463.

21. Michael Gard, *Men Who Dance*, 62–63.

22. West and Zimmerman,"Doing Gender." In *Bodies That Matter*, philosopher Judith Butler develops a similar argument in which gender is performative.

23. See *Gender & Society* 23, no. 1 (February 2009) for a symposium on the concept of "doing gender."

24. To account for the ways class, race, and sexuality define ideals of masculinity within local contexts Connell, writing with Messerschmidt, reconsidered the concept of a singular masculine ideal and shifted from the use of hegemonic masculinity to the plural hegemonic masculinities. These are competing and interacting constructions of dominant masculinity that may exist at local, regional, and global levels. See Connell and Messerschmidt, "Hegemonic Masculinity," 849.

25. Bederman's *Manliness and Civilization* and Summers's *Manliness and Its Discontents* are notable for their incorporation of race and class into historical analyses of masculinity. Bederman specified the emergence of a particular formation of white middle-class masculinity in the United States in the years 1880–1917 and demonstrated that a belief in the superiority of whiteness was central to it. Martin Summers's history of early twentieth-century black middle-class masculinity argues that black men shaped masculinity in reference to other blacks.

26. Bourdieu, *Bachelor's Ball*, 85.

27. Ibid.

28. Wacquant, *Body and Soul*, 16.

29. For the theorization of intersectionality see Kimberlé Crenshaw, "Mapping the Margins"; Patricia Hill Collins, *Black Feminist Thought*; and Evelyn Nakano Glenn, *Unequal Freedom*.

30. Garber, *Vested Interests*, 372.
31. Dyson, "Be Like Mike?" 410.
32. For anti-performative see Halberstam as quoted in Jagose, "Masculinity without Men," paragraph 4.
33. Stein and Plummer, "I Can't Even Think Straight," 185.
34. Dyer, *Matter of Images*, 134.
35. The phrase "physical sense of masculinity" was inspired by Connell's description of the physical sense of maleness in *Gender and Power*, 84.
36. I borrow the concept of bodily aesthetic from Gard, who used bodily aesthetic to describe "the ways in which people use, feel and describe the things they do with their body." See Gard, *Men Who Dance*, 175.
37. Ibid., 46–48.
38. Burt, *Male Dancer*, 24–28.
39. Chauncey, *Gay New York*, 25.
40. See Mary Louise Adams, "'Death to the Prancing Prince'," 78; Gard, *Men Who Dance*, 62–63; Doug Risner, *Stigma and Perseverance in the Lives of Boys Who Dance*, 9.
41. W. G. Anderson, "Dancing: For Young and Old Seen by a Physiological Psychologist," *New York Times*, April 30, 1914, 10.
42. Shawn, "A Defence of the Male Dancer." For another of his attempts to distance dance from femininity see Shawn, "Principles of Dancing for Men."
43. Cultural historian Andrew Hewitt describes Shawn's choreography as an attempt to stage a "hysterical enclosure of the otherwise uncontainable energies of virility." Hewitt, *Social Choreography*, 149. A video clip of Ted Shawn's choreography "Kinetic Molpai" may be viewed on YouTube. See http://www.youtube.com/watch?v=sqWjm7BHEkI.
44. Quoted in Susan Manning, *Modern Dance, Negro Dance*, 24.
45. See Emily Kane, "'No Way My Boys Are Going to Be Like That!'," 161, 166, 170.
46. Verna Arvey, "Control, Not Grace: Richard Cromwell."
47. John Martin, "The Dance: A Man's Art: Increasing Interest Noted in Masculine Circles—Programs of the Week," *New York Times*, February 3, 1935, section X, p.8.
48. Walter Ware, "In Defense of the Male Dancer."
49. It was diluted but did not disappear. Historian Allan Bérubé reports that in 1943 being a professional dancer was treated as an indicator of homosexuality on a psychiatric instrument developed for selective service screening. See Bérubé, *Coming Out Under Fire*, 20.
50. Phyllis Battelle, "The Manly Art of Dancing," *Journal-American*, New York, May 17, 1964, 41-L.
51. Albin Krebs, "Gene Kelly, Dancer of Vigor and Grace, Dies," *New York Times*, February 3, 1996, 1.
52. After the death of her husband and dance partner Vernon, Irene Castle published her memoir and said "Vernon had no intention of going on the stage. That he did go on was largely a matter of accident." See Castle, "My Memories of Vernon Castle," 23. Aaron Cota's autobiographical essay provides a contemporary example of a dancer describing his career as an accident. He wrote, "I became a dance major almost by accident, because I filled in my application to be a film major wrong. I went to the audition anyway, and once I was accepted, I thought, why not?" See Cota in "Aaron Cota," 49.
53. See Nazgol Ghandnoosh, "'Cross-cultural' Practices," 1597, footnote 12 and Joseph Schloss, *Foundation*, 65.

54. I am grateful to my student Ruth Levine for explaining that the popularity of dancing in this manner is such that many youths refer to it simply as dancing. The terms "freaking" and "grinding" are used by adults and by youths when speaking to adults. (Ruth Levine, personal communication).

55. See Shelly Ronen, "Grinding on the Dance Floor," for a study of this type of dancing among college students.

CHAPTER 2

1. In the historical literature "new woman" is used to refer to feminists of the late nineteenth century and to women of the 1910s and 1920s who challenged gender norms through new forms of leisure, appearance, and consumption. I use new woman in the latter sense. According to historian Mary Ryan, "the new woman entered into the sporting world with her male chums, smoking, drinking, dancing lasciviously, and necking openly." See Ryan, *Womanhood in America*, 153. Julie Malnig summarizes the multiple meanings of new woman in "Apaches, Tangos, and Other Indecencies," 77.

2. See Henry Louis Gates, Jr., "The Trope of a New Negro and the Reconstruction of the Image of the Black," for the image of the new Negro. Martin Summers, in *Manliness and Its Discontents*, demonstrates that new forms of black masculinity emerged during this period.

3. The history I present is an urban one that does not account for the dance practices of rural areas. Dance provided recreation in rural areas but was practiced and organized in different ways in specific rural locations. See for example Susan Spalding, "Frolics, Hoedowns and Four-Handed Reels."

4. Susan C. Cook's scholarship on the ways in which ballroom dancers Vernon Castle and Maurice Mouvet embodied masculinity is an important exception. See Cook, "Tango Lizards and Girlish Men" and "Passionless Dancing and Passionate Reform." Russel B. Nye's "Saturday Night at the Paradise Ballroom" and Lewis Erenberg's *Steppin' Out* opened the field of scholarship on twentieth-century popular amusements. This chapter, and to a certain extent the entire book, has been inspired by Lewis Erenberg's pathbreaking work on urban nightlife and gender, as well as that of Susan C. Cook and Kathy Peiss. *Cheap Amusements*, by Peiss, established a foundation for the exploration of gender and popular dance. I followed the footsteps of these historians in archives and discuss figures, including Eugenia Kelly, Vernon Castle, Belle Moskowitz, and Maurice Mouvet, introduced by them. My goal in providing another look at dance in this period is to give greater attention to men, masculinities, and masculine embodiment than the subjects have yet received.

5. Historian Randy D. McBee's work is exceptional in the sustained attention it gives to the experience of men on dance floors. His study of Eastern and Southern European immigrants in the 1910s to 1930s describes dance halls as spaces in which wary and clumsy men competed for scarce female dance partners. McBee assumes rather than explains their inability to dance well. He makes use of Cressey's field notes from his research on taxi dance halls and so may have been describing a particularly insecure group of men who went to halls in which women were available as dancing partners for hire. See McBee, *Dance Hall Days*, especially p. 92.

6. Ann Ferguson discusses Leslie A. Fiedler's concept of the "Good Bad Boy" in her book *Bad Boys*, 86.

7. See Bederman, *Manliness and Civilization*, and Kasson, *Houdini, Tarzan, and the Perfect Man*, for Tarzan creator Edgar Rice Burrough's influence on U.S. masculine

culture and for astute gender analyses of *Tarzan of the Apes*. See John Pettegrew, *Brutes in Suits*, for the image of the brute in the U.S. between 1890 and 1920 in popular masculine literature, including *The Virginian*.

8. The term "sissy" came into use in the nineteenth century. While sissy as an affectionate term for a sister was used in the 1840s, by the 1890s the term sissy was being used to describe an effeminate man. See "Sissy," *Oxford English Dictionary*, online edition.

9. For the popularity of dance for working-class men see George Bevans, "How Workingmen Spend Their Time," 27 and Ann Wagner, *Adversaries of Dance*, 294–98. For its popularity among middle-class young men see Paula Fass, *Damned and the Beautiful*, 199.

10. "Reports of Council," *American Physical Education Review* 10, no. 1 (1905): 47–51. Luther H. Gulick, "Rhythm and Education."

11. Henry Ling Taylor, "The Dancing Foot."

12. "Athletes to Dance as Part of Training: Physical Education Association to Discuss Plan: Gymnasts Favor Scheme," *New York Times*, March 3, 1905, 7; "The Dance and the Child: Dancing Now a Recognized Factor in Education—Its Popularity Growing Steadily," *New York Times*, August 12, 1905, 2; "Says Work and Play Should Come in Turn: Dr. Gulick Favors Frequent Periods of Rest: Dancing as an Educator: Value of Rhythm Is Emphasized by Speakers at Convention of Physical Culturists," *New York Times*, April 18, 1905, 7.

13. "American Physical Education Association: Convention," *American Gymnasia and Athletic Record* 1, no. 9 (1905): 236–42. The quotation is on page 236.

14. Alfred Moseley. "Education in the United States," *The Independent* 56, no. 2881, February 18, 1904, 362; "Mr. Mosely on American Schools," *New York Times*, February 21, 1904, 6.

15. Luther H. Gulick, "The Alleged Effemination of our American Boys."

16. Luther H. Gulick, "Athletics from the Biologic Viewpoint."

17. "Editorial Note and Comment," *American Physical Education Review* 11, no. 3 (1906): 212–13.

18. Luther H. Gulick, "Exercise Must Be Interesting."

19. Dudley. A. Sargent, "What Athletic Games, If Any, Are Injurious for Women in the Form in which They Are Played by Men?"

20. Frances A. Kellor, "Ethical Value of Sports for Women"; Clara Fitch, "The Influence of Dancing Upon the Physique." Martha Verbrugge argues that women physical education teachers were ambivalent regarding the issue of sexual difference. Though they were dedicated to promoting physical activity for women, their professional niche depended on a continuing belief in sex differences. See Verbrugge, "Recreating the Body," 294–95.

21. Gulick, *Healthful Art of Dancing*, 7.

22. Tomko, *Dancing Class*, 191–95.

23. "7,000 Girls Enjoy Dance Fete in Park," *New York Times*, June 9, 1914, 11; "10,000 Girls Dance in Central Park," *New York Times*, May 12, 1915, 13. "9,000 Pupils Dance on Sheep Meadow; Girls' Branch of the Public School League Has Its Annual Fete in Central Park," *New York Times*, May 10, 1916, 13.

24. Tomko, "Fete Accompli," 172.

25. Ward C. Crampton, "New York City Syllabus of Physical Training." This pattern was in practice before the curriculum revision formalized it. Folk dance instruction was made a regular part of elementary school education in New York City under Elizabeth Burchenal's leadership, and her programs were only for girls. See Gulick, *Healthful Art of Dancing*, 28.

26. "Compelled to Dance with NEGRO, She Says: Daughter of Flushing Banker Complained to Father of School Teacher's Order. Civic Association Inquiry: Incident Occurred in the Waltz Part of the Regular Physical Culture Exercises," *New York Times*, January 17, 1911, 1; "Would End School Dancing: Flushing Hopes Thus to Prevent White and Negro Pupils Mingling," *New York Times*, February 22, 1911, 8.

27. Bederman, *Manliness and Civilization*, 17.

28. Chauncey, *Gay New York*, 111; Bederman, *Manliness and Civilization*, 12.

29. For the emergence of men's interest in self-expression, consumption, and leisure see Erenberg, "Everybody's Doin' It," 158 and Bederman, *Manliness and Civilization*, 13.

30. Cook, "Watching Our Step," 191.

31. Elizabeth Aldrich, "Civilizing of America's Ballrooms," 52.

32. "What is Doing in Society," *New York Times*, August 15, 1900, 7; "Mrs. Ogden Goelet's Ball," *New York Times*, August 29, 1900, 7.

33. "Elisha Dyer Dies," *New York Times*, June 3, 1917, 19.

34. Elizabeth Lehr, *"King Lehr" and the Gilded Age*, 58.

35. John Cobbs, *Owen Wister*, 4, 12.

36. Wister. *The Virginian*, 7.

37. Ibid., 11.

38. Ibid., 31.

39. For the statistic regarding unmarried mothers see "The Common Welfare: Regulating Dance Halls," *The Survey*, (New York) [The Charity Organization Society of the City of New York] 26 (1911): 346. For the belief that upper class dancers bestowed legitimacy on bad dances see "Welfare Inspector at Society Dance," *New York Times*, January 4, 1912.

40. Elisabeth Perry, *Belle Moskowitz*, 56.

41. On the popularity of dance as a working-class amusement see Peiss, *Cheap Amusements*, especially 88–98 and Tomko, *Dancing Class*, 21–22.

42. Malnig, *Dancing Till Dawn*, 37; Tomko, *Dancing Class*, 22.

43. Gulick, *Dynamic of Manhood*, 83.

44. William Skarstrom, "Social Centers Instead of Dance Halls."

45. "SUNDAY WOULD NOT START NEW CHURCH; Woman Offered Him $25,000 a Year, He Said, but He Declined. DANCERS 'DRUNK OR CRAZY' Card Playing and Racing for Profit Also Placed Under the Ban by the Evangelist," *New York Times*, May 26, 1917, 8; see also Wagner, *Adversaries of Dance*, 384 for a brief discussion of middle-class masculine culture and Protestant anti-dance attitudes in the United States.

46. Social Advisory Committee, Church of Jesus Christ of the Latter-day Saints, "Practical Hints to Teacher: Extracts From Social Dancing," *American Physical Education Review* 25, no. 5 (1920): 202–8.

47. The California Civic League, San Francisco Center, Public Dance Hall Committee records, 1918–1950, show decades of concern with girls and women's activities and give scant attention to boys and men. See also Rheta Childe Dorr's *What Eight Million Women Want*.

48. Perry, *Belle Moskowitz*, 43.

49. Israels, "Way of the Girl," 495.

50. "East Siders like Model Dance Hall: Popularity of Experiment Shows That the Young Folks Prefer Wholesome Amusements. The Master a Martinet: No 'Freshness' Tolerated Among the Patrons—Dancers Don't Know They are Experimental Subjects," *New York Times*, February 6, 1910, 8; "Dance Hall Evils Being Wiped Out: Mrs. Israels Tells of Model Places Now Being Run Under Philanthropic Auspices," *New York Times*,

May 28, 1910, 13; "To Stop Dance Hall Evils: Assembly Passes a Bill Prohibiting Liquor Selling Among Other Things," *New York Times*, March 11, 1908, 5.

51. Israels, "Way of the Girl," 495.
52. Dorr, *What Eight Million Women Want*, 214.
53. Bevans, "How Workingmen Spend Their Time," 27, 33.
54. Louise De Koven Bowen, "Dance Halls," *The Survey* (New York) [The Charity Organization Society of the City of New York] 26 (1911): 383–87. See p. 385 for the preponderance of men at dances.
55. Israels, "Way of the Girl," 495.
56. Bowen, "Dance Halls," 384–85.
57. "Social Workers See Real 'Turkey Trots': Shudder at 'The Shiver,' Gasp at 'The Bunny Hug,' and Then Discuss Reforms," *New York Times*, January 27, 1912, 1; Perry, *Belle Moskowitz*, 51.
58. "To Bar Turkey Trot in Their Ballrooms: Managers of Dance Halls Agree on That, But How to Do It Is a Problem," *New York Times*, February 3, 1912, 20.
59. Maurice Mouvet, Letter to the Editor, *New York Times*, January 25, 1912, 10.
60. Erenberg, *Steppin' Out*, 158–71 and Cook, "Tango Lizards and Girlish Men," 42; "Passionless Dancing and Passionate Reform," 134; and "Watching Our Step."
61. "The Midnight Sons," *Blue Book*, September 1909.
62. Castle and Castle, *Modern Dancing*.
63. Montgomery Phister. "People of the Stage. Mrs. Vernon Castle and the Great Hippodrome Castle Farewells—Those Special Trains and Her Hurried Rushes to and from Gotham—Her Spectacular Labors in Behalf of Her Patriotic Husband, Who Would Be an Aviator in Defense of His Country—Vernon's Reported Depleted Pocketbook and the Dillingham Method of Setting Him on His Financial Pins Again—Dancing Farewells as a Prelude to Glorious Deeds in Air—Mrs. Castle as the Terpsichorean Star of 'Watch Your Step,'" *Cincinnati Tribune*, February 6, 1916.
64. "Castle Still Dashing Away," *New York Telegraph*, February 9, 1916.
65. "Dancer 'Quite Excited' About Her Husband's Joining the British Aviation Corps for War Service—He Sails Wednesday," *Minneapolis News*, February 11, 1916.
66. "Vernon Still Farewelling," *Toledo Blade*, February 24, 1916.
67. Cook, "Tango Lizards and Girlish Men," 41, 50–51 and "Passionless Dancing and Passionate Reform," 146–48.
68. Erenberg, *Steppin' Out*, 166–67.
69. Cook, "Watching Our Step," 177–212.
70. Edward Scott, "Manner in Social Dancing," *The Dancing Times*, December 1917, 66–67. *Dancing Times* was a British publication and Scott's focus was the amateur dancers of Europe. His comments remain relevant because British ballroom dance culture served as a model for ballroom dancers in the United States.
71. Burroughs, *Tarzan of the Apes*, 54.
72. Pettegrew, *Brutes in Suits*.
73. Reid Badger, *A Life in Ragtime*, 116; see also remarks by Irene Castle in "In the Ball-Room To-Day," 35.
74. Stearns and Stearns, *Jazz Dance*, 128.
75. "The Turkey Trot and Tango Arouse London to Protest," *New York Times*, August 23, 1913, 5.
76. "All New York Now Madly Whirling in the Tango: Every Day New Places Where You May Dance Are Springing Up and Older Establishments Yielding to the Craze, Which Apparently, Has Come to Stay," *New York Times*, January 4, 1914, SM8.
77. Cook, "Passionless Dancing and Passionate Reform," 142–46.

78. "Race is Dancing Itself to Death," *New York Age*, January 8, 1914, 1. See also Summers, *Manliness and Its Discontents*, 175, who quotes from a 1923 letter written by black poet Countee Cullen to a black friend in which Cullen notes that he "danced decorously" even when aroused to "wild, primeval, uncivilized" emotion by jazz music. The letter shows a middle-class black man's commitment to controlled bearing in the 1920s.

79. "The Castles in New York," *The Chicago Defender*, April 11, 1914, 4; Badger, *A Life in Ragtime*, 100–4.

80. "Dancer from Paris Introduces New Steps to Society: M. Maurice, Famous at the Cafe de Paris and Elsewhere in Europe, Comes Here to Teach New Yorkers. Curiously Enough He is Not a Parisian, but a New Yorker," *New York Times*, December 10, 1911, SM10.

81. Richard Barry, "Dancing Teas Are Society's Latest Attempt to Kill Time: Practically All the Smart Restaurants Advertise Them Now and Smart, Semi-smart, and Would-be Smart People Are Among the Patrons," *New York Times*, March 23, 1913, X1.

82. "The Mayor Dooms Afternoon Dancing," *New York Times*, April 4, 1913, 1. Further criticism of the dangers of dancing arose from the medical profession. In 1913 the *Journal of the American Medical Association* published warnings that the new dances were too strenuous for the weak hearts of the aged. "Dancing," *Journal of the American Medical Association* 61, no. 22 (November 29, 1913): 1991. "Dancing for the Aged," *Journal of the American Medical Association* 61, no. 23 (December 6, 1913): 2074–75.

83. "Slandering the Tea Dance," *New York Times*, April 5, 1913, 14.

84. "All New York Now Madly Whirling in the Tango; Every Day New Places Where You May Dance Are Springing Up and Older Establishments Yielding to the Craze, Which Apparently, Has Come to Stay," *New York Times*, January 4, 1914, SM8.

85. Erenberg, *Steppin' Out*, 77–85, provides a detailed description and analysis of this case as an example of the way in which dancing men threatened middle- and upper-class white men.

86. "Miss Kelly in Court on Mother's Charge," *New York Times*, May 23, 1915.

87. "Miss Kelly Sorry," *New York Times*, May 26, 1915, 8.

88. "Miss Kelly Gives Up Trottery Life; Police Hunt On," *The World* (New York), May 26, 1915, 1, 5.

89. "Take Steps to End Afternoon Dances," *New York Times*, May 28, 1915, 9.

90. "Women Aroused by Dance Evils: Mrs. Moskowitz Will Ask McAneny to Drive Out Men Parasites Serving as 'Partners': Want Inspectors Named: Mayor Has Not Appointed Supervisors Provided by Law Governing Tango Resorts," *New York Times*, May 27, 1915, 11.

91. Richard Barry, "Tango Pirates Infest Broadway: Afternoon Dances Develop a New Kind of Parasite Whose Victims Are the Unguarded Daughters of the Rich," *New York Times*, May 30, 1915, SM16.

92. "Eugenia Kelly Wed to Dancer Al Davis," *New York Times*, November 18, 1915, 1.

93. "Ballen, Eugenia Kelly," *New York Times*, April 10, 1937, 32.

94. "Once Rich Woman Slain in Hotel: Secret Patron of 'Tango Parlors' Found Strangled and $2,500 in Jewels Missing: Man Companion Sought: Had Made a Practice of Dancing in Afternoons While Husband Was at Business," *New York Times*, March 18, 1917, 1.

95. "Sternberg Admits Lies in Hilair Case: Coroner Sends Him to Tombs and Gives Police a Day to Find Stronger Evidence: Not a Mercenary Tangoist: Prosecutor

Fails to Produce Proof Other Than Prisoner's Own Admissions," *New York Times*, March 23, 1917, 10.

96. "Ban on Married Dancers: Maurice Will Not Teach Wife or Husband Without Other's Consent," *New York Times*, April 16, 1917, 13.

97. Malnig, *Dancing Till Dawn*, 41.

98. According to Chad Heap "recent immigrants from southern and eastern Europe—especially Italians and Jews—[were perceived] as a sort of nonwhite 'in between' group of peoples, situated above blacks in the racial hierarchy of the United States but beneath old-stock whites." See Heap, *Slumming*, 10.

99. Erenberg, *Steppin' Out*, 83.

100. "Practical Hints to Teachers: Physical Education Pageant," *American Physical Education Review* 32, no. 6 (1927): 448–50.

101. All descriptions of Oakland High School dances are from *The Aegis* yearbook, which changed its name in 1932 to *The Oaken Bucket*.

102. Both of the high schools that I describe were in the San Francisco Bay Area; however, dances were popular among high school students nationwide. See Robert S. Lynd and Helen Merrell Lynd, *Middletown*, 83 for the importance of dances for high school students in a city in the Midwest. All descriptions of Lowell High School dances are from *The Red & White* yearbooks.

103. Alice Hackett, *70 Years of Best Sellers*, 125, 127.

104. "Babbitt," *Oxford English Dictionary*, online edition.

105. Kelly Schrum, *Some Wore Bobby Sox*, and Beth L. Bailey, *From Front Porch to Back Seat*, 10. I am grateful to an anonymous reviewer who encouraged me to place the category of youth in historical perspective.

106. Lewis, *Babbitt*, 80.

107. Ibid., 173.

108. Lynd and Lynd, *Middletown*, 281–82.

109. During this period the earliest college dance programs began. In 1917 a physical education teacher named Margaret H'Doubler started the country's first academic dance program at the University of Wisconsin. See Janice Ross, *Moving Lessons*. Women's leadership in dance education and the preponderance of women in these new college majors was a product of and contributed to sustaining the feminization of dance in the public's mind. These programs generally excluded social dance from their curricula.

110. Fass, *Damned and the Beautiful*, 199, 201–2, 300.

111. Arthur Murray, "This Student Earns $15,000 A Year."

112. National Center for Education Statistics, *120 Years*, 65.

113. "College Athletics Cure Effeminacy: Knute Rockne, Notre Dame Athletic Director, Urges Compulsory Boxing and Football," *New York Times*. April 2, 1922, 29 SPORTS.

114. Stearns and Stearns, *Jazz Dance*, 112.

CHAPTER 3

1. I do not have data on the gender composition of the audience for Astaire's films in the 1930s. Drawing on 1940s survey research music historian Todd Decker reports that Astaire had equal appeal for male and female viewers. See Decker, *Music Makes Me*, 21.

2. Stearns and Stearns, *Jazz Dance*, 228; Decker, *Music Makes Me*, 25. Decker argued that because Astaire incorporated piano and drum-playing into his performances "audiences watched him dance in the same way they watched Goodman, Shaw, or

Krupa play. All displayed the masculine power of jazz." In other words, his engagement with music masculinized him in a way that dance alone could not. See Decker, *Music Makes Me*, 123. In *The Fred Astaire and Ginger Rogers Book*, 11, dance and film critic Arlene Croce wrote that Ginger Roger's "genial resistance . . . brought out his toughness and his true masculine gallantry." Her explanation of Astaire's masculinity is an example of how masculinity is produced through feminine cooperation.

3. Quoted in Peter Levinson, *Puttin' on the Ritz*, 423.

4. For the comment on his pairing with Rogers see John Mueller, *Astaire Dancing*, 313. For discussions of Astaire's aversion to love scenes see Levinson *Puttin' on the Ritz*, 110, 199, 207. Astaire's characters were often men of less-than-upper-class standing who rise in status in the films through the performance of "classy" dance. The lower- or middle-class origins of these characters contribute to the perception of Astaire's masculinity. I am grateful to an anonymous reviewer for this insight.

5. See Cressey, *Taxi-Dance Hall*, for an in-depth look at "taxi" dance halls. The minutes of the Public Dance Hall Committee of the San Francisco Center of the California Civic League contain the observations of reformers who wished to regulate or shut halls where women were paid to dance with men.

6. Carol Martin, *Dance Marathons*, 49.

7. Lynd and Lynd, *Middletown in Transition*, 269; "3,000 Dance in Park as the Season Opens," *New York Times*, June 10, 1936.

8. "Dancing Teachers Need Action," *The American Dancer* (September 1930): 16.

9. Thomas E. Parson, "The Ballroom Observer," *The American Dancer* (October 1934): 10, 23.

10. "Students Set Pace in Dance Invention," *New York Times*, July 12, 1932, 19.

11. Juliet E. McMains, *Glamour Addiction*, 86.

12. "Old-School Dancing Master is Vanishing; Survey Shows 99 percent of Teachers Are Women," *New York Times*, August 6, 1934, 11.

13. Christine Williams developed the concept of glass escalator in her 1992 *Social Problems* article, "The Glass Escalator."

14. Chauncey, *Gay New York*.

15. Verna Arvey, "Dance for Beauty's Sake."

16. Louis Chalif, "Men and Boys Should Dance," 25.

17. According to historian Gena Caponi-Tabery, during World War II "the Lindy was no longer considered black vernacular dance but rather served as a symbol of America itself." *Jump for Joy*, 66.

18. "Wartime America," *Yank* 1, no. 7 (July 29, 1942): 10.

19. "Life Goes to a Swing Shift Dance," *Life* (January 19, 1942): 86–89. Bobbie was a woman.

20. The contrast between larger men and smaller women is not an inevitable or natural phenomena but a conventional one. Among the professional dancers at the Savoy were the couple George "Shorty" Snowden and Beatrice "Big Bea" Gay. Beatrice Gay was taller than George Snowden, and this violation of the norms of gendered partnering was used in their choreography for comic effect. See Frankie Manning and Cynthia Millman, *Frankie Manning*, 246.

21. Bérubé, *Coming Out Under Fire*, 77.

22. Janice Kent, "Dancing Has Its Place in the Physical Education Program," *Journal of Health and Physical Education* 2, no. 6 (1931): 20–21, 50.

23. "Minstrel Land," *The American Dancer* (March 1932): 32–33.

24. Large-scale black northern migration began in the 1910s, slowed in the 1930s, and dramatically increased in the 1940s. See Stephen Steinberg, *Ethnic Myth*, 204–5. The black populations of northern cities were also augmented in those years by Caribbean immigration. See also Summers, *Manliness and Its Discontents*, 5.
25. Katrina Hazzard-Gordon, *Jookin'*, 80.
26. Chad Heap, *Slumming*.
27. Part of the appeal of "slumming" for those who engaged in it was the opportunity to behave in ways that they would not in a venue closer to home. See Heap, *Slumming*, 195–97.
28. Ibid., 8.
29. Stearns and Stearns, *Jazz Dance*, 323–34.
30. Manning and Millman, *Frankie Manning*, 98–99.
31. Joel Dinerstein, *Swinging the Machine*, 26.
32. Gunther Schuller, *Swing Era*, 292, 301.
33. Manning and Millman, *Frankie Manning*, 105.
34. Paul Lopes, *Rise of a Jazz Art World*, 102–3.
35. Caponi-Tabery, *Jump for Joy*, 53.
36. Robert Baral, "Dumbo Dances Hot Harlem Jive," *Dance* (October 1941): 10.
37. In 1941 and a portion of 1942, the publication that would later adopt the title *Dance Magazine* was titled *Dance*.
38. Dinerstein, *Swinging the Machine*, 276.
39. See Dominic J. Capeci, Jr., "Walter F. White and the Savoy Ballroom Controversy of 1943"; Caponi-Tabery, *Jump for Joy*, 62; Russell Gold, "Guilty of Syncopation, Joy, and Animation"; and Heap, *Slumming*, 280 for somewhat differing accounts of the 1943 closure of the Savoy.
40. Arthur Murray, "Conquer That Inferiority Complex," *The American Dancer* (1940): 21. He also directed advertisements to parents in which he encouraged them to send their children to dance class and did not specify gender. As the U.S. moved closer to war and the possibility of mass mobilization of young men, Murray's ads avoided gender references. See, for example, Arthur Murray, "The World's Finest Dance Instruction," *Dance* 9, no. 2 (March 1941): inside front cover.
41. *Educational Dance* was a short-lived journal, edited by women, which sought to reach an audience of school and college dance teachers. *Educational Dance* began in 1938 and ceased publication with its August/September 1942 issue.
42. Shawn, "Masculine American Dancing."
43. Paul Mathis, "Letter to the editor," *The American Dancer* (May 1941): 6–8.
44. Donald Sawyer, "Ballroom Dancing and the Draft."
45. John Martin, "John Martin on Conscription."
46. "There Will Always Be Dancing in the Land of the Free," *The American Dancer* (January 1942): 25.
47. "Dance For Defense," *The American Dancer* (March 1942): 32.
48. The Joint Army and Navy Committee on Welfare and Recreation, "Conference of Morale Officers: Summary of Statements on Control of Venereal Diseases," Munitions Building, Washington, D.C., February 25–28, 1941, p.6. Contained in United States, Joint Army & Navy Committee on Welfare and Recreation, Miscellaneous Publications 1941–42.
49. Ibid.; Meghan Winchell, *Good Girls, Good Food, Good Fun*, 68–70.
50. Anthony H. Leviero, "DANCING PROGRAM EXPANDED FOR 27TH: Welfare Officer Enlists Groups of Anniston Women Sponsors as in World War Days,"

New York Times, November 16, 1940, 6; United States, Joint Army & Navy Committee on Welfare and Recreation, Miscellaneous Publications 1941–42, 1; Jim Marshall, "Dates for Defense," *Colliers* (1941): 66; "600 SOLDIERS AT PARTY: First of Dancing Series Held at Fort Hamilton," *New York Times*, January 8, 1942, 12.

51. Ben Sommers, "Keep Em Dancing," *The American Dancer* (March 1942): 30.
52. L. T. Carr, "Step Out, Soldier!," *Dance Magazine* (1942): 20, 32.
53. Irwin Caplan, "Migawd, Sarge," *Yank* 2, no. 3 (July 23, 1943): 24. The Women's Army Auxiliary Corps (WAAC) soon became the Women's Army Corps (WAC).
54. Recreation Services, Inc., *"A Good Leave Town"; A Brief History of the War Hospitality Committee, Washington, D.C.* (1947); Recreation Services, Inc. (Operating Agency for the War Hospitality Committee), Women's Voluntary Services for Civil Defence (1942–1947); *A.B.C. of British Welcome Clubs* (London, 1944); *New York City's Recreation and Welfare Program for Service Men and Women, 1941–1948*; New York, [New York Committee for Service Men, 1948?]. Winchell, *Good Girls, Good Food, Good Fun*, 60.
55. Studs Terkel, *Good War*, 117.
56. Winchell, *Good Girls, Good Food, Good Fun*, 119.
57. "Northampton Services Dance," *The Stars and Stripes* (London), 3, no. 99 (February 26, 1943).
58. "Dancing for Our Boys," *Dance Magazine* (November 1942): 31.
59. *New York City's Recreation and Welfare Program for Service Men and Women, 1941–1948*. New York, [New York Committee for Service Men, 1948?].
60. "Dancing for Our Boys," 31.
61. Dick Ericson, "Stolen from U.S.O.," *Yank* (April 27, 1945): 22.
62. Winchell, *Good Girls, Good Food, Good Fun*, 32.
63. Roeder, *Censored War*, 57.
64. "In Iceland, Too!," *Yank* 1, no. 11 (1942): 13.
65. Dick Wingert, "Yanks," *The Stars and Stripes* (London) 2, no. 7 (May 30, 1942): 2.
66. The principal exceptions are stories and images about US soldiers attempting to learn Irish dances.

CHAPTER 4

1. George Baker, "The Sad Sack: 'Plans'," *Yank* (June 1, 1945): 18.
2. "Victory," *Yank* (September 7, 1945): 5.
3. Elaine Tyler May, *Homeward Bound*, 1; Steven Mintz and Susan Kellogg, *Domestic Revolutions*, 180.
4. Stearns and Stearns, *Jazz Dance*, 1.
5. In *Adversaries of Dance*, 337, Ann Wagner summarizes reasons for the postwar decline in public social dancing.
6. Larry Starr and Christopher Waterman, *American Popular Music*, 139, 159.
7. Frances Herridge, "Social Dancing's Behind Times," (1948), *PM* Clipping File, New York Public Library, Dance Division.
8. Stearns and Stearns, *Jazz Dance*, 1.
9. Starr and Waterman, *American Popular Music*, 176–78. For an extended discussion of jump bands see Caponi-Tabery, *Jump for Joy*, 68–80.
10. David Garcia, "Embodying Music/Disciplining Dance," 168, 170.
11. César Rondón, *Book of Salsa*, 1.
12. Beth Bailey, *From Front Porch to Back Seat*, 43 and Mintz and Kellogg, *Domestic Revolutions*, 178, 183.
13. John Jackson, *American Bandstand*, 9–10.

14. All descriptions of Lowell High School dances are from *The Red & White* yearbooks. For additional information about the school, see Paul Lucey and Barbara Dahl, *Lowell High School San Francisco*.

15. All descriptions of Oakland High School dances are from the yearbook, which was originally named *The Aegis* and was renamed *The Oaken Bucket* in 1932.

16. Starr and Waterman, *American Popular Music*, 210.

17. For size of the audience for *American Bandstand* see Wagner, *Adversaries of Dance*, 338, and for the general popularity of television, see Starr and Waterman, *American Popular Music*, 158.

18. For example, rock and roll programs were broadcast in Los Angeles in the early 1950s. See George Lipsitz, "Land of a Thousand Dances," 274. *American Bandstand* first appeared as a local Philadelphia program in 1952. See Jackson, *American Bandstand*, 18.

19. David Nasaw, *Going Out*, 244–45.

20. "Television Programs," *New York Times*, July 7, 1957.

21. "On Television," *New York Times*, July 19, 1957.

22. Jackson, *Big Beat Heat*, 168; Jackson, *American Bandstand*, 55–56; Nasaw, *Going Out*, 246; Starr and Waterman, *American Popular Music*, 200.

23. The exact details of the interaction are disputed, but all accounts agree that it did not involve physical contact.

24. "The White Negro" is included in Mailer's 1959 collection *Advertisements for Myself*.

25. Mailer, *Advertisements for Myself*, 340.

26. Baldwin, *Price of the Ticket*, 290.

27. For the participation of black musicians and black teenagers in *American Bandstand*, see pages 26 and 56–58 of *American Bandstand*, John A. Jackson's detailed 1997 history of the program. Though a very small number of blacks were included in the early years of the show, Jackson mentions no instance of a black and white dancing couple.

28. J. P. Shanley, "TV: Teen-Agers Only: 'American Bandstand,' a Daytime Disk Jockey Show, Bows on Channel 7," *New York Times*, August 6, 1957, 42.

29. Starr and Waterman, *American Popular Music*, 216.

30. John Briggs, "The Savoy Era of Jazz Closes on Auctioneer's Brief Reprise," *New York Times*, October 1, 1958, 39.

31. Though the Savoy closed, dancers in Harlem continued to patronize less grand ballrooms. See Lynn Emery, *Black Dance From 1619 to Today*, 348.

32. May, *Homeward Bound*, 179.

33. Clark is quoted in Jackson, *American Bandstand*, 69.

34. "Dancing—A Man's Game" is available for viewing at the New York Public Library Performing Arts Library.

35. Bailey, *From Front Porch to Back Seat*, 102–3; May, *Homeward Bound*, 85.

36. May, *Homeward Bound*, 16; William Graebner, *Coming of Age in Buffalo*, 29; Elizabeth Wheeler, *Uncontained*, 1.

37. Burt, *Male Dancer*, 125. See also May, *Homeward Bound*, 91.

38. Bérubé, *Coming Out Under Fire*, 258.

39. Wheeler, *Uncontained*, 8.

40. Graebner, *Coming of Age in Buffalo*, 22.

41. Hazel Nickola v Russell S. Munro, 162 Cal. App. 2d 449; 328 P.2d 271 (1958).

42. Pearl Kershaw v Department of Alcoholic Beverage Control, 155 Cal App. 2d 544; 318 P. 2d 494 (1957). Albert Vallerga v Department of Alcoholic Beverage Control,

1 California Reporter 494 (1959). For an overview of legal cases involving same-gender dancing see Paul Siegel, "A Right to Boogie Queerly."

43. Mintz and Kellogg, *Domestic Revolutions*, 199. This is not to say that there was a single homogenous youth culture, but only that youth and adult cultures were increasingly distinct. Graebner's 1990 history of postwar youth, *Coming of Age in Buffalo*, demonstrates the heterogeneity of youth cultures.

44. McBee, *Dance Hall Days*, 52; Schrum, *Some Wore Bobby Sox*, 33.

45. "Teeners' Hero," *Time*, May 14, 1956, 53–54.

46. "Elvis A Different Kind of Idol," *Life*, August 27 1956, 101–9.

47. Ibid., 108.

48. Barbara Ehrenreich, in *Dancing in the Streets*, 209, and Marjorie Garber, in *Vested Interests*, 367, make the argument that black performer Little Richard was able to perform in a sensual way because of his histrionic performance of ambiguous gender. His performance read as parody and thus seemed to be harmless.

49. Garber, *Vested Interests*, 366.

50. "Elvis Presley . . . He can't be . . . but he is," *Look*, August 7, 1956, 82.

51. "Hillbilly on a Pedestal," *Newsweek*, May 14, 1956, 82. James and Annette Baxter, "The Man in the Blue Suede Shoes," *Harper's Magazine*, January 1958, p. 45.

52. Gerald Weales, "Movies: The Crazy, Mixed-up Kids Take Over," *The Reporter*, December 13, 1956, p. 40, 41. A female reviewer of *Love Me Tender* was more sympathetic and praised Presley's acting, noting that in the film Presley was not lewd. See Janet Winn, "A Star is Borne," *The New Republic*, December 24, 1956, 22.

53. James and Annette Baxter, "The Man in the Blue Suede Shoes," *Harper's Magazine*, January 1958, p. 45.

54. Vernon Scott, "Elvis: Ten Million Dollars Later," *McCall's*, February 1963, p. 128.

55. For examples of the representation of Elvis as a hillbilly, see "A Howling Hillbilly Success," *Life*, April 30, 1956, 64; "Teeners' Hero," *Time*, May 14, 1956, 53–54; "Hillbilly on a Pedestal," *Newsweek*, May 14, 1956, 82.

56. Starr and Waterman, *American Popular Music*, 238–39.

57. Hopper is quoted in Vernon Scott, "Elvis: Ten Million Dollars Later," *McCall's*, February 1963, 128.

58. Bailey, *From Front Porch to Back Seat*, 61.

59. Cvetkovich, "White Boots and Combat Boots," 336.

60. Ibid., 338.

61. Descriptions of specific men's lives and quotations from them are drawn from interviews and participant observation. All names used are pseudonyms. The age, race or ethnicity, sexual identity, and occupation of each man interviewed are provided in the Methodological Appendix. The occupations of some interview subjects have been changed to ones of equivalent status to protect subjects' anonymity.

62. Steven. D. Stark, "The Last Tango: Isn't Anybody Out There Dancing?" *New York Times*, August 12, 1987, 1, 4.

63. Wilkins, *Wannabes, Goths, and Christians*, 112.

64. Bederman, *Manliness and Civilization*; Pettegrew, *Brutes in Suits*.

65. Hazzard-Donald, "Dance in Hip Hop Culture," 224.

66. Desmond, *Dancing Desires*, 25.

67. Anthony Thomas, ""The House the Kids Built," 439.

68. Joshua Gamson, *Fabulous Sylvester*, 138.

69. Lorraine Kreahling, "Writer Flies High, Then Tumbles but Gets Back Up Again," *New York Times*, June 8, 1997.

70. Price, *Blood Brothers*, 19.
71. Ibid., 20.
72. Cvetkovich, "White Boots and Combat Boots," 337.
73. Starr and Waterman, *American Popular Music*, 344.
74. Anna Quindlen, "What's New in the Discotheques," *New York Times*, November 11, 1977, 52, C18.
75. Dyer, "In Defence of Disco," 22.
76. Román, "Theatre Journals: Dance Liberation," ix, xi.
77. See Gamson, *Fabulous Sylvester*, 184–85 and Gillian Frank, "Discophobia."
78. See Graebner, *Coming of Age in Buffalo*, 6, for the diversity and importance of subcultures during the postwar period.
79. I became aware of the "no dancing" notes through Starr and Waterman, *American Popular Music*, 288.
80. Starr and Waterman, *American Popular Music*, 318, 331.
81. My description of the riot is drawn from Gamson, *Fabulous Sylvester*, 184; Frank, "Discophobia," and an interview with a witness to the event.
82. Gamson, *Fabulous Sylvester*, 184.
83. Ibid., 185.

CHAPTER 5

1. Desmond, *Dancing Desires*, 7.
2. Burt, "Dissolving in Pleasure," 229.
3. Bull, "Sense, Meaning, and Perception in Three Dance Cultures," 274.
4. Thomas, *Body, Dance and Cultural Theory*, 100.
5. Susan Leigh Foster makes a similar point when writing about modern dance choreographers such as Merce Cunningham whose asexual presentation of "intimate contact" distanced choreography from its sexual potential. See Foster, "Closets Full of Dances,"174.
6. See Kyra Gault, *Games Black Girls Play*, 98 and Stephanie Sears, *Imagining Black Womanhood*, 140–41, for discussions of the ways in which dance that may appear sexy to a viewer may have an entirely different meaning to the dancer.
7. Graham, *Blood Memory*, 122.
8. Pascoe, *Dude You're a Fag*, 86.
9. Ibid., 63. Later in the book Pascoe qualifies this statement when she notes that "Dancing was another arena that carried distinctly fag-associated meanings for white boys but masculine meanings for African American boys who participated in hip-hop culture." See Pascoe, *Dude You're a Fag*, 73.
10. In a study of parental responses to gender nonconformity of very young boys, many fathers were troubled by their son's interest in ballet. See Kane, "'No Way My Boys Are Going To Be Like That!'," 160. The popular film and musical *Billy Elliot*, while ostensibly about this prejudice, does not challenge the underlying gender binary that associates masculinity with athleticism and femininity with grace. For an analysis of the gender dynamics of this film see Gard, *Men Who Dance*, 199–202.
11. Michael Ventura, *Shadow Dancing in the U.S.A.*, 45.
12. Maria Pini, *Club Cultures and Female Subjectivity*, 117. Similarly Wilkins's women informants preferred Goth clubs to what they deemed "regular" clubs because subcultural norms meant that women could dance without being ogled or subjected to uninvited touch by men who were present. See Wilkins, *Wannabes, Goths, and Christians*, 62–63.

13. Kimmel, *Manhood in America*, 5.
14. Sociologist Peter Hennen refers to this dimension of a gender order as its polarity. See Hennen, *Faeries, Bears and Leathermen*, 35.
15. In "Grinding on the Dance Floor," 365, a study of dances at a majority white and Asian private college, Shelly Ronen found that women danced suggestively as they danced together in groups, and that men never danced with each other at all.
16. In the context of analyzing cinematic representations of white men, cultural studies scholar Richard Dyer wrote, "A sense of separation and boundedness is important to the white male ego." See Dyer, *White*, 152. I am indebted to Eileen Otis for encouraging me to think about the dancing body in interaction with others and a related conceptualization of masculinity as isolated and corporeally discrete. (Eileen Otis, personal communication).
17. Roth, *Human Stain*, 26.
18. Pascoe, *Dude You're a Fag*, 63.
19. Best, *Prom Night*, 95; Kimmel, *Manhood in America*, 5.
20. Halberstam is quoted using the term "anti-performative" in Annamarie Jagose, "Masculinity Without Men." See also Halberstam, *Female Masculinity*, 234–35.

    In a study of drag king performances Halberstam found that the most successful impersonations of white masculinity involved parody while performances of black masculinities could strive for authenticity. See Halberstam, "Mackdaddy, Superfly, Rapper," 111.
21. Dyson, "Be Like Mike?," 410.
22. Best, *Prom Night*, 95.
23. Gottschild, *Black Dancing Body*, 104.
24. Eduardo Obregón Pagán describes a similar gender differentiation of dance styles among Mexican American youths in California during the 1940s. Mexican American young men minimized their movement while the women with whom they danced flaunted improvisational talent. See Pagán, *Murder at the Sleepy Lagoon*, 54.
25. Hunter, "Shake it, Baby, Shake It," 26.
26. The butterfly and tootsie roll are dances performed by young black women that involve rapidly raising and lowering the buttocks.
27. Schloss argues that the masculinity of the form is apparent in its name. "B-girls often refer to what they do as 'b-boying,' but b-boys *never* call their dance 'b-girling.'" See Schloss, *Foundation*, 65.
28. Ibid., 107.
29. Ghandnoosh, "'Cross-Cultural' Practices," 1597, note 12.
30. Shawn, "Masculine American Dancing," 2–3. See also L. E. Hutto, "Rhythmic Activities for High School Boys," *Journal of Health and Physical Education* 5, no. 1 (1934): 32–33, 60–61. Herman Hagedorn's 1930 biography of Theodore Roosevelt, *Roosevelt in the Badlands*, describes him performing an "Indian wardance" after killing a buffalo. Even if the description is not factual, it contributes to the popular belief that it is acceptable for white men to dance when they perform the dances of Native Americans. Cited in Pettegrew, *Brutes in Suits*, 352, note 22.
31. Robinson, "Race in Motion," 114.
32. See Garber's *Vested Interests* for a sustained discussion of the frequent coincidence of racial appropriation and cross-dressing.
33. McMains, "Brownface," 57, 59.

34. Sedgwick, *Between Men*, 1–2.
35. I use gender rather than sex because I am referring lived identities rather than biology or physiology.
36. McBee, *Dance Hall Days*, 92.
37. "HARDER CONDITIONS FOR GIRL WORKERS; And Miss Hamilton Finds That Their Social Clubs Are Starving for Leaders. SO DANCE HALLS FLOURISH Secretary of League of Women Workers Deplores Lack of Interest of Women of Leisure," *New York Times*, November 20, 1909, 4.
38. "3,000 Dance in Park as the Season Opens: 15,000 Others Gather on Mall to Watch—Rules Are Stricter Than Last Year's," *New York Times*, June 10, 1936.
39. See Jennifer Donlin, "Rendering Grinders Toothless," *New York Times*, August 14, 2011, 14, ST10 for a report of young women's discomfort being approached in this way. One was quoted saying "we dance in a circle with our butts facing inside instead of out. That way it's really hard for guys to dance on us." Using the phrase "dance on" rather than dance "with" suggests that the man's approach feels more like an imposition than an invitation.
40. Leib and Bulman, "Choreography of Gender," 11.
41. Román, "Theatre Journals," ix.
42. Gard, *Men Who Dance*, 127.
43. Bollen, "Queer Kinesthesia," 295, 305.

CHAPTER 6

1. Savigliano, *Tango and the Political Economy of Passion*, 74.
2. Beverley Skeggs, *Formations of Class and Gender*, 104. See also Adams, "'Death to the Prancing Prince'," 67–69 for a discussion of men dancing on stage and the problem of being looked at.
3. Mulvey, "Visual Pleasure and Narrative Cinema,"11. In a study of Western art and advertising John Berger wrote, "men act, and women appear. Men look at women. Women watch themselves being looked at." Berger, *Ways of Seeing*, 47.
4. Ehrenreich, *Dancing in the Streets*, 19.
5. Ibid., 9.
6. Kimmel, *Manhood in America*, 5.
7. Media theorist Rosalind Gill argues that when the quality of to-be-looked-at-ness is bestowed upon men in advertisements, it is managed in ways that restore the active masculinity of the objectified man's body. See Gill, "Beyond the 'Sexualiza-tion of Culture' Thesis."
8. Bourdieu, *Outline of a Theory of Practice*, 72–73.
9. E. Ann Kaplan, "Is the Gaze Male?"
10. I am indebted to Tyson Smith for this insight. (Tyson Smith, personal communication).
11. The division of a dance class into rows of men and women is an enduring convention within the United States. It tends to reinforce beliefs in innate sex differences while contributing to the production of distinctly gendered movement. Once divided into separate rows men and women are often instructed to apply different movement styles to the same choreography. For example men are typically asked to let all of the women's rows go first and then are expected to cover more space as they move across the floor.
12. Connell, *Gender and Power*, 84.
13. Messerschmidt, "'Doing Gender'"; West & Zimmerman, "Doing Gender."

14. Families take many forms. I use "parent" here to mean an adult who raises a child.

15. I adapt the phrase "generative foundation" from dance historian Jurretta Jordan Heckscher. Heckscher used the longer phrase "common generative foundation" to describe the shared cultural structures of West and Central Africa that slaves in the Chesapeake area of the United States drew upon as they developed African American dance forms. See Heckscher,"Our National Poetry," 21.

16. See Jonathan Jackson, "Improvisation in African American Vernacular Dancing," 42.

17. Thorne, *Gender Play*, 46.

18. Biologist Anne Fausto-Sterling reports that "boys with older sisters kept the same level of male-typed play while also playing more often in female typical ways." Fausto-Sterling, *Sex/Gender*, 56.

19. Messerschmidt "'Doing Gender'," 86.

20. I am indebted to an anonymous reviewer, who led me to this insight by giving the example of his or her own experience of parenting a white son.

21. May, *Homeward Bound*, 166.

22. Thomas, *Body, Dance and Cultural Theory*, 202.

23. In another interview, Tyler, a twenty-year-old man of Chinese and white ancestry, felt embarrassed watching his parents dance because, he said, "I'm used to being *raised* by them."

24. Ehrenreich, *Dancing in the Streets*, 212.

25. I am inspired here by Susan B. Kaiser's use of the concept of "minding appearances." See Kaiser, "Minding Appearances."

26. According to music and dance scholar Joseph G. Schloss, many dancers strongly reject the term "breakdance" and favor the term "b-boying." See Schloss, *Foundation*, 58. My subjects used "breakdance" and for the sake of consistency, in this section and others where subjects employed the term, I use it as well.

27. Pascoe, *Dude You're a Fag*.

28. Halberstam is quoted in Annamarie Jagose, "Masculinity Without Men."

29. Richard Dyer, "In Defence of Disco," 22.

CHAPTER 7

1. Bourdieu, *Outline of a Theory of Practice*, 164.

2. West and Zimmerman, "Doing Gender," 146.

3. West and Zimmerman, "Doing Gender," 135–37.

4. In ethnographies of masculinity in school settings, Ferguson and Pascoe found that performances of masculinity that teachers considered normative for white boys were deemed social violations when performed by blacks. See Ferguson, *Bad Boys*, 86 and Pascoe, *Dude You're a Fag*, 76–77.

5. Both race and ethnicity are cultural constructs that draw on discourse and perceptions regarding geographic origins, culture, and physical appearance. The socially constructed boundaries of racial categories generally include members of multiple ethnic groups, and many ethnic groups include members of multiple racial categories. In many cases the categorization of groups as racial or as ethnic has shifted over time. I use both terms because in the periods I describe some identities were perceived as races, and others as ethnicities.

6. Amina Mama, *Beyond the Masks*, 82.

7. In particular local contexts in the United States where there are few blacks, the term "ghetto" is pejoratively applied to other communities of color. Within black communities "ghetto" may be used to make class distinctions.

8. I became aware of this quotation through Katrina Hazzard-Gordon's writing on the role of dance in establishment of black community inclusion. See Hazzard-Gordon, *Jookin'*, 118.
9. See Chad Heap's 2009 *Slumming* for a detailed history and analysis of slumming.
10. Karen Hubbard and Terry Monaghan, "Negotiating Compromise on a Burnished Wood Floor," 139.
11. Heap, *Slumming*, 277.
12. Wilkins, *Wannabes, Goths, and Christians*, 156.
13. William Perkins, *Droppin' Science*, ix. See George Lipsitz, *Footsteps in the Dark*, 51, for the close interaction of Asian and black diasporic music cultures.
14. Wilkins, *Wannabes, Goths, and Christians*, 104.
15. Kyle Kusz makes a similar argument in an analysis of representations of white youth in books about raising boys. See Kusz, "'I Want To Be the Minority'," 402. See also Beverley Skeggs, who wrote "plundered attributes have to remain associated with the 'originary' group in order to guarantee the attribution of 'the real' and the authentic." Skeggs, *Class, Self, Culture*, 187.
16. Rodriguez, "Color-Blind Ideology and the Cultural Appropriation of Hip-Hop," 649.
17. Maira, "Belly Dancing," 329.
18. Marlon Ross, "In Search of Black Men's Masculinities," 599.
19. Kimmel, *Manhood in America*, 31 describes how, in the mid-nineteenth century, men felt that masculinity required self-control.
20. Rogin, *Blackface, White Noise*, 25.
21. Tomko, *Dancing Class*, 215–16.
22. Cook, "Watching Our Step," 191.

CHAPTER 8

1. Scott Korb, "The Right Moves: What Every White Guy Like Me Owes to Michael Stipe," *New York Times Magazine*, October 16, 2011, 106.
2. Kate Phillips, "Schwarzenegger Apologizes for Hot Tape," *The Caucus, New York Times*, September 8, 2006.
3. As an example of how elements of the dancer's habitus may be acquired through play that is not strictly dancing, see Gault's *Games Black Girls Play*, esp. 29.
4. Pascoe, *Dude You're a Fag*, 86.
5. Bederman, *Manliness and Civilization*, 7.
6. West and Zimmerman, "Doing Gender," 136.

SELECTED BIBLIOGRAPHY

Adams, Mary Louise. "'Death to the Prancing Prince': Effeminacy, Sport Discourses and the Salvation of Men's Dancing.'" *Body and Society* 11, no. 4 (2005): 63–86.

Aldrich, Elizabeth. "The Civilizing of America's Ballrooms: The Revolutionary War to 1890." In *Ballroom, Boogie, Shimmy Sham, Shake: A Social and Popular Dance Reader*, edited by Julie Malnig, 36–54. Urbana: University of Illinois Press, 2009.

Anderson, Eric. "Inclusive Masculinity in a Fraternal Setting." *Men and Masculinities* 10, no. 5 (2008): 604–20.

Arvey, Verna. "Control, Not Grace: Richard Cromwell." *The American Dancer*, September 1931, 12.

———. "Dance for Beauty's Sake." *The American Dancer*, January 1931, 12.

Badger, Reid. *A Life in Ragtime: A Biography of James Reese Europe*. New York: Oxford University Press, 1995.

Bailey, Beth L. *From Front Porch to Back Seat: Courtship in Twentieth-Century America*. Baltimore: Johns Hopkins University Press, 1989.

Baldwin, James. *The Price of the Ticket: Collected Nonfiction: 1948–1985*. New York: St. Martin's, 1985.

Bederman, Gail. *Manliness and Civilization: A Cultural History of Gender and Race in the United States, 1880–1917*. Chicago: University of Chicago Press, 1995.

Berger, John. *Ways of Seeing*. New York: Penguin, 1972.

Bérubé, Allan. *Coming Out Under Fire: The History of Gay Men and Women in World War Two*. New York: The Free Press, 1990.

Best, Amy. L. *Prom Night: Youth, Schools, and Popular Culture*. New York: Routledge, 2000.

Bevans, George Esdras. "How Workingmen Spend Their Time." Ph.D. diss., Columbia University, 1913.

Bollen, Jonathan. "Queer Kinesthesia: Performativity on the Dance Floor." In *Dancing Desires: Choreographing Sexualities On and Off Stage*, edited by Jane C. Desmond, 285–314. Madison: University of Wisconsin Press, 2001.

Bonilla-Silva, Eduardo. "The Linguistics of Color Blind Racism: How to Talk Nasty about Blacks without Sounding "Racist." *Critical Sociology* 28, no. 1 (2002): 41–64.

Bourdieu, Pierre. *Bachelor's Ball: The Crisis of Peasant Society in Bearn*. Chicago: University of Chicago Press, 2008.

———. *Outline of a Theory of Practice*. New York: Cambridge University Press, 1977.

Brand, Max. *Destry Rides Again*. New York: A. L. Burt, 1930.

Bull, Cynthia Jean Cohen. "Sense, Meaning, and Perception in Three Dance Cultures." In *Meaning in Motion: New Cultural Studies of Dance*, edited by Jane C. Desmond, 269–87. Durham: Duke University Press, 1997.

Burroughs, Edgar Rice. *Tarzan of the Apes*. New York: Buccaneer Books, 1914.

Burt, Ramsay. "Dissolving in Pleasure: The Threat of the Queer Male Dancing Body." In *Dancing Desires: Choreographing Sexualities On and Off the Stage*, edited by Jane. C. Desmond, 209-41. Madison: University of Wisconsin Press, 2001.

———. *The Male Dancer*. 2nd ed. New York: Routledge, 2007.

Butler, Judith. *Bodies That Matter: On the Discursive Limits of "Sex."* New York: Routledge, 1993.

Cain, James M. *The Postman Always Rings Twice*. New York: Vintage, 1934.

Capeci, Jr., Dominic J. "Walter F. White and the Savoy Ballroom Controversy of 1943." *Afro-Americans in New York Life and History* 5, no. 2 (1981): 13–32.

Caponi-Tabery, Gena. *Jump for Joy: Jazz, Basketball and Black Culture in 1930s America*. Amherst: University of Massachusetts Press, 2008.

Castle, Irene. "My Memories of Vernon Castle." *Everybody's Magazine*, November 1918, 22–27.

Castle, Vernon, and Irene Castle. *Modern Dancing*. New York: World Syndicate Co, 1914.

Chalif, Louis. "Men and Boys Should Dance." *The American Dancer*, May 1932, 25.

Chauncey, George. *Gay New York: Gender, Urban Culture, and the Making of the Gay Male World, 1890–1940*. New York: Basic Books, 1994.

Cobbs, John L. *Owen Wister*. Boston: Twayne Publishers, 1984.

Collins, Patricia Hill. *Black Feminist Thought*. New York: Routledge, 2000.

Connell, R. W. *Gender and Power*. Stanford: Stanford University Press, 1987.

———. *Masculinities*. Berkeley: University of California Press, 1995.

———, and James W. Messerschmidt. "Hegemonic Masculinity: Rethinking the Concept." *Gender & Society* 19, no. 6 (2005): 829–59.

Cook, Susan C. "Passionless Dancing and Passionate Reform: Respectability, Modernism, and the Social Dancing of Irene and Vernon Castle." In *The Passion of Music and Dance: Body, Gender and Sexuality*, edited by William Washabaugh, 133–50. New York: Berg, 1998.

———. "Tango Lizards and Girlish Men: Performing Masculinity on the Social Dance Floor." In *Proceedings: Society of Dance History Scholars*, New York, June 19–22, 1997, compiled by Linda J. Tomko, 1997, 41–55.

———. "Watching Our Step: Embodying Research, Telling Stories." In *Audible Traces: Gender, Identity, and Music*, edited by Elaine Barkin and L. Hamessley, 177–212. Los Angeles: Carciofoli Verlaghaus, 1999.

Cota, Aaron. "Aaron Cota." In *When Men Dance*, edited by Jennifer Fisher and Anthony Shay, 49–52. New York: Oxford University Press, 2009.

Crampton, Ward C. "The New York City Syllabus of Physical Training." *American Physical Education Review* 19, no. 9 (1914):647–57.

Crenshaw, Kimberlé. "Mapping the Margins: Intersectionality, Identity Politics, and Violence against Women of Color." *Stanford Law Review* 43, no. 6 (1991): 1241–99.

Cressey, Paul G. *The Taxi-Dance Hall: A Sociological Study in Commercialized Recreation and City Life*. 1932. Reprint, New York: Greenwood Press, 1968.

Croce, Arlene. *The Fred Astaire and Ginger Rogers Book*. New York: Dutton, 1972.

Cvetkovich, Ann. "White Boots and Combat Boots: My Life as a Lesbian Go-Go Dancer." In *Dancing Desires: Choreographing Sexualities On and Off the Stage*, edited by Jane. C. Desmond, 315–48. Madison: University of Wisconsin Press, 2001.

Decker, Todd. *Music Makes Me: Fred Astaire and Jazz*. Berkeley: University of California Press, 2011.

Demetriou, Demetrakis Z. "Connell's Concept of Hegemonic Masculinity: A Critique." *Theory and Society* 30, no. 3 (2001): 337–61.

Desmond, Jane E. *Dancing Desires: Choreographing Sexualities On and Off Stage*. Madison: University of Wisconsin Press, 2001.

Dinerstein, Joel. *Swinging the Machine: Modernity, Technology, and African American Culture between the World Wars*. Amherst: University of Massachusetts Press, 2003.

Dorr, Rheta Childe. *What Eight Million Women Want*. Boston: Small, Maynard & Company, 1910.

Dyer, Richard. "In Defence of Disco." *Gay Left* (London), no. 8 (1979): 20–23.

———. *The Matter of Images*. New York: Routledge, 1993.

———. *White*. New York: Routledge, 1997.

Dyson, Michael Eric. "Be Like Mike? Michael Jordon and the Pedagogy of Desire." In *Signifyin(g), Sanctifyin', and Slam Dunking*, edited by Gena Dagel Caponi, 407–16. Amherst: University of Massachusetts Press, 1999.

Ehrenreich, Barbara. *Dancing in the Streets: A History of Collective Joy*. New York: Metropolitan Books, 2007.

Emery, Lynne Fauley. *Black Dance from 1619 to Today*. 2nd rev. ed. Princeton: Princeton Book Co., 1988.

Erenberg, Lewis A. "Everybody's Doin' It: The Pre-World War I Dance Craze, the Castles, and the Modern American Girl." *Feminist Studies* 3, no. 1 (1975–1976): 155–70.

———. *Steppin' Out: New York Nightlife and the Transformation of American Culture, 1890–1930*. Chicago: University of Chicago Press, 1984.

Fass, Paula. *The Damned and the Beautiful: American Youth in the 1920's*. New York: Oxford University Press, 1977.

Fausto-Sterling, Anne. *Sex/Gender: Biology in a Social World*. New York: Routledge, 2012.

Ferguson, Ann Arnett. *Bad Boys: Public Schools in the Making of Black Masculinity*. Ann Arbor: University of Michigan Press, 2000.

Fitch, Clara. "The Influence of Dancing Upon the Physique." *American Physical Education Review* 11, no. 4 (1907): 324–32.

Foster, Susan Leigh. "Closets Full of Dances: Modern Dance's Performance of Masculinity and Sexuality." In *Dancing Desires: Choreographing Sexualities On and Off the Stage*, edited by Jane C. Desmond, 147–207. Madison: University of Wisconsin Press, 2001.

Frank, Gillian. "Discophobia: Anti-Gay Prejudice and the 1979 Backlash against Disco." *Journal of the History of Sexuality* 16, no. 2 (2007): 276–306.

Gamson, Joshua. *The Fabulous Sylvester: The Legend, the Music, the Seventies in San Francisco*. New York: Henry Holt, 2005.

Garber, Marjorie. *Vested Interests: Cross-Dressing and Cultural Anxiety*. New York: Routledge, 1992.

Garcia, David. "Embodying Music/Disciplining Dance: The Mambo Body in Havana and New York City." In *Ballroom, Boogie, Shimmy Sham, Shake: A Social and Popular Dance Reader*, edited by Julie Malnig, 165–81. Urbana: University of Illinois Press, 2009.

Gard, Michael. *Men Who Dance: Aesthetics, Athletics, and the Art of Masculinity*. New York: Peter Lang, 2006.

Gates, Jr., Henry Louis. "The Trope of a New Negro and the Reconstruction of the Image of the Black." *Representations* 24 (1988): 129–55.

Gault, Kyra D. *The Games Black Girls Play: Learning the Ropes from Double-Dutch to Hip-Hop*. New York: New York University Press, 2006.

Ghandnoosh, Nazgol. "'Cross-Cultural' Practices: Interpreting Non-African-American Participation in Hip-Hop Dance." *Ethnic and Racial Studies* 33, no. 9 (2010): 1580–99.

Gill, Rosalind. "Beyond the 'Sexualization of Culture' Thesis: An Intersectional Analysis of 'Sixpacks,' 'Midriffs' and 'Hot Lesbians' in Advertising." *Sexualities* 12, no. 2 (2009): 137–60.

Glenn, Evelyn Nakano. *Unequal Freedom: How Race and Gender Shaped American Citizenship and Labor.* Cambridge, MA: Harvard University Press, 2002.

Gold, Russell. "Guilty of Syncopation, Joy, and Animation: The Closing of Harlem's Savoy Ballroom." *Studies in Dance History* 5, no. 1 (1994): 50–64.

Gottschild, Brenda Dixon. *The Black Dancing Body: A Geography from Coon to Cool.* New York: Palgrave Macmillan, 2003.

Graebner, William. *Coming of Age in Buffalo: Youth and Authority in the Postwar Era.* Philadelphia: Temple University Press, 1990.

Graham, Martha. *Blood Memory.* New York: Doubleday, 1991.

Grindstaff, Laura, and Emily West. "Hegemonic Masculinity on the Sidelines of Sport." *Sociology Compass* 5 (2011): 859–81.

Gulick, Luther H. "The Alleged Effemination of our American Boys." *American Physical Education Review* 10, no. 3 (1905): 213–20.

———."Athletics from the Biologic Viewpoint: Athletics Do Not Test Womanliness." *American Physical Education Review* 11, no. 3 (1906): 157–60.

———. *The Dynamic of Manhood.* New York: Association Press, 1917.

———. "Exercise Must Be Interesting." *American Physical Education Review* 12, no. 1 (1907): 60–63.

———. *The Healthful Art of Dancing.* New York: Doubleday, Page & Co., 1910.

———. "Rhythm and Education." *American Physical Education Review* 10, no. 2 (1905):164–69.

Hackett, Alice Payne. *70 Years of Best Sellers: 1895–1965.* New York: R.R. Bowker, 1967.

Halberstam, Judith. *Female Masculinity.* Durham: Duke University Press, 1998.

———. "Mackdaddy, Superfly, Rapper: Gender, Race, and Masculinity in the Drag King Scene." *Social Text* 52/53 (1997): 104–31.

Hazzard-Donald, Katrina. "Dance in Hip Hop Culture." In *Droppin' Science*, edited by William E. Perkins, 220–35. Philadelphia: Temple University Press, 1996.

Hazzard-Gordon, Katrina. *Jookin': The Rise of Social Dance Formations in African-American Culture.* Philadelphia: Temple University Press, 1990.

Heap, Chad. *Slumming: Sexual and Racial Encounters in American Nightlife, 1885–1940.* Chicago: University of Chicago Press, 2009.

Heckscher, Jurretta Jordan. "Our National Poetry: The Afro-Chesapeake Inventions of American Dance." In *Ballroom, Boogie, Shimmy Sham, Shake: A Social and Popular Dance Reader*, edited by Julie Malnig, 19–35. Urbana: University of Illinois Press, 2009.

Hennen, Peter. *Faeries, Bears and Leathermen: Men in Community Queering the Masculine.* Chicago: University of Chicago Press, 2008.

Hewitt, Andrew. *Social Choreography: Ideology as Performance in Dance and Everyday Movement.* Durham: Duke University Press, 2005.

Hubbard, Karen, and Terry Monaghan. "Negotiating Compromise on a Burnished Wood Floor: Social Dancing at the Savoy." In *Ballroom, Boogie, Shimmy Sham, Shake: A Social and Popular Dance Reader*, edited by Julie Malnig, 126–45. Urbana: University of Illinois Press, 2009.

Hunter, Margaret. "Shake it, Baby, Shake It: Consumption and the New Gender Relation in Hip-Hop." *Sociological Perspectives* 54, no. 1 (2011): 15–36.

"In the Ball-Room To-Day." *The Dancing Times*, November 1918, 31 – 39.

Israels, Belle Lindner. "The Way of the Girl." *The Survey* [The Charity Organization Society of the City of New York,] 22 (1909): 486–97.

Jackson, John A. *American Bandstand: Dick Clark and the Making of a Rock 'n' Roll Empire*. New York: Oxford University Press, 1997.

————. *Big Beat Heat: Alan Freed and the Early Years of Rock and Roll*. New York: Schirmer Books, 1991.

Jackson, Jonathan David. "Improvisation in African American Vernacular Dancing." *Dance Research Journal* 33, no. 2 (2001): 40–53.

Jagose, Annamarie. "Masculinity Without Men: Annamarie Jagose Interviews Judith Halberstam about Her Latest Book *Female Masculinity*." *Genders* 29 (1999).

Kaiser, Susan B. "Minding Appearances: Style, Truth, and Subjectivity." In *Body Dressing*, edited by Joanne Entwistle and Elizabeth Wilson, 79–102. New York: Berg, 2001.

Kane, Emily W. "'No Way My Boys Are Going To Be Like That!': Parents' Responses to Children's Gender Nonconformity." *Gender & Society* 20, no.2 (2006): 149–76.

Kaplan, E. Ann. "Is the Gaze Male?" In *Feminism and Film*, edited by. E. Ann Kaplan, 119–38. New York: Oxford University Press, 2000.

Kasson, John F. *Houdini, Tarzan, and the Perfect Man: The White Male Body and the Challenge of Modernity in America*. New York: Hill and Wang, 2001.

Kellor, Frances. "Ethical Value of Sports for Women." *American Physical Education Review* 11, no. 3 (1906): 168.

Kimmel, Michael. S. *Manhood in America: A Cultural History*. New York: Oxford University Press, 2006.

Kusz, Kyle W. "'I Want To Be the Minority': The Politics of Youthful White Masculinities in Sport and Popular Culture in 1990s America." *Journal of Sport and Social Issues* 25, no. 4 (2001): 390–416.

Lehr, Elizabeth Drexel. *"King Lehr" and the Gilded Age*. 1935. Reprint, New York: Arno Press, 1975.

Leib, Allison Yamanashi, and Robert C. Bulman. "The Choreography of Gender: Masculinity, Femininity, and the Complex Dance of Identity in the Ballroom." *Men and Masculinities* 11, no. 5 (2009): 602–21.

Levinson, Peter J. *Puttin' on the Ritz: Fred Astaire and the Fine Art of Panache*. New York: St. Martin's Press, 2009.

Lewis, Sinclair. *Babbitt*. New York: Harcourt, Brace & Co, 1922.

Lipsitz, George. *Footsteps in the Dark: The Hidden Histories of Popular Music*. Minneapolis: University of Minnesota Press, 2007.

————. "Land of a Thousand Dances: Youth Minorities, and the Rise of Rock and Roll." In *Recasting America: Culture and Politics in the Age of the Cold War*, edited by Lary May, 267–84. Chicago: University of Chicago Press, 1989.

Lopes, Paul. *The Rise of a Jazz Art World*. New York: Cambridge University Press, 2002.

Lucey, Paul A., and Barbara A. Dahl. *Lowell High School San Francisco: A History of the Oldest Public High School in California*. Sesquicentennial Ed. Lowell Alumni Association, 2007.

Lynd, Robert S., and Helen Merrell Lynd. *Middletown: A Study in Contemporary American Culture*. New York: Harcourt, Brace & Co., 1929.

————. *Middletown in Transition: A Study in Cultural Conflicts*. New York: Harcourt, Brace & Co., 1937.

Mailer, Norman. *Advertisements for Myself*. New York: G.P. Putnam, 1959.

Maira, Sunaina. "Belly Dancing: Arab-Face, Orientalist Feminism, and U.S. Empire." *American Quarterly* 60, no.2 (2008): 317–45.

Malnig, Julie. "Apaches, Tangos, and Other Indecencies: Women, Dance, and New York Nightlife of the 1910s." In *Ballroom, Boogie, Shimmy Sham, Shake: A Social and Popular Dance Reader*, edited by Julie Malnig, 72–90. Urbana: University of Illinois Press, 2009.

———. *Dancing Till Dawn: A Century of Exhibition Ballroom Dancing*. Westport: CT: Greenwood Press, 1992.

Mama, Amina. *Beyond the Masks: Race, Gender and Subjectivity*. New York: Routledge, 1995.

Manning, Frankie, and Cynthia R. Millman. *Frankie Manning: Ambassador of Lindy Hop*. Philadelphia: Temple University Press, 2007.

Manning, Susan. *Modern Dance, Negro Dance*. Minneapolis: University of Minnesota Press, 2004.

Marsh, Agnes L. "Social Dancing as a Project in Physical Education." *Journal of Health and Physical Education*. 4, no. 2 (1933):28-30, 54.

Martin, Carol. *Dance Marathons: Performing American Culture of the 1920s and 1930s*. Jackson: University Press of Mississippi, 1994.

Martin, John. "John Martin on Conscription." *The American Dancer*, December 1941, 9, 27.

May, Elaine Tyler. *Homeward Bound*. New York: Basic Books, 2008.

McBee, Randy A. *Dance Hall Days: Intimacy and Leisure among Working-Class Immigrants in the United States*. New York: New York University Press, 2000.

McMains, Juliet. E. "Brownface: Representations of Latin-ness in DanceSport." *Dance Research Journal* 33, no. 2 (2001): 54–71.

———. "Dancing Latin/Latin Dancing: Salsa and DanceSport." In *Ballroom, Boogie, Shimmy Sham, Shake: A Social and Popular Dance Reader*, edited by Julie Malnig, 302–22. Urbana: University of Illinois Press, 2009.

———. *Glamour Addiction: Inside the American Ballroom Industry*. Middletown, CT: Wesleyan University Press, 2006.

Messerschmidt, James. W. "'Doing Gender': The Impact and Future of a Salient Sociological Concept." *Gender & Society* 23, no. 1 (2009): 85–88.

Messner, Michael A. "The Masculinity of the Governator: Muscle and Compassion in American Politics." *Gender & Society* 21, no. 4 (2007): 461–80.

Mintz, Steven, and Susan Kellogg. *Domestic Revolutions: A Social History of American Family Life*. New York: Free Press, 1988.

Mosely Educational Commission to the United States of America. *Reports of the Mosely Educational Commission to the United States of America, October–December, 1903*. 1904. Reprint, New York: Arno Press, 1969.

Mueller, John. *Astaire Dancing: The Musical Films*. New York: Alfred A. Knopf, 1985.

Mulvey, Laura. "Visual Pleasure and Narrative Cinema." *Screen* 16, no. 3 (1975): 7–18.

Murray, Arthur. "This Student Earns $15,000 A Year." *Forbes*, April 17, 1920, p. 22, 25

Nasaw, David. *Going Out: The Rise and Fall of Public Amusements*. Cambridge, MA: Harvard University Press, 1999.

National Center for Education Statistics. *120 Years of American Education: A Statistical Portrait*, edited by Thomas D. Snyder, 1993.

Nye, Russel B. "Saturday Night at the Paradise Ballroom: Or, Dance Halls in the Twenties." *Journal of Popular Culture* 7, no. 1 (1973): 14–22.

Pagán, Eduardo Obregón. *Murder at the Sleepy Lagoon: Zoot Suits, Race, and Riot in Wartime L.A.* Chapel Hill: University of North Carolina Press, 2003.

Pascoe, C. J. *Dude You're a Fag*. Berkeley: University of California Press, 2007.

Peiss, Kathy. *Cheap Amusements: Working Women and Leisure in Turn-of-the-Century New York*. Philadelphia: Temple University Press, 1986.

Perkins, William Eric. *Droppin' Science: Critical Essays on Rap Music and Hip Hop Culture*. Philadelphia: Temple University Press, 1996.

Perry, Elisabeth Israels. *Belle Moskowitz: Feminine Politics and the Exercise of Power in the Age of Alfred E. Smith*. New York: Oxford University Press, 1987.

Pettegrew, John. *Brutes in Suits: Male Sensibility in America, 1890–1920*. Baltimore: Johns Hopkins University Press, 2007.

Pini, Maria. *Club Cultures and Female Subjectivity: The Move from Home to House*. New York: Palgrave, 2001.

Price, Richard. *Blood Brothers*. Boston: Houghton Mifflin Company, 1976.

Risner, Doug. *Stigma and Perseverance in the Lives of Boys Who Dance: An Empirical Study of Male Identities in Western Theatrical Dance Training*. Lewiston, NY: The Edwin Mellen Press, 2009.

Robinson, Danielle Anne. "Race in Motion: Reconstructing the Practice, Profession, and Politics of Social Dancing, New York City 1900–1930." Ph.D. diss., University of California, Riverside, 2004.

Rodriguez, Jason. "Color-Blind Ideology and the Cultural Appropriation of Hip-Hop." *Journal of Contemporary Ethnography* 35, no. 6 (2006): 645–68.

Roeder, George H. *The Censored War: An American Visual Experience during World War Two*. New Haven, CT: Yale University Press, 1993.

Rogin, Michael. *Blackface, White Noise: Jewish Immigrants in the Hollywood Melting Pot*. Berkeley: University of California Press, 1996.

Román, David. "Theatre Journals: Dance Liberation." *Theatre Journal* 55, no. 3 (2003): vii–xxiv.

Rondón, César Miguel. *The Book of Salsa*, translated by Frances R. Aparicio. Chapel Hill: University of North Carolina, 2008.

Ronen, Shelly. "Grinding on the Dance Floor: Gendered Scripts and Sexualized Dancing at College Parties." *Gender & Society* 24, no. 3 (2010): 355–77.

Ross, Janice. *Moving Lessons: Margaret H'Doubler and the Beginning of Dance in American Education*. Madison: University of Wisconsin Press, 2000.

Ross, Marlon. "In Search of Black Men's Masculinities." *Feminist Studies* 24, no. 3 (1998): 599–626.

Roth, Philip. *The Human Stain*. New York: Vintage, 2000.

Rotundo, E. Anthony. *American Manhood: Transformations in Masculinity from the Revolution to the Modern Era*. New York: Basic Books, 1993.

Ryan, Mary P. *Womanhood in America: From Colonial Times to the Present*. 2nd ed. New York: New Viewpoints, 1979.

Sargent, Dudley A. "What Athletic Games, If Any, Are Injurious for Women in the Form in which They Are Played by Men?" *American Physical Education Review* 11, no. 3 (1906): 174–81.

Savigliano, Marta E. *Tango and the Political Economy of Passion*. San Francisco: Westview Press, 1995.

Sawyer, Donald. "Ballroom Dancing and the Draft." *The American Dancer*, November 1940, 7, 22.

Schloss, Joseph G. *Foundation: B-boys, B-girls, and Hip-Hop Culture in New York*. New York: Oxford University Press, 2009.

Schrum, Kelly. *Some Wore Bobby Sox: The Emergence of Teenage Girls' Culture, 1920–1945*. New York: Palgrave Macmillan, 2004.

Schuller, Gunther. *The Swing Era: The Development of Jazz, 1930–1945*. New York: Oxford University Press, 1989.

Sears, Stephanie D. *Imagining Black Womanhood: The Negotiation of Power and Identity within the Girls Empowerment Project*. Albany: State University of New York Press, 2010.

Sedgwick, Eve Kosofsky. *Between Men: English Literature and Male Homosocial Desire*. New York: Columbia University Press, 1985.

Shawn, Ted. "A Defence of the Male Dancer." *New York Dramatic Mirror*, May 13, 1916, 19.

———. "Masculine American Dancing." *Educational Dance* (February 1941): 2–3.

———. "Principles of Dancing for Men." *Journal of Health and Physical Education* 4, no. 9 (1933): 27–29, 60–61.

Siegel, Paul. "A Right to Boogie Queerly: The First Amendment on the Dance Floor." In *Dancing Desires: Choreographing Sexualities On and Off the Stage*, edited by Jane C. Desmond, 276–83. Madison: University of Wisconsin Press, 2001.

Skarstrom, William. "Social Centers Instead of Dance Halls: Sage Foundation Promotes Use of Schoolhouses for Dancing by Means of Photoplay." *American Physical Education Review* 17, no. 5 (1912): 401–3.

Skeggs, Beverley. *Class, Self, Culture*. New York: Routledge, 2004.

———. *Formations of Class and Gender: Becoming Respectable*. Thousand Oaks, CA: Sage, 1997.

Spalding, Susan Eike. "Frolics, Hoedowns, and Four-Handed Reels: Variations in Old-Time Dancing in Three Southwest Virginia Communities." In *Communities in Motion: Dance, Community, and Tradition in America's Southeast and Beyond*, edited by Susan Eike Spalding and Jane Harris Woodside, 11–29. Westport, CT: Greenwood Press, 1995.

Starr, Larry, and Christopher Waterman. *American Popular Music: From Minstrelsy to MP3*. New York: Oxford University Press, 2010.

Stearns, Marshall Winslow, and Jean Stearns. *Jazz Dance: The Story of American Vernacular Dance*. New York: Macmillan, 1968.

Stein, Arlene, and Ken Plummer. "I Can't Even Think Straight: 'Queer' Theory and the Missing Sexual Revolution in Sociology." *Sociological Theory* 12, no.2 (1994): 178-187.

Steinberg, Stephen. *The Ethnic Myth: Race, Ethnicity, and Class in America*. Boston: Beacon Press, 1989.

St. Louis, Brett . "Sport, Genetics and the 'Natural Athlete': The Resurgence of Racial Science." *Body and Society* 9, no. 2 (2003): 75–95.

Summers, Martin. *Manliness and Its Discontents: The Black Middle Class and the Transformation of Masculinity, 1900–1930*. Chapel Hill: University of North Carolina Press, 2004.

Tarkington, Booth. *Penrod: His Complete Story*. Garden City, NY: Doubleday, 1913.

Taylor, Henry Ling. "The Dancing Foot." *American Physical Education Review* 10, no. 2 (1905): 137–45.

Terkel, Studs. *The Good War: An Oral History of World War II*. New York: MJF Books, 1984.

Thomas, Anthony. "The House the Kids Built: The Gay Black Imprint on American Dance Music." In *Out in Culture: Gay, Lesbian and Queer Essays on Popular Culture*, edited by Corey K. Creekmur and Alexander Doty, 437–45. Durham: Duke University Press, 1995.

Thomas, Helen. *The Body, Dance and Cultural Theory*. New York: Palgrave Macmillan, 2003.

Thorne, Barrie. *Gender Play: Girls and Boys in School*. New Brunswick, NJ: Rutgers University Press, 1993.

Tomko, Linda J. *Dancing Class: Gender, Ethnicity, and Social Divides in American Dance, 1890–1920*. Bloomington: Indiana University Press, 1999.

———. "Fete Accompli: Gender, 'Folk-Dance,' and Progressive-Era Political Ideals in New York City." In *Corporealities: Dancing Knowledge, Culture and Power*, edited by Susan L. Foster, 155–76. New York: Routledge, 1996.

Ventura, Michael. *Shadow Dancing in the U.S.A.* New York: St. Martin's, 1985.

Verbrugge, Martha H. "Recreating the Body: Women's Physical Education and the Science of Sex Differences in America, 1900–1940." *Bulletin of the History of Medicine* 71, no. 2 (1997): 273–304.

Wacquant, Loic. *Body and Soul: Notebooks of an Apprentice Boxer*. New York: Oxford University Press, 2004.

Wagner, Ann. *Adversaries of Dance: From the Puritans to the Present*. Urbana: University of Illinois Press, 1997.

Ware, Walter. "In Defense of the Male Dancer." *The American Dancer*, May 1938, 15, 48.

West, Candace, and Don H. Zimmerman. "Doing Gender." *Gender & Society* 1, no. 2 (1987): 125–51.

Wheeler, Elizabeth A. *Uncontained: Urban Fiction in Postwar America*. New Brunswick, NJ: Rutgers University Press, 2001.

Wilkins, Amy. *Wannabes, Goths, and Christians: The Boundaries of Sex, Style, and Status*. Chicago: University of Chicago Press, 2008.

Williams, Christine. "The Glass Escalator: Hidden Advantages for Men in the Female Professions." *Social Problems* 39, no. 3 (1992): 253–67.

Winchell, Meghan K. *Good Girls, Good Food, Good Fun: The Story of USO Hostesses*. Chapel Hill: University of North Carolina Press, 2008.

Wister, Owen. *The Virginian: A Horseman of the Plains*. 1902. Reprint, with an introduction by Robert. B. Parker, New York. Signet Classics, 2010.

INDEX

adolescence, 50–53, 187

African Americans. See blacks

Africans, representations of, 41–42, 171

aging and dance, 52, 122–23

Aldrich, Elizabeth, 30

All-American boy, 6, 11, 51, 188–89; jitterbug and: 58, 70, 72, 188

American Bandstand, 15, 76, 78–80, 83–84

anti-performative, 11, 113, 158

Astaire, Fred, 14, 54–55, 60, 171–72

athletics: contrasted to dance, 133, 142, 157, 189; and defenses of dance, 9, 80–82; and gender difference, 25–28; and masculine dominance, 8

Babbitt, 22, 51–52

Bailey, Beth, 88

Baldwin, James, 78

ballet: and ballroom, 57; as discourse, 106; femininity of, 12–13, 107, 189; and gaze, 8, 12; masculinity of, 80–81; in physical education, 25

Barry, Richard, 45–47

b-boys: masculinity of, 8–9, 117–19, 131, 191; racialization of 164, 178–79

Bederman, Gail, 28, 189

Bérubé, Allan, 59

Best, Amy, 114

Big Beat, The, 76–78

blackbody, 181

blackface, 60, 181

blacks: dance ability presumed, 59, 166, 169–70; as dance creators, 33, 43, 56, 61, 64; represented as primitive, 24, 43, 63, 77–78, 171; sexualized, 77–78, 111, 185. *See also* Africans, representations of

bodies, mental disconnects from, 151–54

Bollen, Jonathan, 131

Bourdieu, Pierre, 9–10, 135, 164

Bowen, Louise De Koven, 36–37

Brand, Max, 6

Brown, James, 89, 90, 145

brute, 42–43 see also wildness

Bull, Cynthia, 106

Burchenal, Elizabeth, 27

Burroughs, Edgar Rice, 42

Burt, Ramsay, 8, 12, 82, 106

Cain, James M., 6

Castle, Irene and Vernon, 38–41, 43–44

Chalif, Louis, 58

Chauncey, George, 12, 28, 57

civilization, 26, 43, 78, 204n78

Cohn, Nik, 97–98

college student dances, 50, 52–53

color-blind speech norms, 4, 181

Connell, Raewyn, 7, 9–10, 139

Cook, Susan C., 30, 38, 40–41, 181

cotillion: early 20th century, 31–32, 34, 42; mid-20th century, 143; contemporary 141

Crampton, C. Ward, 24, 28

Cressey, Paul G., 5

Cvetkovich, Ann, 89

dance, initiating a, 124–26

dance instruction, 90, 92–93, 148

dance partners, separated, 86–88. *See also* men partnering men; women partnering women

dance, popularity of: early twentieth century, 36; post-WWII decline: 74–75

(227)

Printed in the USA/Agawam, MA
April 21, 2014

588202.077